CABIN PRESSURE

CABIN PRESSURE

One Man's Desperate Attempt to Recapture
His Youth as a Camp Counselor

Josh Wolk

HYPERION

NEW YORK

Library of Congress Cataloging-in-Publication Data

Wolk, Josh

Cabin pressure : one man's desperate attempt to recapture his youth as a camp counselor / Josh
Wolk.—1st ed.

  p. cm.

ISBN 1-4013-0260-2

ISBN-13: 978-1-4013-0260-3

1. Wolk, Josh, 1969– 2. Camps—Anecdotes. 3. Camps—Humor. I. Title.

GV192.7.W65A3 2007

796.54—dc22   2006049730

Hyperion books are available for special promotions and premiums.
For details contact Michael Rentas,
Assistant Director, Inventory Operations,
Hyperion, 77 West 66th Street, 12th floor,
New York, New York 10023,
or call 212-456-0133.

Design by Laura Drew

Chapter opening illustrations by Tristram Drew/TD Fine Arts

FIRST EDITION

10 9 8 7 6 5 4 3 2 1

For Christine, of course

AUTHOR'S NOTE

ONE OF THE THINGS THAT MADE MY SUMMER CAMP SO SPECIAL WAS THE LIB-
eration from self-consciousness. For eight glorious weeks, boys were free
of the intimidating, judgmental scrutiny that they had to tiptoe around for
an entire school year. They could finally be comfortable with their own
personalities, likes, and dislikes, at ease knowing that no one was staring at
them, analyzing their actions.

Which was kind of at odds with my writing a book about them.

No camper or counselor asked to have their summer chronicled and interpreted by me. When I told the director my intentions while applying to
return to work at camp, he said, "All I care about is getting a good staff.
What you do with the experience is up to you." When I arrived, people
saw me as a counselor. When I disclosed my memoir "side project" to
people, camper and counselor alike asked a few questions and then got distracted by the diving board, sailboats, mountains, bows and arrows, or
tennis courts and dashed off to have a good time, quickly forgetting about
my book. Fortunately, it didn't stop them from being themselves. Which is
all the more reason not to punish them for it.

All the events that appear in this memoir did happen, but I have
clouded people's identities, composited some, and changed all their names,

as well as the name and location of the camp itself. This last part was a decision I struggled over, as I wanted my camp to be recognized as the beloved spot it is, but I didn't want to leave anything that would make the people involved recognizable. Everyone I had the pleasure to spend the summer with left camp with idyllic memories, memories I didn't want to confuse by making these wonderful kids and dedicated counselors feel retroactively self-conscious. This goes most of all for my hilarious, sometimes maddening, but always incredible cabin of fourteen-year-old campers: I can think of few people in this world, including myself, who would be willing to be immortalized as their adolescent self.

CABIN PRESSURE

PROLOGUE

A DOUCHEBAG SAYS "WHAT."

I had learned this helpful fact in junior high, but—much like algebra and the capitals of foreign countries—I had forgotten it sometime over the last twenty years. Now, at thirty-four years old, standing on the edge of a dock, I got a refresher course from the three twelve-year-olds splashing in the green lake water below me.

"Come on, I want to see your backstroke," I begged them.

"Adubagsaywhuh?" mumbled a lumpy, shaggy-haired boy whose dense pattern of freckles made him look like he'd been shot in the face with an orange paintball. He bounced on his toes, spinning himself in a slow circle in the water, making tiny waves with his cupped hands. His two swim-classmates had their backs to me, looking out at a couple of sailboats slowly inching toward their moorings on this windless day.

"I don't know what you're saying." I stared at him. "Get moving."

"Adubagsaywhuh?"

"*What?*" I said.

"Ahhhhhh!" he sprang up in the water, laughing and spraying my feet with water. His friends turned around to see what happened. "*I* said 'a douchebag says "what,"'" and *you* said 'what!' Guess you're a douchebag! Hey, guys, dja hear what I just did?"

One of his friends said, "Ahomosaywhuh."

"What?" asked the freckled one.

"Ahhhhh! Homo!" Hoisted by his own petard. Gratifying, sure, but it didn't bring me any closer to my goal of getting these three to swim. And now a frenetic splash fight had broken out. Pinwheeling their arms into the water for maximum dousing, they turned their heads from each other to keep their faces protected. Preventing their mouths from filling with water allowed them to take the "what" game to the next level while still keeping up an aquatic assault.

"Adickheadsayswhat!"

"I can't hear you. Afartfacesayswhat!"

"Apoopeatersayswhat!"

"Enough!" I yelled, taking a step back to avoid the crossfire. In the distance I heard a bugle honk, signifying the end of the class, and the end of another morning at Camp Eastwind. "All right, you win! Now get out of the water!" The splashes petered out and they scrambled up the dock ladder, stopping only to shake and spray me like wet dogs before scurrying to get their towels. I sat down on the edge of the dock, dangling my feet in the water and looking out at the lake that stretched beyond our cove. Shadowing the far coast were low, green Maine hills and mountains. The summer air was fresh—the only trace of anything unnatural was the faux-beachy smell of the sunscreen trapped in my untrimmed beard and mustache. When I first got to Eastwind this summer, I was convinced this spot was the most restful in the world. After six weeks, I believed roughly the same thing, provided all the kids were removed.

My co–swim counselor, Helen, wandered up behind me. "So what's this I hear about you being a douchebag?"

"I can't deny it. I said 'what.' "

"What?"

"Welcome to the club, douchebag." I hopped off the dock into the water and submerged, enjoying the deadened underwater silence, where there were no lake trout muttering, "Abottomdwellersayswhat?"

Lunch was characteristically hectic and deafening, the dining hall full of flailing arms all trying to get the last slice of bacon for their BLTs. This sparked a philosophical debate at my table of five kids that lasted for the duration of the meal: Can vegetarians drink bacon grease? While trying to moderate this discussion, an orange gob of French dressing dripped off my salad fork onto my T-shirt. I halfheartedly wiped it away with my thumb, leaving a rusty streak. My normal fastidiousness had gone the way of my need for privacy this summer; my T-shirts and shorts were Jackson Pollocks of meal stains. The water left after I finally did my laundry would provide scientists with the precise DNA of my diet.

By the time lunch ended, we'd agreed to disagree on the bacon conundrum, at least until we could find a vegetarian. Now it was Rest Hour, time for everyone to return to their cabins and count the minutes until they were no longer forced to sit still. I went to gather the mail, and made the slow walk back to the cabin, orbited by four of my fourteen-year-old camper roommates demanding to know if they got any letters.

"Nobody gets mail until everyone's on his bed," I said.

"OK, fine, but just tell me: Did I get any?"

"Nobody gets mail until everyone's on his bed."

"I'm not asking to have it, just tell me, did I get any?"

"Nobody gets mail until everyone's on his bed."

This loop continued until I pushed open the wide screen door of our one-room pine cabin. I strode down the aisle between two rows of metal cots, neck ducked forward so as not to smack my forehead on a rafter. I passed the bed of Lefty, the cabin's biggest wiseass. He was showing off a tiny class photo of a girl to his wide-jawed sheepdog of a pal visiting from a different cabin, who took it in admiringly. "So she sent me a letter and I wrote her back, but I made her wait a little bit. She'll totally write back."

"She's cute," said the sheepdog, nodding. His helmet of thick, curly hair flopped atop his head like a bleacher-bum's rainbow wig. "Really cute. You should totally *do* her."

I interrupted. "Are you pulling out that picture again? How can we be sure that's not your sister?"

"Haaaaa, your sister!" the sheepdog said, laughing and pointing at Lefty.

"It's not your sister, 'cause I already did her," Lefty volleyed back at me.

"Haaaaa, he did *your* sister!" the sheepdog said, laughing and pointing at me. Any port in a storm.

3

"Hey!" I barked. "I will *not* have talk like that in my cabin." I leaned forward and snatched the picture out of his hand. "Especially around my new girlfriend. Helloooooo, sweet thing! Four more years till you're eighteen and *mine*." Lefty pounced off his bed and grabbed at the picture, yelling for the sheepdog's help, who then jumped on my back. With the picture in one hand and the mail in the other, I could only twist back and forth, attempting to throw them off. Just before we were about to topple to the floor, I yelled, "If you guys don't get off me right now I'm not giving out the mail! Maybe a certain girlfriend is trying to get through!"

Lefty let go—but not without poking me in the chest first—and ordered the sheepdog to heel. I winked at the picture and whispered "Call me" before handing it back. I banished the sheepdog to his own cabin, then walked up and down the center aisle, distributing the mail. Boys gleefully ripped open envelopes with skateboard magazines and comic books; they weren't yet totally jaded teens—they still grinned happily when they got a letter from Mom, too. When the mail was all gone except for a large envelope for me, there was nothing from Lefty's "girlfriend." "Sorry, man," I said. "She's probably just trying to come up with the right words. Sometimes, 'Dear Stinky, stop writing to me' just isn't enough."

I dumped my envelope out on my bed. Forwarded mail from home—a bunch of bills, a few magazines. Lefty appeared over my shoulder and reached in to grab my new copy of *Harper's*. "There any hot chicks in this?" he said, thumbing through it.

"Yeah, go crazy." I thumbed through the stack of mail, a flip-book of metered envelopes. One thicker and taller envelope stood out. It was made of rough, textured paper. It wasn't stamped, but it had my name and camp address written in a florid script. I tore it open and pulled out a rectangle of thick, creamy card stock. Handpressed in red letters, it read:

James and Ann Schomer Would Be
Extremely Happy to Have You Witness and
Celebrate the Marriage of Their Daughter
Christine to Josh
Son of Richard and Linda Wolk
Saturday, September 13, 2003, at 6:00

The biggest day of my life, just—I looked over at a conspicuously blank desk calendar on my shelf—six weeks away. I stared at the invite for a while. The precise, elegant lettering felt out of place in this emporium of dirty socks and damp towels. But it was inarguably exciting. This was the staple of all future scrapbooks. My most-prized souvenir-to-be. I was getting married. I needed to share the moment.

"Hey, Lefty . . ." I got up off my bed, just in time to catch a fluttering *Harper's* in the chest.

"That magazine *blows*," he said. "It's all words and crap. Give me bikinis, Josh. *Bikinis*."

"Josh has dirty magazines?" Someone down the bunk perked up.

"No, he sucks," yelled Lefty.

"What are you, gay?" hollered someone else. "What about *Maxim*?"

"What about *Big Dorky Swim Counselor Monthly*?" cracked Lefty. "I bet you've got a subscription to that."

I rolled my eyes and laid back down on my bunk, staring at the invite. Six weeks? It felt so close. And as I inhaled deeply the smell of sweat and forest and mildew and lake breeze, it felt so far away.

CHAPTER ONE

EVER SINCE I MOVED TO NEW YORK CITY IN 1991 AFTER GRADUATING FROM college, the word "summer" lost all of its verve. Manhattan is many things—vibrant, thrilling, propulsive—but it most certainly is not a summer paradise. It isn't all New York's fault: Most adults have to come to terms with the fact that summer is no longer an extended vacation. But the city rubs it in your face. The giant skyscrapers lean over you, daring you to just try to get a glimpse of nature. The only oasis is Central Park, but as you squeeze in on weekends to claim a little patch of lawn, the buildings still loom around the edges like sentries; you and your fellow parkgoers are the prisoners who have been given a couple hours out in the "yard." Just try to swim in a pond and you'll be shot on sight. I resented everyone's forced exuberance as they trekked from their tiny apartments to convene in the Park. It wasn't a real summer; we were just playing summer, the way you played doctor or post office as a kid.

Through eleven years of working in the city in television production and then in magazines, each summer I devoted at least fifteen minutes a day to closing my eyes and drifting into a reverie about the place that best idealized what a summer should be: Camp Eastwind. From 1980 to 1988, as a camper and counselor, I attended this all-boys camp on Maine's

Sebago Lake. (Judging by the number of camps that ringed its 105-mile shoreline, I assumed that "Sebago" was an Indian word for "land of friendship bracelets and wedgies.") The more I thought about camp, the more it seemed insane that I would choose to be in New York. At camp, I spent every day standing on a dock, a fleet of sailboats available for a post-dinner jaunt, surrounded by my closest friends. In New York, I sat under an air-conditioning vent, attempting to store up as much chill as possible to hold me for the muggy trek home. At camp I was never more than forty yards away from a refreshing dip in a lake. In New York I debarked from the subway smelling like I had been soaking in a marinade of my co-commuters' sweat. When I really wanted to torture myself, I would recall that in one of the camp bathrooms, you could pee while watching a glorious sunset through the window above the urinal. Just try to find a urinal with a view in New York.

Eastwind was the repository of approximately 87 percent of my greatest memories. I had thrived as a camper there; during those summers I replenished all the self-confidence that was lost during the previous year spent in the ego-shooting gallery that was public school. Eastwind is a noncompetitive camp, which isn't the coddlefest it sounds like. It concentrates on one-man sports like boating, archery, and rock climbing, so you are able to better yourself without worrying about being crushed by others. The us-versus-them bloodlust of other camps' Color Wars is anathema to Eastwind. I was an extraordinarily tall kid ("extraordinarily" being a euphemism for "freakishly"), six feet tall by age thirteen, and six-seven by eighteen. When you're growing that fast, you have to give up all dreams of excelling at team sports. You concentrate on smaller goals, such as bending over to tie your shoes without tumbling into a ditch. But without the scrutiny of a scorekeeper, I threw myself into activities like archery and canoeing until I became quite good. At camp I was recognized for what I could do, as contrasted with school, where on a daily basis I was angrily confronted with why I couldn't dunk a basketball. I even had my first kiss at a dance with a neighboring girls' camp. Everything I couldn't get during the school year, I got at Eastwind.

At seventeen I became a counselor, hired by the director and assistant director who watched me grow up; I couldn't ask for a more official handstamp into adulthood. Now I was in charge, and part of a staff I had revered for the past six years. I was finally the one whom the campers looked to for guidance, even idolized. And as it was my first "real" job with a regular salary, I embraced the image of myself as a working man. When I'd hang out at the Staff Lounge after the kids went to sleep, getting drunk with my friends, we saw ourselves as dads who relaxed after work with a drink. Granted, those dads weren't playing Quarters with Milwaukee's Best—the cheapest case we could buy—and then stumbling home at two A.M. over an obstacle course of tree roots, mumbling mushmouthedly about how that bastard Tom cheated by taking too-small sips when his quarter missed. And yet, hangover be damned, we'd still—incomprehensibly—be able to get up at seven A.M. and ably deal with the next fourteen hours of screaming kids. These truly were the salad days.

The summer of 1989, after my sophomore year at Tufts University, I decided to seek out more adult jobs and internships. I could sense the dreaded "real life" crouching in wait for me in just two years, and it would require a résumé with entries that involved more than greased-watermelon races. Nonetheless, I was certain that I would eventually be back. Nobody ever left Eastwind for good. Long-gone counselors were constantly reappearing, taking one last Eastwind summer before or after attending graduate school. A couple of alumni in their fifties had actually returned to work for a session alongside their second-generation-Eastwind-counselor sons. While they might have been a little out of place, no one begrudged their intentions, because no one wanted bad karma out there in case years later he wanted to do the same thing. If and when I did go back, I was confident I wouldn't be alone. In '88 I was a counselor alongside guys who had been campers with me at age eleven, of course, but I also had coworkers who had been *my* counselor when I was eleven. With that kind of constancy, I could always count on camp to be exactly as I remembered it.

Years passed, and I never found the opportunity to return for an entire summer. I visited regularly for the first couple of years, and then only sporadically for special reunions. These occasional gatherings, attended by dozens of familiar faces who would travel any distance to breathe their childhood air, always hit the "restart" button on my urge to return for a whole summer. But there was never a realistic time; either my career severely lacked momentum and I was too panicky to take two months off from obsessing about it, or professionally I *was* gaining momentum and I didn't want to risk derailing myself. Besides, I thought, as another June came and went, camp will always be there, and I'll try again next year. If it never changed, and I never changed, what was the hurry?

Then, in the summer of 2002, I got engaged to Christine and we set a date for September 2003. It was an exhilarating time, an enormous life landmark. And suddenly everything that was once in the hypothetical realm of "someday we'll have hovercars and live on the moon"—a house, kids, family vacations—was now becoming real. At thirty-three, I had long considered myself an adult, but as I prepared to cross the line of marriage, I realized that *this* was real adulthood. Everything before was just the Epcot Center version: It simulated all of the trappings (independence, career progress) but had none of the real ramifications. Now I was entering a phase not only rife with exciting possibilities, but also riddled with weighty responsibilities.

I come from a family with a proud tradition of worrying, so while other grooms-to-be might busy themselves, say, obsessing over the end of their promiscuity or time lost with their male friends, my hand wringing was more big-picture. I figured that after marriage, everything needed to be thought of in terms of a thirty-year plan, not a three-month plan. This was a time when money should be saved for something more than a big-screen TV. Mortgages, 401(k)s, IRAs, day care, preschools, college funds . . . it would all soon be a part of my daily consciousness, and the many colors of my fret palette. The staples of my life up until now were screwing around, acting immature, and having ample time to watch TV or just stare off into space; they were the key elements of the innocent frivolity of childhood, and I was about to lose them. My silver hair would no longer be considered prematurely gray: it would be appropriately gray. And not only was this the next phase of my life, it was the last phase. The schedule from the wedding on would be worry-worry-worry-worry-death. I decided now was the time to give my life's carefree first act a farewell party. And where better to do it than Eastwind, the place I most closely associated with the joys of childhood?

Planning our wedding had been the catalyst for countless arguments between Christine and me. Our opinions differed on every aspect of our wedding except who the bride and groom would be, and if I suggested vanishing off to summer camp for the two months prior to the event, she might change her mind on that, too. But she was surprisingly open to my idea. Perhaps some of this was a naive underestimation of how much work would be involved in planning the wedding, but a big part of it was her desire to live vicariously through me. Now a TV producer, she too had once been a devoted camper and counselor, up in New Hampshire. As a fellow too-tall teenager, she cherished those summers as a time when she was noticed for other qualities than her height, a happening that actually made her stand taller. She still had good friends from her camp days and could summon the lyrics of hundreds of her old dining-hall songs on command.

Getting a job at Eastwind used to be effortless for an old-timer. All you'd have to do was call up the director and announce your intentions, and you'd be hired. It was as informal as asking if you could swing by for a beer. Once you'd proven your worth, you had a lifetime pass. Now that the director I'd worked for was retired, I had to apply to his successor, Frank Mason, whom I had never met. In November of 2002 we had a long chat on the phone, and it felt strange having to sell myself for the job. I figured it would be no problem, since Frank, too, had started as a camper in the 1970s, become a counselor, and then left for seventeen years before returning in the early '90s with a family and eventually becoming director. This made him the ultimate camp recidivist, and he'd surely embrace my quest.

Frank was receptive, although businesslike. We talked about my desire to return to teach my old activity, swimming, and he seemed to be listening but waiting for a catch. Startled by the absence of an immediate "come on down!", my pitch became more fervent. As I filled him in on my life since 1988, I played down the journalism experience and stressed the patches of volunteer tutoring and big-brothering I'd done in college and afterward. The maxims came fast and furious. *I believe that the children are the future! You never stand so tall as when you bend down to help a small child! A stranger is a friend you haven't met yet! You can lead a horse to water, but if you think you can get him to drink, I've got a moss-gathering rolling stone I'd like to sell you!* I felt a familiar real-world professional anxiety take over, which was alien to my camp experience. If he accepted me, I hoped I could shake it off when summer came. I didn't want to be over-achieving down at the swim dock, trying to invent new strokes to impress Frank with my initiative. ("The butterbackstroke, eh? That shows the kind of spunk, moxie, and grit I want on my team, Wolk. How does the title *head* of swimming grab you?")

A few weeks later I received a letter from Frank confirming my employment as a swimming counselor with a salary of $3,000 for the summer. Eight weeks of camp, preceded by a week of precamp orientation . . . it averaged out to around $330 a week. Considering this included room, board, and all the refreshing dips in the lake I could take, this was very fair compensation indeed.

The cool June night before I left for camp, I stood in the bedroom of our apartment, surveying the piles of clothes that covered our bed. I was still unable to commit to what I would stuff in the empty duffel bag crumpled and waiting on the floor.

Every summer, Camp Eastwind used to send a packing checklist to each camper recommending what to bring: five pairs of shorts, seven T-shirts, two bathing suits, one flashlight, three packs of DD batteries, etc. The powers-that-be seemed to have arrived at this formula by averaging out the clean laundry requirements of the most vain, finicky camper and the stinkiest, the camper who would wear the same yellowing T-shirt every day until the only remnant of its original color was a small white dot that lay over a blocked sweat duct on the left shoulder. The numbers always worked for me, apparently putting me in the fiftieth percentile of filthiness.

By the end of my camp career, I had the formula memorized. Everything practically jumped into my trunk, as if lured by the familiar musty smell that puffed out when the box was swung open. Since then, my brain had dumped some of its old, long-unused inventory, and that included my camp packing list. As I stood in our Manhattan apartment, staring blankly at the heaps of T-shirts, shorts, and jeans on my bed, I had no idea what I needed. I knew how to pack for business trips, for wedding weekends, for funerals, for ski and beach vacations, for holidays home, for company retreats. But nothing that involved bug spray, a towel, and a canteen. I asked Christine to come look.

She walked in, twisting her long, brown, wavy hair into a ponytail, her reflexive getting-down-to-business hairstyle for anything from painting a room to picking out a book to read. She is an excellent problem solver, which comes in handy, as I am often stymied by the simplest of decisions. Her brows furrowed over her dark eyes as she stared at the tiers of clothes for a long moment. "What about a pair of nice pants?" she asked.

"Nice pants?"

"Yeah. You always need one nice set of clothes," she said.

I paused. "Really?"

"You never know what might come up, so why not be prepared?"

It was a sensible point. And so I went into my closet and browsed my sensible clothes. Maybe one pair of black, creased pants. And maybe my purple, point-collared dress shirt. Just in case. And then I stopped, remembering that nobody in the history of Camp Eastwind has ever needed nice clothes. Archery would not be going semiformal. The dining hall would not institute a dress code. Sure, I could have brought a couple of button-down shirts, but only to be used on cool nights, and chosen by the rule "Only pack something you don't mind getting a macaroni-and-cheese stain on." Trying to slide back into the camp mentality meant suppressing eons of social training. It was like trying to remember all the best strategies for Freeze Tag.

I wished I had my old trunk again. I had regretfully gotten rid of it in 1993, when a girlfriend instructed me that it no longer cut it as a coffee table, no matter what color sheet I draped over it. I knew if I could just open it, lean in, and huff that moldy scent, I'd be instantly reminded of every lesson, emotion, and experience I ever had at camp. The smell evoked pancakes in the dining hall and campfires, as well as the way to rig a sailboat and the most effective method to convince a twenty-one-year-old cocounselor to buy you beer. In essence, it would conjure up Utopia, which is the way I remembered Eastwind. It was the experience against which I graded all others: pure, refreshing, innocent, exhilarating, uplifting. And that's why I was going back.

The night before leaving, I lay awake thinking about Christine. Up until now, I hadn't been overly concerned with our time apart. The occasional separation was healthy, I thought. I still loved everything about her: Her ability to infuse the most quotidian task with creativity (early in our dating life, she sent me a letter from Nantucket written mazelike over a flattened fried-clam box), her ebullient and contagious passion for books, movies, and art (the word "feh" was not in her vocabulary), her flexible sense of humor (she tittered at the most urbane of bon mots, and yet never minded the many variations I came up with for pleas to pull my finger). She was the first woman I had ever realistically imagined moving in with, let alone committing to for life. And, considering that life—if it went according to plan—would go on for a long time, I hadn't worried about cheating us of a precious few weeks together. Sure, some would argue that life is so fleeting that every day is a blessing, but we can all admit that in long-term relationships, no matter how loving, some days are more blessed than others.

Part of what kept things lively for us was my pesty nature, or at least that's the way I saw it. A few days earlier, I had followed her around the house, prodding her, "So how much are you going to miss me? Put it on a scale of 'Super Miss Me' to 'Holy Crap, I Miss You So Much, It Burns, It Burns.' Will you be able to eat? How many meals? Will eggs taste differently when missing me? What *does* missing me taste like?" Finally, she turned to me in a moment of candor and said, "I'll miss you, but to be honest, I'm kind of looking forward to some alone time."

Which was why, on my last night before going away to camp, I lay awake, listening to the occasional car beeping outside—my last traffic sounds for nine weeks. "Looking forward to some alone time" didn't sound like something a future wife should say. We weren't even married yet, and our life together was seeming more complicated. Thank God for my upcoming festival of simplicity.

CHAPTER TWO

I AM AN EXTREME NOSTALGIST. AFTER I SEE, OWN, HEAR, OR EXPERIENCE something, it entrenches itself into a special place in my memory, and I can be sure that within a few years just the mention of it will make me sigh and slip into a wistful reverie. It could be anything from an old TV show to a pair of shoes. You could show me the sadistic orthodontic headgear that terrorized my jaw for far too many childhood years and I'd gaze at it as if I were Charles Foster Kane and you'd handed me Rosebud.

This overwhelming affection for old touchstones has resulted in an unfortunate penchant for anthropomorphism. I assume that everything feels the same way about me as I do about it. For example, when it's time for a triannual closet cleaning, I find it nearly impossible to throw out old clothes. And when I do, I need to bring them to Goodwill immediately, because otherwise, when I go to sleep, I imagine a soft, frightened voice emanating from the shopping bag of discards, an old flannel shirt calling my name in panic. I once put an old, ratty armchair that was never comfortable to begin with out on the street, and I couldn't leave the apartment until either the trash truck or a garbage picker scooped it up, because I couldn't bear to see it abandoned, betrayed and alone.

Returning to camp, where every single activity, cabin, tree root, or toilet is tied to a fond childhood memory was like injecting me with nostalgia heroin. As I drove up Interstate 95 toward New England, my brain constantly shuffled through a playlist of disparate experiences, showcasing all the different and wonderful pleasures I'd be reexperiencing. My counselor days were many things—silly, wild, emotional, soul-searching, tender, outrageous, and maturing—so driving toward Eastwind I felt a delirious sense of anticipation, as if heading to a tropical island where there would be pizza, DVDs, massages, my high-school crush waiting in a bikini to confess her lust, and a chorus of my childhood idols, including but not limited to Steve Martin, Larry Bird, and the Who, all waiting to sing "For He's a Jolly Good Fellow" upon my arrival. Oh, and the ghost of my grandmother would be there to give me a hug, tell me she was proud of me, and bake me her cherished stuffed potatoes. And she wouldn't be sitting near the bikini'd crush so I wouldn't even have to feel awkward.

I've always had a horrific sense of direction. When I was a Cub Scout, the badge I had the hardest time earning was not for fire starting or knot tying, but rather for memorizing how to get to my local police and fire stations. As intently as I had studied my town map, whenever quizzed my directions would land a driver straight into the ocean. And we didn't even live in a coastal town. Yet driving up to camp from my childhood home, I felt entirely confident in where I was going.

Once I hit Maine and my route slowly devolved from interstate to local highway to rural road, the landmarks became more potently evocative, climaxing as I sped into the familiar desolate rotary on the edge of town. On it sat a gas station/grocery mart. When we successfully begged legal counselors to buy us beer, this is where they came. I could practically taste the low-priced ale we'd happily settled for. It tasted like freedom! And piss. But mostly freedom. Say, 83 percent freedom, 17 percent piss. But that was good enough.

The sun was dimming, and I drove a few miles more along an unremarkable strip of local road, then made the turn by another, dingier gas station, still in the exact state of arrested decomposition that it had always been. Cutting down that side street, Eastwind's large green-and-white sign appeared, nailed to a tree and pointing down the camp road. This was the final chute into childhood. This road would lead me right to the main parking lot, and, if I were to keep the wheel steady and drive over some rocks and trees, straight into the lake. I was almost at my safest place on earth: all the comfort of the womb, but with plenty of room to water-ski.

For two miles the road sloped gently downhill, giving my car added momentum and propelling me faster and faster toward camp, and then I hit the fork that served as Eastwind's unofficial entrance. Bear left and you hit the Office, the Dining Hall, and the three cabins where the youngest campers—aged eight to ten—lived, while to the right stood the cabins for the older boys. (All of the cabins had animal names. The older ones were mighty and lumbering—Lions, Pumas—while the youngest were less intimidating and more cutesy, like the Otters and Rabbits. It was a welcome miracle that no one took the food-chain symbolism of the cabin titles too close to heart, or we would have suffered mortal cabin raids where the thirteen-year-old Tigers would return for Rest Hour with the gristle of nine-year-old Possums stuck between their teeth.) As I followed the road downward to the left, the shading trees over the road parted and I found myself coasting into the dirt parking lot, big enough for about five camp vans. Loose gravel crunched under my tires, sounding to my overeager ears like an old mountain man with a deep voice muttering "rustic-rustic-rustic-rustic." Looming to my left was the Office, a long, dark-brown pine structure (an unspecific description, as nearly all of camp's buildings were dark brown and made of pine) built against the back side of a hill.

Staff orientation didn't begin until the next day, but I had decided to arrive a night early to get acclimated. I got out of the car, and it was quiet, the only sound the hum from a couple of motorboats taking night jaunts out on the lake. The Office was dark, but there were lights on in the Dining Hall, which sat below it, alongside the lakeshore. I pushed through its twin swinging screen doors, an act I usually associated with an entrée into cacophony. The wide-open room was lined with three rows of wood tables with metal folding chairs, normally filled with boys screaming to be heard over boys screaming to be heard over boys screaming to be heard, the auditory equivalent of a nesting doll: the deeper you went, you'd always find another headache. But tonight it was silent.

I surveyed the rest of the room. To the right was the bay of screen windows looking out on the lake ten yards away. This was not only a pastoral mealtime view, it also proved helpful when energetic sailing counselors laid out a fervent sales pitch to get kids sailing that day. You could look behind you and check the water's surface for signs of wind to see if it jibed with the counselor's promise of high-seas adventure.

On the opposite wall was a stone fireplace, which would be lit on cold, clammy, rainy days. It also marked the backdrop for the director's post-meal announcements; next to the fireplace hung a small metal bell that, when clanged, settled the boys. On its left stretched a long, rectangular window that looked into the industrial kitchen, from which the kitchen crew dispensed food and refills.

The door to the kitchen swung open, and a reedy guy with an apron ambled out. He had a matted-down bush of light blond hair on top and a goatee that was four shades darker. He stopped when he saw me, and stared. Wiping his hands on his apron, he walked over.

"Josh?" he asked.

This was just what I'd hoped for. Proof that Eastwind never forgot its boys. "Yes?" I said.

"Hey," he said, sticking out his hand. "I don't know if you remember me, but I'm Zach Simmons."

Good Lord. Zach Simmons had been one of Eastwind's youngest campers when I was last here. He was tiny and adorable, with big eyes and a perpetual smile, the kind of kid who everybody protected, even though there was no need because everyone loved him. You had to be careful with the small, fawnlike campers. Often the cutest kids had parents who thought they were flawless, which bred in them a mean streak that offered a wild disconnect the first time you witnessed it, like getting bit by an adorable puppy. But as I looked at Zach, mentally subtracting his facial hair to reconstruct the tiny boy I once knew, I remembered that he had been nothing but good.

"Holy shit, Zach!" I said, grabbing his hand, perhaps a bit too enthusiastically. "Of course! Great to see you!" And it was. Granted, I'd probably not thought of him once in the past fifteen years, but it was great to see anyone who confirmed that I had once been there. This was his eighteenth year at camp, he told me. He spent winters teaching gym in a private school in Vermont and returned to Eastwind early every summer to help set up. He'd be a counselor in the oldest campers' cabin, but he no longer taught an activity; now he was in charge of supervising and training the counselors-in-training, or CITs.

As we talked, I noticed someone else shyly approaching. "Oh," said Zach, noticing him. "Do you remember this guy?"

He was burly with a square, genial face topped by a dirty Red Sox cap. "I'm Jim Rogerson," he said. The name sounded very familiar, but unlike Zach, who looked like his younger self with a goatee slapped on, I couldn't place Jim's face.

"I was kind of trouble back then," he said with a nervous laugh.

Jim Rogerson. Suddenly I remembered. He was one of those puppies who bit. Literally. He had once gotten in trouble for biting another camper. And if it wasn't biting, it was something else. A hyperactive kid, he was constantly being dragged away from one activity or another down to the Office by a fed-up counselor. As I later learned, after his last camper year, he had applied to be a CIT, and Frank had answered with a firm no. But a few years later he convinced Frank he'd grown up, and when allowed to return, he'd proved himself responsible. Now, at age twenty-four, he was marking his fifth summer as a staff member, and every year Frank trusted him to join Zach to set things up.

I was overjoyed to see the both of them. Sure, I was nearly ten years older than they, and the last time I had seen them I was a counselor and they were tiny campers, but hey, we were all adults now. I wouldn't be patronizing about it, either; no "I remember when you were just a tiny little brat who cried at lunch." It would just be the three of us hanging out at the Staff Lounge, telling the newer staff about the old days, maybe pointing ourselves out in the old camp pictures that hung framed in the Office. We would be revered as living history.

All of this flashed through my head as I peppered them with questions about their lives and played the nostalgist's favorite game: "Do you remember that guy who . . . ?" They weren't quite as enthusiastic, though. They were friendly and happy to chat, but there was something stiff, guarded, even nervous about their demeanor. They carried themselves like they'd just bumped into their high school science teacher in a strip club. Damn my graying hair! How could they look upon me as a peer when my hair said "Dad"?

I consoled myself with the fact that this was only the first night. Over time they'd learn that the gray hair was just a cosmetic difference. Inside, I didn't feel much different from fifteen years ago. I excused myself to drive over to the Bears cabin to move in. It would be home to a bunkful of fourteen-year-olds, and I had asked Frank to be stationed there because not only had I been a counselor there for my last summer, but also I'd lived there as a camper in 1983 and '84. I figured, if you're going to try to relive your youth, why risk messing with the formula?

The cabin was located at the far north end of Eastwind, twenty yards up a hill from the idyllic Senior Cove: Windsurfing lessons were held in this calm, wide inlet, and the entire camp gathered at its beach on Saturday nights for cookouts. Right next to the Cove, the Tigers, Pumas, and Antelope cabins stretched in a line, as if lumped together as tract housing for teens. The Bears loomed above them all, although the Lions—the cabin for the oldest boys, fifteen-year-old teens—was even higher up the hill. But that was set back, nearly hidden in the woods, so they could feel removed in their own cool. If the Bears acted like the wise middle brothers who bossed around the younger siblings, the Lions were the oldest brother who occasionally came home from college and hid out in his room smoking pot.

Entering the familiar pine building, I went straight for my old corner bed and dropped my duffel. I inhaled the familiar, thick, woody odor. This was cabin smell at its purest, before it took on the very specific scents of that summer's campers: by early July the youngest cabin might have a faint scent of pee thanks to its bedwetters, while the oldest might reek of BO and mildewed bathing suits.

I fished out a flashlight and looked across the boxy cabin, with its six screened windows on each side, an empty cot under each, two of them bunkbeds. Scanning my halogen circle around the ceiling, I passed over a riot of scribbled signatures. At every session's end, the campers scrawled their name and year all over the walls. I found my name in three places, but after nearly twenty years the thick ink had faded to a light fuzz. I was tempted to trace over them before the kids got here.

That would have to wait. It was only nine P.M., but I was exhausted from all the adrenaline of anticipation. I laid out my sleeping bag and sat down on the cot to shuck off my pants. I felt my butt instantly compress the three-inch-thick foam mattress until I was sitting directly on the squeaky springs, which sank down toward the wood floor. As I slithered into my sleeping bag, I instantly discerned a problem. This cot was six-feet, one-inch long, six inches shorter than I.

It was beginning to look like a fetal-position kind of summer. And with my legs bent to fit on the bed, it was a physical feat to turn over without either falling off, getting my head or feet wedged in the metal ends of the bed, or suffocating in the sleeping bag as it clung to the worn, prison-striped, waterproofed mattress cover like a Colorform. I hoped I never succumbed to insomnia this summer, as tossing and turning was not an option.

The soft crinkling sound of my settling sleeping bag subsided a minute after I stopped moving, and all I could hear was the sound of tiny waves flopping onto the shore below me, while a bracing early-summer breeze whispered through the trees around me and through the cabin window. There could be no noise more calming and somnolent: It was the aural equivalent of drinking a mixture of Sominex, warm milk, and roofies right after getting a blow job. It was the soundtrack for the greatest sleeps of my life, and, small cot be damned, I was unconscious immediately.

CHAPTER THREE

AT FIVE THIRTY A.M., I WAS JOLTED AWAKE BY A LOUD HONKING. THE EIGHTH Avenue traffic outside my Manhattan apartment had nothing on this. It was the loons, ducklike lake residents who seemed a lot more exotic when they weren't waking me up with their squawking. They were joined by a blasting chorus of other birds. This was a parody of pastorality. A lone chickadee sweetly rousing me from its tree just outside my cabin would have been fine. But this was nature's car alarm. And soon another, more modern sound joined the birds: motorboats. Back and forth they cruised across the lake in their early-morning joyrides, their motors growing louder and then fading as they passed our cove. The only buzzing I remembered interrupting my sleep years ago as a camper were mosquitoes, and a little Off cured that. When had all this water traffic started? I remembered nothing but placid waters, maybe the occasional cigarette boat whizzing by in the afternoon to gently rock our canoes and rowboats with a bit of novelty wake.

I didn't really mind the early awakening, since I was so eager to see the camp's grounds. After grabbing a bowl of cereal in the empty dining hall, I dashed past all the activity hubs: the waterfront, the tennis courts, the wood shop, the arts-and-crafts and nature shacks, the archery range. I could spot some surface improvements, but mostly it was all so reassuringly . . . the same. Camp is such a reliable touchstone because you never have to worry about it modernizing and underscoring how dated you are. When you revisit, say, your old elementary school and see computers in every classroom, you feel prehistoric, remembering the day in fifth grade when everyone gaped in awe at a classmate's new solar calculator. But there is nothing anyone can do to a tennis court that will make you feel like you're in a different era. There are no digital nets or rackets that work by laser. I didn't have to worry about getting to the archery range and finding incredulous kids saying, "Wait, you had to aim the bow and arrow *yourself*? Then what did the robots do?" Everything was so constant, so consistent, that the more I saw around the quiet camp, the more logical it felt that soon a bugler would blow reveille and my old friends would tumble blearily out of their cabins, scratching their bedheads, scuffing down the steps in worn Teva sandals striped with dirt, while wearing stained college T-shirts inside out and backward, a Hanes Beefy-T tag flapping under their chin: the uniform of boys with no girls around to impress. We would grunt at each other, addressing each other by last names or an impromptu nickname composed of random profanity ("Hey, cockshit." "What's up, dickfuck?"). The wood shop had the same bandsaw, the sports lawn had the same soccer nets, the same kickboards were stacked at the swimming dock, so why shouldn't the same friends be lined up on their bunks?

I returned to the cabin to find another car parked next to mine. I pushed open the door, nearly slamming it into someone who yelped and hopped out of the way.

"That was close! We oughta put a bell on that thing!" he said, sticking out his hand to shake after regaining his balance. "I'm Trevor." Barrel-chested with short brown hair so precisely parted and combed that it looked like he had snapped it on like a Lego scalp, he had the blinding smile of a flight attendant, even though he was a junior high teacher from Pennsylvania. He'd been looking for something different to do with his summer break, he told me, found Eastwind, and was hired to teach rock climbing. He spoke of his love for outdoorsmanship in a way that should have said "rebel," but his polite diction and rigid, serious personality said "science teacher." He looked to be in his early thirties as well, a pleasant surprise. No doubt we were of the same mind: two men spitting in the face of maturity, hungry for the opportunity to regress.

While unpacking, he pointed out some of the books he had brought for the kids; it was a long-standing tradition that counselors read to their cabin before turning the lights out, all the way up to the Bears. The theory was that it calms the kids down after evening activities so it's easier for them to transfer into sleep mode. If you abruptly turn out the lights on a cabin full of boys whose pulses are still racing from playing soccer for evening activities, then you'll get the opposite of sleep. You'll get flipped bunks and two hours of fart noises. Being read to was one of the secret camper pleasures that kids never mentioned to their friends at home. No fourteen-year-old wanted to tell his friends that he had a bedtime story read to him before night-night, and yet there was something undeniably restful about this ritual, provided the counselor picked the right reading material. Trevor proudly waved one of his selections, a worn paperback with cover art of microscopes and molecules that could scream "No Fun" from a distance of fifty yards.

"They're four-page stories about famous scientists," he happily explained.

Hmmm. Apparently he didn't like to waste time, so he planned to alienate all the kids on the first night. Sure, in a perfect world, the campers would go to sleep inspired and illuminated by the life of Sir Isaac Newton, dreaming dropped-apple dreams and waking up with a new respect for gravity. But this was summer. Kids were coming off ten months of being lectured at by teachers. Anything that even hinted of education was going to cause a mass rebellion. If you're going to mention Jonas Salk, it had better involve the little-known part of his life when he hunted down ninjas with a chainsaw.

So perhaps we weren't both striving for immaturity this summer. But this could be a good thing. I'd feared that when the kids got here, they'd ridicule me as old and out of touch. Now at least they'd have someone worse to mock first.

Following Trevor's lead, I put away the contents of my duffel bag. My personal space consisted of a fifteen-inch-wide alley of floor next to my cot. Wood shelves lined the corner wall, a perk of being staff, while each camper got only six cubbyholes next to his bed that climbed to a shelf that ran all around the cabin over the headboards. For kids, it was a small patch of land, but sacred. When a boy was feeling petulant or cranky and someone stepped even a toe in his territory, he would yell, "Get out of my *aaaaaAAArea!*", a warning cry that rose and dipped like a siren and was heard hundreds of times a day all over camp.

I heard other counselors' cars crunch down the camp road to their nearby cabins, and the calm of the forest was punctured as they plugged in their portable stereos to give their unpacking a soundtrack. I heard occasional yells of happy reunion and saw people I'd never met looking excited to see each other. Back in the '80s, it took hours to unpack, because I was constantly interrupted by the arrival of old friends. Today I got it done in twenty minutes.

As I rearranged piles of underwear to kill time, the door swung open again and the camp director, Frank, walked in. Thin with sinewy muscles that rearranged themselves with every movement, he had a thick red beard that framed a tight smile. He greeted Trevor, then the two walked over to me.

"Hey, Frank," I said. "Good to see you. Thanks for having me up this summer."

"No problem," he said, nodding. "I think it's gonna be a great one." He clapped me on the back. In the world of male gestures, it's one of the more heartfelt signs of welcome: less formal than a handshake, more resonant than a high five. "So," he said, looking over at Trevor. "You guys have already got two-thirds of your staff together."

"Yes, we do," Trevor said peppily. "And who else are we waiting for to complete the Bears team?"

"Mitch Donelly. You probably know him, Josh."

I smiled weakly and swallowed. Oh, I knew Mitch. Suddenly I was feeling very much like a teenager again. Unfortunately, it wasn't the carefree, goofy side; it was the insecure, painfully self-aware symptoms of adolescence. And it looked like it would now be lasting for nine weeks.

Mitch's first year as a counselor was 1985, my first as a CIT. He was twenty-four years old and worked as a private-school sports coach during the year. Though he was hired as a tennis instructor, what he really wanted to do was teach kayaking. At that point the kayaking program wasn't very popular and was considered a wild, niche skill, like juggling hatchets. Mitch loved kayaking. He loved all outdoor sports: He owned his own kayak and sailboat and rock-climbing gear. He was lean with a muscular chest, and kept his shoulders hunched and his chin jutted forward as if he were a dog trying to sniff for traces of adventure. Mitch was the first of his kind to be exposed to most campers and staff, and his macho lifestyle quickly mesmerized most of them. In the staff lounge, he told stories of his adventures to an enthralled audience of coworkers. Eastwind was always an outdoorsy camp, but a couple of whitewater canoe trips were as extreme as it got. Mitch showed the counselors that there was a whole new world of adrenaline beyond hiking up and down a mountain or paddling down a bouncy river in a flooded canoe.

He started taking staff with him on his days off to go rock climbing, and quickly got them addicted. During Free Swims, he showed counselors how to do more effective and quicker rolls in a kayak, and campers gathered around to watch these tutorials. Over the next few years, I watched the staff transform into action-sport junkies, and, like crack dealers, they'd give campers a free taste and get them hooked, too. When I was first a counselor in 1986, all anybody wanted to do on a day off was go to a beach or a mall or the trashy arcade complex across the lake that had a drive-in movie theater, a go-cart track, and all the overly made-up girls you could ogle at. But by 1988, many staff were using their free time to conquer rock faces or rivers with their own ropes and boats.

I was never big into trips. I'd tackle the occasional mountain or river as a camper, but I was a homebody at heart; I loved the cozy insularity of camp and didn't like to miss its daily life. As a counselor, I first taught archery and then moved to swimming, two activities that rarely necessitated leaving camp. If Eastwind were a production of *Our Town*, I'd be the Stage Manager, sitting on the porch, keeping tabs on the camp's predictably placid life. As the number of trips grew, the camp emptied out more and more during the week. On those desolate days, with most of my friends gone, I'd sometimes get a gnawing feeling that there was a big party in the wilderness and I was the guy asked to stay behind and guard everybody's stuff. But those moments were fleeting, and certainly not enough to get me to beg for backpack duty.

At those times in the Staff Lounge when the conversation turned to all things extreme, I'd just tune out and talk instead to someone who didn't give a crap about risking his life. Sure, many of my old buddies may have come to love things that I had neither the interest nor the guts to try, but I wasn't intimidated by it. They could show me all the dented crash helmets they wanted; I still remembered them as the wee dorks who played Dungeons & Dragons on a rainy day and cried when their wizards got killed by an orc.

But Mitch was a full-grown, fully functioning man's man when I first met him, and he made me nervous. He didn't do it on purpose. I just couldn't relate to him, nor he to me. He was a natural athlete who was all about the outdoors. I was an uncoordinated teenager who loved Monty Python and quoting *Saturday Night Live*. He kept a mattress in the back of his van for conquests. I got so nervous around girls that I sweated through *their* shirts. He was all about taking life by the balls. I was perfectly happy to leave life's balls alone.

My self-consciousness around Mitch got worse every year. When he'd walk in on a bunch of us loudly horsing around in the Staff Lounge, I'd find myself quieting down and slouching deeper into one of the lounge's ratty, moldy couches. Every instance we'd find ourselves alone together would find me more tongue-tied. He remained for many years after I left in '88, and his number of followers only grew. Kayak-loving campers grew into kayak-loving counselors who taught new campers how to look into the eye of a whitecap with no fear. Even as he aged, he still had a crowd of teenage acolytes hoping to meet him out west in the fall to conquer a river or a rock face. At the occasional reunions, I'd return to camp, hugging every single person I saw, but that unabashed ebullience would abruptly pause when I'd see him; we'd formally greet each other, shake hands, stare at each other for a few moments, and then go our separate ways. If camp was the escape from all of school's rules about what a guy should be, Mitch was the reminder.

"So," continued Frank. "With you two old-timers and Trevor, you guys are my all-star cabin."

"Rock on, Bears!" said Trevor, not at all rockingly.

I forced a smile as Frank left to greet more staff. Just the night before, talking to Zach and Jim, I had felt very old indeed, and I had wished they could see how I still thought young. Now the very thought of bunking with Mitch made me feel like an awkward teenager. Somewhere in between Manhattan office life and eighth-grade gym class lay comfort: I just needed to find it.

CHAPTER FOUR

MITCH WASN'T AT DINNER WHEN THE WHOLE STAFF CONVENED FOR THE FIRST time. I was surprised that everyone looked a bit older than I expected, many in their midtwenties. This was heartening. I would only be ten years older than most, and that might back me out of the "father" demographic and into "older brother."

Many of the guys seemed to know each other, and I hung on the periphery until I was approached by a blond, athletic twenty-two-year-old with wide-open eyes that displayed a perpetual sense of giddy disbelief, as if everyone she talked to had just pulled a coin out of her ear. She introduced herself as Anne, my boss as head of swimming. I had heard that there were more female counselors here these days. There had always been a few in camp, but usually they were older than most of the staff, there with their husbands or children. (No matter their looks or age, by the end of a mostly male summer, they became, by default, the Most Beautiful Women in the World.) Through the '90s, more and more counselors started asking to bring their girlfriends, and now it had gotten to the point where women comprised about one-sixth of the staff. Plus, now they were integrated right into the cabins with boys younger than thirteen. They had their own separate quarters, but when they had cabin duty, they slept overnight there with the boys on an empty cot. Frank thought having women around was a calming presence to the younger boys, a soothing maternal force among all this testosterone. I supposed that females might help the male staff, too, the distaff presence reminding guys not to pull down their shorts and pee on the side of the camp road whenever the urge struck them. It would make the reentry into polite, coed society at summer's end less jarring.

Anne welcomed me enthusiastically, which was reassuring. She introduced me to the third member of our swim team, Helen, a compact, muscular twenty-year-old Australian who was in America for the first time. After an endless flight and bus and car rides that finished deep in Maine late the night before, Helen was suffering from a mix of crippling jet lag and culture shock, making her capable of only brief smiles and grunts of greeting.

"We may've switched things around a bit from when you were last here," Anne told me. "But that just means that we can switch it around again. If you have any ideas for ways you think we can do lessons better, let me know." Ideas? I didn't know anything—she shouldn't listen to me. It had only been a couple of weeks ago that I'd completed a Red Cross recertification course to teach swimming, and that had been the first time in fifteen years that I'd given the task a moment's thought. When I thought about the coming classes, it was with an ever-growing panic as to whether I could do this job. I didn't have suggestions, I had questions. Hundreds of them, and they all came tumbling out. How did she teach a different combination of kids each day? Which strokes should I start out with? Could she refresh my memory on some swim games so the kids wouldn't get bored with just swimming laps? What SPF sunscreen should I wear? Who would put it on my back?

She looked a little surprised by my panic. She told me not to worry, but her confused look said, "Aren't you, like, ten years older than I? Shouldn't you have your shit slightly more together about a job that you did just fine when you were a teenager?" It was true, I didn't remember having any troubles when I taught it last. Over the past few days I had feverishly searched my memories for my old secrets to teaching. I couldn't come up with any, and that was likely because I had no secrets, I just did it. But now, after more than a decade in the professional work-force, that approach was anathema. You didn't just *do* a job. You agonized over it, worried about whether your superiors noticed if you did some-thing wrong, and obsessed about whether they noticed that you'd done something right.

Along with my vanished teaching skills, tonight I was also at a loss over what happened to my social skills. After Anne hopped off to greet her old friends, I looked around at the flurry of happy reacquaintances around me. I could think of no entrée, and to the few people who intro-duced themselves, I demonstrated the wit and charisma of a life jacket. When a buffet dinner of salad and pork chops was brought out, I filled my plate and sat next to Helen, since we had two things in common: we were both teaching swimming and we were both friendless. Plus, I had been to Australia two years prior, so right there we had *loads* to talk about. Unfor-tunately, I was so eager to have a conversation that I forgot that the rules of dating apply to any first-time social interaction: when you show your-self as being needy, the other person will walk away. On and on I went about Australia: *I've been to Sydney! What about that Great Barrier Reef, huh? I find Vegemite to be quite disgusting. And boomerangs: what's up with them?*

After ten more minutes of this, she excused herself to get seconds. Or to kill herself. Either would have been understandable, really. Sitting near me were the kitchen girls. Frank often found his kitchen workers through a company that helped young foreign people who wanted a summer job opportunity in America. This year they had come from Latvia, Kazakh-stan, and Poland, and they barely spoke English. They huddled together shyly, and I looked at them and smiled. They smiled weakly back, and we all shrugged at each other. And then we spent the rest of the meal speaking the international language of awkward silence.

After we'd all cleared our plates, Frank had us push back the tables and arrange our metal folding chairs in a giant circle. "It's great to see every-body here tonight," he said, leaning against a table. "We've got a really great staff this year and it's going to be a fantastic summer. I know a lot of you folks, and a lot of you know each other, but we've also got a lot of new faces. So why don't we just go around the room and everybody can share a little bit about yourself."

I listened to everyone's dossier. One I recognized—Chas, a wild-haired sailing instructor whom I remembered as a small, theater-loving camper who was obsessed with knights. That fascination with all things swordplay had turned into a career: Now he often worked at Renaissance festivals and Medieval Manors as a jouster and duelist. Some were familiar by proxy, like Ethan the tennis counselor, whose older brother I had once taught to dive. There were a few seventeen-year-olds, coming off their CIT summer to be counselors for the first time. You could see them attempting to look grown-up amidst all the college graduates. To me, they looked uncamouflageably young. I wondered if seeing such a young face on their kids' summer guardian would make parents ill at ease on opening day. Then again, would it be any less off-putting to drop their kids off with me? At least it made sense for a teenager to be a camp counselor. But when a gray-haired thirty-three-year-old greeted you at a cabin door, that raised more disturbing questions than it answered. I had to remember never to use the phrase, "Your son will be in good hands." No sense panicking anyone.

As the intros went round and round, I rehearsed mine in my head. I knew the dangers of a bad introduction. I had once seen a new nature counselor show up the first day wearing a jaunty, green-felt Peter Pan hat. I was aware of how difficult it was for a first-timer to fit in, so I generously gave his cap the benefit of the doubt. And then came his turn to speak.

"Hi!" he said. "I'm Ned. I'll be teaching nature, and I like kites!"

Maybe I could have forgiven the Lost Boy headgear, but he lost me and everyone else at kites. Needless to say, for the rest of the summer, nobody was lining up to take his day off with Ned. Especially on windy days.

My turn came and went anticlimactically. My mention of being here from 1980 to 1988 elicited neither gasps nor applause, especially coming after Zach announced that this was his eighteenth summer. Even mentioning that I was a writer for *Entertainment Weekly* did nothing for people. In a new crowd, that revelation is usually met with pleas for celebrity gossip or stories about stars I've met. I'm not proud when what makes me interesting is only the fact that I've encountered interesting people, but with new faces I'd pimp out whatever I needed. However, in the Venn diagram of life, the circles of camp people and pop-culture addicts seemed to overlap only on me. Nobody here was particularly wowed by the fact that I'd chatted with Madonna and Woody Allen. Had I written for *Crevasse Monthly* or *Paddle Fancy*, I would have been swarmed.

When the circle returned to Frank, he said we'd start with something to loosen us all up, and then invited Amit, an Indian wood-shop counselor with a gentle face and shaved head, to come forward. Amit bounced to the center of the room and clapped his hands. "All right, we're gonna do something fun."

That intro could mean only one thing: New Games, the getting-to-know-you staple of camps, youth groups, and nonprofit retreats since the '70s that typically involved asking ten people to balance on a small wooden square, or arrange themselves by birthday without speaking, or extricate themselves from a "human knot" of hands clasped through each other's legs. All this amidst the ubiquitous "trust falls," in which you picked a partner, closed your eyes, and fell backward into a stranger's arms. New Games were ideally meant to teach you that you could count on each other. To me, the trust always seemed predicated on these precisely orchestrated situations. I never extrapolated from these exercises that this particular group of people would always be there for me—just that they would be there when ordered by an authority figure to do so. It didn't exactly make me skip through life confident that I always had a safety net.

Tonight we'd be doing New Games strictly for entertainment purposes. Amit had an encyclopedic knowledge of them. For tonight's kickoff sport, he had selected something called "Toilet Tag." It was a melee where the "It" (Amit) chased everyone around our circle, and when he tagged you, you needed to become a toilet. You did so by getting down on one knee and bending your arm up at an "I'm a little teapot" right angle, flexing your hand 90 degrees to serve as your flusher. To free you from your scatological prison, another player sat on your knee and "flushed" your hand, and away went your troubles, along with your dignity.

I turned to Helen, a stricken look on my face. "But I'm thirty-three years old" was all I could blurt out. She cackled loudly for the first time. I wasn't joking.

The game began, and everyone dashed around, arching their backs to narrowly avoid Amit's flailing arms. I speedwalked around the room, unable to commit to full enthusiasm. I knew the point of games like this was to make everyone loosen up because you're all acting silly together. But that rationale had never been enough for me. It was the same reason I'd always hated Halloween. Instead of making me comfortable looking dumb, I thought, how about I just don't look dumb.

I felt Amit's fingers strafe my back, and I slowly lowered myself to one knee. Now I am a toilet, I thought. No, do not free me, my fellow players. Save yourselves, and leave me in my bathroom ignominy. My flusher hung limp at the end of my arm; I could not bring myself to keep it erect. And as I knelt there, I saw the rear dining hall door swing open, and in came Mitch, looking bemused at the room full of half-man, half-potty chaos that he'd walked in on.

Had I wanted to make the first impression to him that I was no longer the dorky teenager he once knew, I certainly wouldn't have opted to do it while impersonating a toilet. As it was, we picked up where we left off: me feeling foolish, him magically able to arrive at a moment where he was the only one left looking cool. Guys like that always do, while the rest of us are always in the middle of picking loose a wedgie or tidying up a nostril.

CHAPTER FIVE

JUST AS MITCH WALKED IN, AMIT ARBITRARILY CALLED THE GAME TO A HALT, because in Toilet Tag, everybody was a winner. I flushed myself, lifted myself off my knee, and went back to my seat, where Mitch was standing. He looked exactly the same, with maybe a little less hair. He wore shorts and flip-flops even though it was cold, and I could see the ropy muscles traversing his legs. Perhaps he had carried his van all the way from his home in Vermont. He looked surprised to see me, and I wrenched on a huge smile and said hello. Who knew, maybe he would see in me the adult I was and an instant kinship would flower.

"Hey, Mitch!" I said, a little too eagerly.

"Josh, man, how's it going?" We shook hands.

"Wild to be back," I said.

"I'll bet," he said. And then an uncomfortable silence enwrapped us both like a scratchy blanket.

"Yeah, it's been a long time." I wondered if I was more ill at ease now or as a toilet.

"All right," he said, breaking the moment. "Let me go say hey to Frank." Okay, I thought. Bears 2003, best cabin ever!

The rest of the evening, Frank gave us an introductory pep talk. It was

34

his most seasoned staff ever, he crowed, then went over some basic goals for the summer: making sure every kid tried something new, eradicating bullying, and, his one nonnegotiable for the summer, eliminating destructive gossiping among the staff. This last point was intensely important to him, though it seemed naive to me. After twelve years of New York's whisper-prone office life, I thought that asking staff not to gossip seemed as much a fantasy as asking that everyone stay dry while swimming in the lake. But Frank didn't see it that way. He radiated pure idealism. When anyone volunteered his thoughts on making the summer better, he'd shake his head in gleeful wonderment and say, "That's *awesome!*" And in the truest, least Bill-and-Ted sense of the word. The idea of creating a haven where kids couldn't get a bee sting without it being a glorious teaching moment jazzed him immeasurably. He appeared to be a man free of cynicism who longed for simpler times; as we touched on some of the issues we might encounter this summer—precocious sexual talk, violent attitudes, fragile self-image—he attributed many to the damning effects of popular culture. And as someone who worked at a magazine entirely devoted to pop culture, I found it difficult not to stand and apologize.

Before stopping for the night, Frank pointed out that we had a few first-time Eastwinders on the staff this year. "Eastwind's a special place," he said. "It's different, not just a camp. So I was hoping that some of you other guys could explain to them just what makes Eastwind so special. Anyone?"

Many hands went up. This was a question that Eastwinders were dying to answer. "We take the job very seriously." "This is a place kids can come without being judged." "The peaceful beauty of this spot." "Kids leave here better and more confident than when they came." I wondered how this sounded to the newbies: They were out in the woods, surrounded by a bunch of proselytizing strangers extolling the virtues of a wonderland. It followed the Cult Recruitment Playbook to a word. It also felt slightly odd to me that my deep personal kinship with the place was not so unique that it couldn't be shared by a roomful of strangers. But Frank's earnestness worked. I couldn't help feeling more bonded with the group.

After the meeting disbanded, people wandered up to the Staff Lounge to share an inaugural beer. I lagged behind, and I quickly found myself lost in the woods. The lounge was only about forty yards from the Dining Hall, on a path that cut through dense trees. I used to instinctually make that walk in the pitch black without a flashlight. But that internal GPS had broken down, and even with a powerful Maglite and seeing the light from the lounge in the distance, I kept losing the path and finding myself snarled in branches. I grew flushed, wondering how I'd explain to someone who saw my light bouncing in the woods why I was bushwhacking three feet from the footpath.

Once I found it, I saw that the lounge had been significantly improved since my days. It was still a disgusting pit, but a far roomier pit. There was now space enough for four wildly ugly and worn couches arranged in a square around a rickety coffee table littered with playing cards and cribbage boards. A dartboard hung off to the side. When I walked in, staffers were sprawled on the couches, laughing and reminiscing. There was no room to sit, so I leaned against a wall, figuring a diagonal stance would minimize the appearance of lurking. I listened and half-nodded along with a flurry of conversations going on around me, trying to find my way in. I desperately wished Christine were here. I'm a reticent mingler in the best of circumstances, while she can effortlessly chat with any stranger. It was one of the great inequities of our relationship that she was responsible for assisting me into conversations not just at her own office Christmas parties, but at mine, too.

While many of the counselors were drinking beer, the get-together wasn't as boisterous as in the old days. When I was last here, the in-camp drinking age was eighteen, the director's rationale being that if a counselor could be responsible for the lives of ten kids on the side of a mountain, how could he say that staffer wasn't responsible enough to have a beer when he got home? In 1999, Frank, troubled by the amount of partying in camp, had raised it to the state age, a wildly unpopular decision with the younger staff. Though I'd never mention it to any of the more junior counselors sadly sipping their Cokes, I was relieved by this ruling. While there are few things more exciting than being a drunk teenager, there are few things more annoying than being around a drunk teenager. When I got drunk at Eastwind for the first time at seventeen (jumping the gun on camp's "legal" age), I remember actually slurring the words, "There'sh no one I'd rather do thish with than you guysh" to my fellow counselors. "You guysh are the *besht*." To make matters more clichéd, we were listening to Billy Joel and had just put our arms around each other to sing "Piano Man." I didn't need to see that again.

Mitch was hunkered deep into one of the rattiest sofas, his flip-flops planted firmly on the table. He was the epicenter of a group debriefing on river and rock-climbing trips taken over the year. They joked with a shorthand that was alien to me, name-checking a series of rock faces and rivers and classes of rapids that I hadn't heard of. The phrase "shredding the gnar" kept coming up, and I had no idea what that meant. It was clear that my collection of anecdotes about how, say, Nathan Lane was kind of a prick during a film junket I once attended would have no cachet here whatsoever.

Finally, I set down my beer bottle and made my way back to the door. No one noticed when I left. I decided to call Christine, so I thrashed my way through the woods to the Office. The large building was Frank's HQ, but it also had a big, open room with a long table that the staff often hung out around. When I walked in, two of the kitchen girls were morosely tapping out e-mails on the pair of staff computers. They looked as lonely as I felt. They probably didn't know what "shredding the gnar" meant either, which could have been a great bonding topic if only there were other English words they did know. I went to one of the Office's two phones, curled myself into a corner to simulate privacy (cursing the fact that my cell phone didn't get service at camp), and dialed Christine.

She picked up and was happy to hear my voice. I liked that feeling. I whispered quietly, "I think I've made a terrible mistake."

"What's wrong?"

"This whole thing is just wrong. I don't belong here anymore. I don't know anybody here, and nobody knows me. They don't know anything about me. It's like I was never here."

She sighed. "It's only the first night."

"I *know*. It's not like I'm throwing my shit in the car and leaving. It's just really fucking depressing, that's all."

"What did you say? I can barely hear you."

I tried to speak louder, upgrading from a whisper to a mutter. "I said I'm staying, it's just depressing, that's all."

"I know, but it'll get better," she said. "What's been happening?" Just then a few more counselors came in and plunked down around the table. I smiled weakly and then burrowed farther into the corner. Once more than half of the spectators in the room were English-speaking, I didn't feel comfortable complaining aloud.

"Nothing much," I said blandly. "Just met everybody. Good group, good group."

" 'Good group, good group?' That doesn't sound depressing. Seriously, what's wrong?"

I glanced at the computer next to me. I wondered how the kitchen girl was getting crazy Kazakhstanian letters to pop up on Hotmail. I turned back and pressed my forehead harder against the Office wall. If it broke through, I'd have some privacy on the other side. "Look, there are a lot of people here. I don't want to bother them, so let's talk about it later."

"Is it because someone might hear you?"

I changed the subject. "Have you talked to Kate yet?" Kate was a photographer friend of hers who was going to shoot our wedding. As the words came out of my mouth, I felt the receiver grow cold.

"I'm still not sure I want to do that."

I winced. "Please tell me you're kidding." We had disagreed on so much during the wedding planning that even now, three months before the date, the items we'd actually resolved were so few that I cherished them like troubled children we'd finally sent off to college. I'd thought that getting a photographer was one of them. But now it looked like it had flunked out and had come home, asking for its old room back.

The very idea of wedding photos was too traditional and generic for Christine. When I mentioned them, she could only imagine soft-focused mattes of brides nuzzling their bouquets while looking over their shoulders. To her, it was a slippery slope from this to tossing her garter and doing the Macarena. This standoff was indicative of the entire wedding-planning process. We were now expecting around two hundred people at our wedding, but Christine had been against a big ceremony from the very beginning. She initially had wanted to exchange our vows at City Hall. Her view was that getting married was a very personal moment, not a spectator sport. I, on the other hand, loved the idea of gathering all our family and friends together for a big bash. Sitting at camp, awash with lonely self-pity, the idea had never seemed more appealing.

The arguments had gone on for months as we searched for a happy medium. A small wedding? No, that seemed pointless to me. A medium-sized party? No, once we factored in the family that *had* to be invited, it left no room for our friends. A private ceremony, and then a big party later? We couldn't agree on whether we'd elope for the vows, or just have our parents there. (I suggested we have a big wedding, but have the guests put paper sacks over their heads for the ceremony to maintain privacy . . . and quickly learned there was nothing funny about this suggestion.) It all became moot once we made a list of who we both wanted there (her family is especially large), and it became inevitable that ours would be a two-hundred-person affair. Her subsequent panic grew right along with the size of the bash.

Christine's worries always came back to it being an *impersonal* ceremony. She lived in fear of the generic. In even the smallest get-together at our apartment, she made sure there were a few surprise dishes to amaze and delight the guests who, like me, expected only chips and a soup-mix-based dip. She believed there was no sense inviting people over to your house if you weren't going to make it personal. And a wedding was the largest and most personal party she could imagine, and the pressure to keep it that way was overwhelming. When she thought of big weddings, her mind instantly flashed to every identical, bad-bridesmaid-dressing, Pablo-Neruda-reading, some-cousin-with-a-flute-tooting betrothal she'd ever been to. She wanted something unique so passionately that she would explode upon hearing any wedding-related word, or even something that just sounded like one. Mention skiing at Vail and she'd scream, "You'll get me in a veil when you pry it onto my cold, dead head!" It took months of slow, patient pleading to convince her that I didn't want any of that regular wedding crap either: Like her, I didn't want groomsmen or brides-maids (we were too old to worry about ranking our friends), a first dance (too showy), or line dancing (too shitty). I just wanted a fun, happy night.

Fortunately, she trusted her mother, who, having spent the last couple of years traveling in Vietnam, Thailand, and China, floated the idea of fill-ing the reception with Asian touches. What could be less generic than that? (Assuming you're not Asian.) Over the spring, she and her mother spent long phone calls discussing decorations and colors and set-ups and many other things that made me sleepy. But I dared neither complain about nor disagree with any of it lest the whole house of cards tumble.

By the time I had left for camp, some things were shakily certain, but much remained in flux. I had been both thrilled and afraid to be leaving for the final few months before the wedding. Thrilled because I would be out of the way when another wave of doubt came crashing, and fearful because if I wasn't there to break the surf, who knew what could happen: I could return and find out that she had already gotten married to D. B. Cooper on an Arctic ice floe, just to prove to me what a small and private wedding really looked like.

And now yet another thing was being removed from the "done" column. "I feel like I'm being bullied into these photos," she said.

"Bullied?" I squawked. "I'm asking to get pictures taken at our wedding, I'm not trying to get you into donkey porn." Everyone, including the kitchen girls, looked up. I wondered whether "donkey porn" was the same in any language.

"Yeah, well, I'm still not sure."

"Christine," I whispered. "You know Kate. You know better than me that she's incapable of doing tacky work. Even if I got six of my strongest friends to hold you down while I smushed a piece of wedding cake into your face, she'd refuse to take the cap off her lens."

"Don't even *think* that we're going to feed each other cake!"

"That . . . was . . . just . . . an example," I said with a calm inversely proportional to my frustration. "Look, let's talk about this later."

"Later? Why can't we resolve this?"

"We just can't, it'll be fine."

"Is it because people are around?"

"Maybe," I said, speaking only in words that would remain noncommittal to observers on my end. "Yes."

"Is that the way this is going to be all summer?" she said angrily. "Because we've still got a lot to do, and I'd like it if we could have a real conversation."

"We can e-mail."

"E-mail! I've got to plan this thing fast, I can't wait for you to sit down and craft a diplomatic policy paper! We have to talk like normal people."

We sat in mutual, perturbed silence. I continued the argument in my head and was doing quite well until she broke the quiet with a determined calm. "I'm sorry you're having a bad time. I am. But I need you to be patient with me on this. And by 'patient' I mean responsive. We order the invitations next week and then there's no turning back."

"I kind of thought there already was no turning back."

"Don't push it. It's a mental leap. I feel like once these get printed, I'm stuck with this giant party that I'm still not sure what to do with. And you are in camp and I'm glad of that, but while you're bummed out there, I'm completely panicking here. Plus, I leave for Los Angeles in ten days." She was heading west for a five-week freelance job on a TV show. "So I'm a bit stressed, too. And when I think of the photos, it makes me think of a cake, and it makes me think of the dress, and then I think of everybody staring at me wearing the dress, and next thing you know I'm freaking out."

"All right, I get it," I said.

"You get it, and . . ."

"And I get it."

"No, 'I get it and I love you. Dearly.' "

"I get it and I love you."

"I didn't hear 'dearly.' Or if you add an adverb, will the other counselors discover you have emotions and then chase you with torches?"

"I love you dearly."

"All right, now go poop in the woods or whatever you do there to cheer yourself up. Good night."

"Good night. And Christine?"

"Yes?"

"It's gonna be a great wedding."

She exhaled slowly. "You better hope so."

CHAPTER SIX

IN THE WEEK LEADING UP TO THE KIDS' ARRIVAL, WE DIVVIED UP OUR TIME
between setting up our activities, cleaning up the camp, and convening for
counseling workshops. Many of Frank's tutorial themes were familiar, like
the difference between discipline and punishment, and the importance of
identifying and heading off scapegoating. But then we delved into sexuality. The issues were specific and probing: What do you do when your
teenage campers' adolescent joking about women goes from clueless bragging to violent misogyny? What about a kid who is tormented for being
effeminate? Or the overuse of the epithet "faggot"? And what about the
borderline, presexual goings-on we might encounter? One staffer recalled
how in a previous summer he had walked into a cabin and found two nine-
year-olds wrestling naked in a sleeping bag. What was the correct, non-
stigmatizing reaction to *that*?

In the old Eastwind era, sexual issues were touched upon when they
became untenable. My last year as a camper, someone in the Lions smug-
gled in some truly horrific German porn magazines, the kind that simultaneously gave you erections and nightmares. They became such a source of
fascination that the campers barely left their cabin to eat, and the assistant
director had to stage an intervention, giving a long bunkside chat on

pornography and respecting women that convinced them to relinquish their stash of *das Poonenshtup* and continue a more uncorrupted summer. Now, Frank was hyperaware that boys were being overwhelmed by more than just confusing hormones. They spent ten months of the year having movies, TV, and the Internet—Frank's bugaboos—grind sex into their eyeballs and earholes, feeding those hormones until they were fat and angry. When I was a teenager, life was one long search for nudity. Hence the German porn: you took what you could get, no matter how frightening or foreign. This quest for nudity seemed positively Rockwellian compared to the fact that kids today could summon up every possible orifice with one Google search. I remember my parents complaining about sex on television when I was watching *The Love Boat*, but that was nothing compared to a world with www.hotshavednuns.com. And that was the world that our campers would be coming from.

It was a different world when it came to any human contact, too. Like hugging. In my day, a nice manly embrace was a fine way to make a camper feel good about himself. It imbued a feeling of equality and maturity on even the youngest boys. When a counselor greeted me with a big hug in the same way that I'd seen other adults warmly greet each other, it felt like I'd been welcomed into the brotherhood of men. But in today's paranoid and litigious world, *everything* was suspect. All it would take was one kid to misconstrue a congratulatory hug, or one parent to misconstrue a son's happy recollection of a congratulatory hug, and the camp could be buried in a sea of torts faster than you could say "Court TV."

It was painful to watch Frank try to reconcile the realities of what made a kid's day versus what made a lawyer's day. In the midst of a session on how to deal with an unhappy camper, Frank looked pained as he interjected that he thought we shouldn't hug anybody. The staffers murmured and hubbubbed.

"Not at all?" asked Jousting Chas. "I think it really helps these kids. I'm not saying we should paw at them, but what about when a kid is sad? His dad would hug him, and we're kind of his dad here."

"Yeah, I know . . ." Frank grimaced and furrowed his brow. He had been a camper. And he was a dad. He knew from both sides that it was a self-defeating rule. "You just have to be careful today. But I know how important it can be in some moments." He thought. "Then maybe a side hug is OK." He mimed putting his arm around a kid's shoulder and giving him a double shake.

"So that's what we have to limit it to?" asked another staffer. "We have to maneuver ourselves to the side like that?" Perhaps this way one arm could be free to point at hot chicks our own age and prove the embrace had no ulterior motive. The debate continued, with counselors recounting personal experiences when a well-timed hug had increased a bond with a camper. Frank would never argue with any moment that made a kid's summer, and the tight-lipped expression he wore reflected his inner struggle. "Look, I leave it up to your personal judgment," he finally decreed. "I don't want to tell anyone that they can't give a kid what he needs. So you can give a hug, just, uh, no lingering."

The week wore me out. I absorbed all of these workshops with an *Is there going to be a test?* intensity, nervous that if I missed any of the warning signs for a bedwetting camper I would get bumped down to CIT. And between sessions, I exhausted myself attempting to befriend the other counselors. After each night in the Staff Lounge, my muscles ached, as if I'd sprained my gregarious muscle. *Ingratiate with the legs, not with the back.*

On the third night, I felt like I made some progress with Mitch. He had selected the bed on the far corner of the Bears, across from Trevor, and he came over to talk as I was writing in my journal. He sat down and started telling me about his new motorboat that he'd brought up to camp, all the better to dominate land and sea, I guessed. Knowing nothing about boats, I seized on our one commonality, past Eastwind staff, and asked him about some guys I knew he was still in touch with. He then launched into a gripping and salacious rundown of every bit of camp gossip he had accrued in the past fifteen years. It was the greatest bedtime story I'd ever heard in my life, filled with drunken hookups, fistfights, and cuckoldings. I wasn't sure how much of it was actually true and how much was idle rumor elevated to fact in his mind, but it was no less entertaining for it. Mitch was an eager storyteller, although his energy flagged during my stories. The same went after he caught me up to date on his life, and the major river trips he took over the past year; when it was my turn he tuned out for some paddling on the river in his mind.

This was a tiny step forward, although it didn't entirely loosen me up. The next day I was sitting around at the end of lunch when Mitch came out of the kitchen with a giant institutional vacuum cleaner he was trying out on the wood floor. After noticing it wasn't picking up a big spill, he announced, "It doesn't suck anymore," presenting a straight-line setup as tantalizing as a chocolate cupcake. So many options: I could have gone with either an oral-sex zinger ("Try buying it dinner, Mitch") or something more all-purpose ("Look on the bright side: Nobody will ever be able to say that about you"). But instead, stalled with nervousness, I just nodded in sympathetic, literal agreement: Yes, it was a shame that the sucking powers of the vacuum were no longer functioning correctly.

Fortunately, I was slowly finding friends elsewhere. I developed an easygoing rapport with two international counselors: Sean, a sandy-haired, wiry Brit, was unceasingly friendly, the kind of guy who will remain interested in one of your stories long after you yourself have realized it has no point. He was a five-year Eastwind veteran, although this was his return after two years off. He had quit his teaching job in England last year, deciding to pursue a career as a professional windsurfer. "I followed my dream to Australia," he told me, "and left the dream there." He'd decided to take another summer at camp at age twenty-nine to figure out what was next. Reg, another Aussie, sported spiky blond hair and chunky, black, shoelace-less sneakers, but his punky presentation was at odds both with his conservative job back home (tech support for a government agency) and his capitalist dreams: All he wanted was to be an entrepreneur. His business goals didn't get much more specific; at twenty-three he just wanted to create *anything* that would make him a fraction of the fortune of his idol, Bill Gates.

I'm not sure why my personality seemed more appealing to foreigners. (Helen, too, had become more friendly, to the point where she laughed wildly at whatever I said, whether it was a joke or not. "I'm off to get another bowl of cereal" was enough to have her pounding the table in hysterics. I chalked her mania up to withdrawal symptoms from her jet lag.)

Perhaps in their countries, social discomfort was revered as a sign of wisdom. Whatever the reason, I gladly accepted their camaraderie.

On one of our last nights of orientation, Sean assured Reg and me that we were in for a treat. The staff assembled in the Dining Hall for a defensive driving course, and Frank introduced Shelly, a stocky local driving instructor who came in every couple of summers to teach Frank's staff about safety. He was in his fifties and puffed out his chest, the aggressive stance of the middle-aged man determined to prove he can still kick a younger man's ass. I looked around the room and saw that Sean and the other returning counselors all had anticipatory grins on their faces. Perhaps Shelly was the one man in America who could make side-view mirrors entertaining.

The show began. "Let me tell you a little bit about myself," he said forcefully, pacing the floor. "I was an army grunt. I did three tours in 'Nam. I saw a lot of things." This was an odd opener for a driving lesson. Would we be navigating traffic circles or booby-trapped tunnels? As if to answer my question, he explained how it all tied together. "In an accident you don't know what's happening. Like in the jungle, when you don't know whether your next step will be your last." And so began a course I would later refer to as *Apocalypse Rotary*.

According to Shelly's metaphor, once you put yourself in danger—by either sneaking up on Charlie when all you had was a can opener and a shiv you made out of a filling you pried out of your own tooth, or by driving four miles over the speed limit—then all your reflexes couldn't do anything to save you if something went wrong. "Let's say you're driving down a two-lane road and a minivan is suddenly coming right at you," he said, then randomly called Trevor to stand up and join him. Shelly shook his hand, then calmly began asking him questions as if he were Alex Trebek chatting up a *Jeopardy!* contestant. Where you from? How long have you been driving? Do you have a good record? And then in the middle of his next question—BAM!—he abruptly lashed out with a flat hand, stopping with the heel of his palm a centimeter under Trevor's nose.

"Didn't see *that* coming, did you?"

A still-startled Trevor gulped no.

"This is what we call the 'one-hit kill,'" Shelly continued. "Hit the nose, drive it up into the brain. It's over. You're *gone*. But let's do it in slow motion, give you time to react. What do you do when I come at you?" He slowly moved his palm toward Trevor's face, and Trevor bent his neck to the left to dodge it. Shelly shook his head at the predictability of it all. "Well, now you're dead. If you go that way, I come up with my foot"—he swiveled and brought his leg up in a judo move—"and kick your larynx."

I was confused. An oncoming minivan can kick you in the larynx? I didn't know Dodge Caravans could do that. Well, if I ever did get my ass kicked by a minivan, I hoped it would kill me. I'd seen *The Deer Hunter*: I didn't want to get dragged back to its camp and made to play Russian roulette with a bunch of scared Priuses.

I watched in amused disbelief as the lecture continued in this absurdly militant fashion, a mix of war tales and life lessons, including the fact that he was a fierce competitor who never let his kids beat him in sports. "My son didn't beat me at basketball until he was seventeen. When they were six, seven years old? I'd *crush* them!"

When it was all over, Shelly—and what a paradoxically effete name that was, like a serial killer named Timmy—bid us all safe driving and headed back home, presumably to throw a basketball at his son's head and call him a pussy. With everyone feeling like we'd just sat through a four-hour director's cut of *Platoon*, I went up to the Staff Lounge with Sean, Reg, and a few others to decompress. Reg slumped down on a couch, visibly annoyed.

"What's wrong?" I asked.

"This 'one-hit kill' thing, it's bullshit," he grumbled.

The rest of us laughed. "*That's* the only part of it you found stupid?" asked Chas.

"It's daft, mate," he continued. "You cannot kill someone that way." Reg was a born debunker and conspiracy theorist. Shelly's maneuver probably went against every kill-zone how-to he'd read from equally sketchy Internet sources.

Jeannie, a hearty Virginian tennis counselor who was there with her hiking-counselor boyfriend, walked in. "What's going on?"

"Reg's a bit pissed at Shelly for teaching us the one-hit kill. Thinks it's bad info," said Sean.

"That dude was *crazy*," said Jeannie, getting herself a beer.

"Crazy?" I said, standing up and glaring at her while expanding my chest and assuming the Shelly posture. "Crazy is when you're up to your chin in a rice paddy, the enemy's two clicks away, and all you've got to protect yourself is a Saltine cracker and your love for the USA." I paused. "So don't drink and drive."

Everybody laughed. "Oh, you think that's funny?" I said. "We'll see how funny it is when you're in the jungle getting fragged by heavy artillery and the last thing you see before it all goes black is your best friend Schultzy, the one who saved your ass three times for each butt cheek, take one right in the chest. And he's a fucking hero—a HERO!—but who's gonna give a shit, what with all those peaceniks turning Tricky Dick into some pussy who's afraid to give us what we need to win? Who, *you*? I don't think so. And that's why you need to check your rear *and* side-view mirrors before changing lanes."

Stomping around the room, abruptly lashing out with a judo chop that I claimed could circumcise a man (the "one-hit snip"), I had the room roaring, and I felt at ease in the Staff Lounge for the first time that summer. After beating the impression to death, I plopped back onto the couch, woozy with comfort. I was being myself with not just one person, not two people, but seven people. It was as if the stopper that had been jamming up my voice box had been yanked, and I was now comfortably babbling about any random topic. Most-hated foods, guilty-pleasure bands, most painful skin rashes we'd suffered . . . no matter how inane the topic, I could bat it around effortlessly with the group.

Jeannie picked up a deck of cards. "Anyone want to play cribbage?" she asked.

I didn't know how to play, I said. "You've gotta learn," said Sean. "It's the Eastwind card-game addiction."

"I don't need another game as a monkey on my back," I said. Two years before someone had introduced "Speed Scrabble" to Christine and me: By using just the tiles without the board, you raced to create your own grid, adding more tiles as the game went on. Our competitive streak as-

sured that we played endlessly, constantly trying to humiliate the other al-
phabetically. We tried to teach it to other friends, but we'd been unable to
temper our fevered rivalry, which inevitably made the game no fun for any
struggling newcomers.

"I *love* Scrabble," said Jeannie. "That sounds fun. I think there's a
board around somewhere, maybe in the Office."

I leapt off the sofa, vowing to bring it right back. I dashed down the
path to the Office, playing out yet another best-friend-to-all scenario in
my head. Jeannie would love Speed Scrabble and teach it to her boyfriend,
and he would bring tiles on his river trips and teach some campers, and
they would get addicted, and it would become known as "Josh's Game"
and would so consume the camp that the trips department would fizzle
from lack of interest, leaving Mitch paddling down a river alone, a lone
tear dripping into the water so he's *LITERALLY KAYAKING IN A
RIVER OF HIS OWN TEARS!* The kids might go home pale with atro-
phied muscles from playing word games all summer long, but what they
gave up in outdoorsmanship they'd more than make up in spelling acuity.

Rummaging around the Office's storage closet, I found tennis balls,
juggling pins, and Wiffle ball bats, but no Scrabble. I jogged down to the
Dining Hall, which had a game cabinet I rifled through. Othello, Risk,
Monopoly . . . Scrabble! There it was, in a frayed red box with masking
tape on each corner to reattach the split edges. I picked it up and sped back
to the Office. As I got closer to the Lounge, I heard more noise. Hopping
up the steps, I swung open the door and saw that in my absence, most of
the other staff had arrived. My intimate gathering of seven had turned into
an all-staff party in only fifteen minutes. I could see Jeannie sitting on her
boyfriend's lap amidst a gaggle of hikers who had commandeered the sofas, listening to a Mitch adventure tale. Reg and Sean had been absorbed
into a rambunctious darts game, while a few other counselors argued over
the tunes blaring out of the decrepit stereo in the corner.

It was a raucous blast. The older staff looked ready for a long night of
drinking.

And I stood at the door with a Scrabble board.

I couldn't have looked like a bigger buzzkill if I'd been wearing a giant
pin that read THEY CALL IT "DOPE" FOR A REASON. Did I imagine it, or had

everyone at the party whispered "narc" in unison? All of the good cheer I'd built up that night vanished as quickly as if I'd picked a rackful of vowels. I slowly slouched into the corner, sliding the board game on top of the refrigerator.

The kids may have been more complicated these days, with their precociousness and sexual-identity issues and societally twisted psyches, but I still couldn't wait for them to arrive. I may still prove to be old in their eyes, but at least to them the whole staff would be old. From that vantage point, I'd be in the uncool majority.

CHAPTER SEVEN

MONDAY, JUNE 23, WAS CAMPER ARRIVAL DAY. WHICH MEANT BREAKFAST would be the last quiet meal the staff would have for the next eight weeks. I savored the crinkle of the cereal bags, the gentle splash of milk on Cheerios, the soft *phut* of a spoon cleaving through a giant bowl of scrambled eggs. Such subtle noises would soon be drowned out by pleas to go to the bathroom and loudly pinging drum solos with forks and water glasses. Kids would be arriving all day, but it would start early. Some boys wanted so badly to have the best pick of bunks that they made their parents drive up the night before and stay in a local motel so they could be first down the road.

After breakfast, I changed into my bathing suit and headed to my station at the dock. Anne and Helen and I had to stay here all day, waiting for first-time Eastwinders to come demonstrate their swimming skills and be placed in the proper swimming level. We spent the first couple of hours on the bench, watching as the camp got more and more crowded. A bunch of the kids were second-generation Eastwinders, and their dads ran right alongside them, taking turns pointing out every landmark. Two of them had been counselors with me in my last summer. I watched them spin around, shouting out familiar sights, and then abruptly stop when they saw me in the same spot they'd left me—standing by the swimming dock, chewing on a pen, clipboard in hand. *Wow*, I could see them thinking, *this place really doesn't change*. When I explained that yes, I was back, they looked at me with jealousy. Just standing on the dock made them want to call home, quit their job, strip to their boxers, and do cannonballs off the diving board for eight straight weeks. I couldn't bear to tell them that there were times in the past week that I'd considered calling New York to get my old job back. Instead I played the role of the Luckiest Man in the World. Talking to these guys made me feel like everything really hadn't changed . . . even if they weren't dressed as counselors, but rather—sigh—dads. Perhaps I wasn't so bad off after all, I thought. I was young enough to recognize that white socks shouldn't be worn with Top-Siders.

Swimming was the sole mandatory activity at Eastwind, the only broccoli in a camp full of pizza. Campers had to take three lessons a week until they passed out of the Red Cross' level five, after which they'd be proficient at all the major strokes and water safety. Swimming had the reputation of being a chore, so when the new kids finally arrived, we pounced on them, smiling and extolling the wonders of our activity, trying to make our propaganda sink in before the jaded returnees told them our class was a drag.

These new kids came in two types. The shy, overwhelmed ones quietly wandered around the dock clutching their towels, not wanting to ask any questions that might mark them as new. And then there were the Type-A kids who hadn't known a moment of shyness in their lives. They'd announce themselves with a loud, "So is this where we get the swimming test? Because I'm a *really* good swimmer." Inevitably, the shy kids were much better swimmers than they let on, and the loud kids were much worse. When we asked a shy one if he could do the sidestroke, he'd shrug and then do it as seamlessly as if he were a computer simulation. But when we asked a loud boy to show us the elementary backstroke, he'd lean back in the water and flail his arms and legs in a way that looked like a less-coordinated version of drowning. "That was it, right?" he'd boast, hyperventilating after the spasms had stopped. "No? Oh, wait, I know what it is, it's this, right?" And he'd start again, his flailing looking no different except this time he'd whack himself in the face. I never understood this unflagging, deluded confidence. I was openly contemptuous of it when I saw it in frat guys or dim-bulb football stars, but I was also secretly jealous. What would life be like if it never occurred to you that you couldn't do something?

At the end of the afternoon, it was time for the first Free Swim, open to all campers who wanted to baptize their summer. I volunteered to brave the chilly water and swim out to the stationary platform fifteen yards out, called the Raft. On it was a slide, a diving board, and the lifeguard tower, which I climbed to look down on the six boys who hyperactively splashed on and off the Raft. Their eyes were crossed in excitement over the summer's start, as the water washed away the stench of learning and homework. They dashed back and forth, first whizzing down the slide, then running off the diving board, and then back to the slide, wanting to maximize every moment of water fun before someone took it away from them. When one stood at the dock end of the diving board, he pronounced, "This will be a double-kookamonga with a twist." His friends yelled, "Just gooooooo!" and he ran and jumped off the end, spinning three-quarters of the way around and kicking his legs. What trademarked it as a "kookamonga" was the fact that he yelled "kookamonga!" in midair. Technically, he should have yelled it twice to make it a double, but all in all, I gave it a 7.5, and his friends agreed, clapping and declaring it awesome, and waiting to duplicate it themselves. This was the same unadulterated joy over the same exact low-impact acrobatics that I remembered from my youth, down to the word "kookamonga." After the novelty leaps, they took turns play-shooting each other and making "Arrrgh, ya got me!" death falls off the edge of the raft. Today's imitated assassins were the Mr. Smith clones from the Matrix movies. My friends and I had done the same pantomime, except we were taking a laser in the chest from a *Star Wars* stormtrooper. In the '40s, kids probably toppled into the lake after taking a fake arrow while playing cowboys and Indians. I had no idea how kids got into the water before movies.

Other than my lunch break, I had spent the entire day at the dock, and only after the last new kid was assigned a class was I able to steal up to the Bears to meet my ten new campers. I pushed open the screen door and sauntered in as nonchalantly as possible. Should I call them "dudes"? Did anyone use that anymore? How about "Welcome to our crib"? No, the only thing lamer than a white fourteen-year-old saying that was me saying that. "What up, Bears?" I said, which was equally awful.

It was moot, as no one looked up. The cabin that had been empty this morning was now crammed with stuff. Each boy's six shelves were stuffed to maximum capacity, but in a precise order that still reeked of the just-departed mothers' touches. Empty laundry bags hung limp and thin next to each bed, each a different color, deceptively pristine compared to the kickline of stink they'd become in just days. Every bed was made perfectly for the last time, and the boys were hanging out in clumps, showing off their new tennis rackets, fishing poles, or sneakers. I walked down the aisle, smiling at the various groups.

"Hey, guys," I said, stopping at three of them taking turns trying on another boy's superlight backpack. "I'm Josh, one of your counselors." I extended a hand. Eastwind men shook hands.

Being fourteen, they gave me the entire range of handshakes, from firm to boneless. "So, you guys get settled in all right?"

They nodded politely, a little patronizingly. "We've all been here before," said a tall, chunky Bear.

"Hey, me too," I said. Perhaps my longevity would impress them. "Look up there." I pointed to my fading name on the ceiling. "I was a camper in this cabin in '83 *and* '84. Twenty years ago. Wild, huh?"

They squinted up at my name. Not quite with awe. Something else, really. "I wasn't even born yet," said one. They all murmured agreement and then turned back to the backpack.

I took some solace from this reaction. Whether I was too old or unhip was a nonfactor. It was a variation on the philosophical question of a tree falling in the forest: If a man attends camp, but you don't exist at the time, why the hell is the man bothering to make a sound about it when there are new backpacks to be admired?

CHAPTER EIGHT

THE FIRST BLOW OF THE PREDINNER BUGLE SIGNALED THE TRUE BEGINNING of camp. Eastwind's entire schedule was announced by an old tin bugle: Reveille woke us up at seven A.M., Taps quieted everyone down for the night at eight thirty P.M. And in between, different calls marked every period, Free Swim, and meal. This bred such a Pavolvian response into everybody that through November you couldn't listen to Dixieland jazz without wanting to go for a swim or make your bed. I clapped my hands to roust the Bears, but they were all on their way out the door to the assembly ground already, still deep in verbal pissing contests about whose school had the most homework that year.

The dusty assembly ground was a fenceless pen surrounded by the cabins for the middle campers—the Caribou, Coyotes, and Cheetahs. The area was frantic with boys running around and hopping on counselors' backs, crazed with excitement over the departure of their parents and the commencement of camp. The bugler shakily blasted the Assembly tune, indicating that it was time for everyone to line up by cabin between their counselors, facing Frank, where we'd belt out our cabin attendance— "Bears all present and accounted for, Sir!"—and then turn for the lowering of the American flag from its white birch pole. Judging by the excitable snickering and pushing during the ceremony, the line that designated unacceptable behavior during this ceremony had been bumped down. Whereas you used to get pulled aside for poking your neighbor, now it took yanking someone's pants down to be considered a chastisable offense.

Once the flag was lowered and folded, Frank read off the month's table assignments. Boys were dismissed in groups of five, a combination of different-aged kids that they were stuck with for the summer. If their group was a horrible amalgam of atrocious manners and unappetizing personalities, it was one that would fester for weeks.

Reg and I had elected to share a table, facing each other at opposite heads. Over the roar of shouting kids, Reg and I introduced ourselves, and then asked every kid's name, names I immediately forgot, even though two of them were Bears. It had been a day full of introductions, and my memory bank was full. Frank quickly silenced the crowd with a clang of the fireplace bell, recited a short, nondenominational grace, then gave the okay for all the boys designated as waiters to bolt into line by the food window, and grab a tray and main course.

"Where are you from?" a ten-year-old kid with jug ears and giant, M&M-size freckles asked Reg. He was a Rabbit. Pete? Paul? Something like that. He wrinkled his nose at Reg's accent as if trying to decide whether Reg was friend, foe, or from Saturn.

"What do you mean, where am I from?" Reg laughed. "I'm from Australia. Kangaroos? Koala? Greatest country in the world?"

"Yeah, *right*," snorted the eldest, a Lion named Bradley or Brian or something. He wore his stringy hair over his eyes and slumped in his chair, his arms crossed over his private-school T-shirt. In just five minutes he had perceived that we were all the stupidest people on the planet. "Although it's better than this country."

"What are you talking about?" piped up another Rabbit, an African-American boy with a birthmark in the epicenter of his chin. "America is number one!"

The Lion let loose a humorless chuckle worthy of a sixth-year philosophy-major undergrad. He reveled in the superiority of being the oldest camper there, even though he was barely a year older than the two Bears: one, our waiter, was now fighting the line, while the other Bear, a quiet, wispy introvert with wide-spaced, watery eyes, sat in the seat next to his, intent on trying to weave his knife's edge through the tines in his fork. "Yeah, 'number one,' " sneered the Lion, who sat to my right, next to the two Wolves. "We've got the number-one idiot running it, George Bush."

"Maybe you're the number-one idiot," squeaked back his opponent. "He's beating the terrorists."

"Oh, yeah, an ex-boozer is beating the terrorists," he scoffed. "The only thing he loves more than booze is oil."

It was political debate at its most incisive: A ten-year-old who got his opinions from his father at the dinner table versus a fifteen-year-old who got his opinions from a college-freshman brother who'd just attended his first peace march. I was curious to hear a third opinion: Didn't we have an eleven-year-old who could only recite a mangled anti–Dick Cheney joke he misheard the night his babysitter let him stay up late and watch *The Daily Show*? Then we'd really have a *Crossfire*.

We were interrupted by our waiter's arrival back at our table. He plunked down his tray in front of me, a platter of roast beef slices clattering against bowls of green beans and mashed potatoes. "I was the eighth person in line!" he crowed.

"Big deal," snorted the Lion. "I've been first before."

"It *is* a big deal," I said, lifting the food off the tray and pulling a stack of multicolored plates closer to me. "Eighth is perfect. Quick enough for the food to still be hot, but long enough so it cools and nobody burns their mouth. I think we should all personally thank . . . I'm sorry, what's your name again?"

"Jackson." Our waiter beamed, scratching his tight, curly blond hair as he stared hungrily at the food. He had an athletic build and a downy My First Mustache, but radiated the refreshing naïveté of a teenager who hadn't yet learned that he could be cocky about it. He clearly hadn't learned the wardrobe of a smug jock; the collar of his polo shirt was stretched out so far that one end practically hung over his shoulder, *Flashdance*-style.

After serving Reg, I pointed to each kid, then spooned him a plate of whatever he wanted, passing it down the table. "See? Perfect food temperature. Who wants to start the summer with a burned mouth?"

"I'm not eating that stuff anyway," grumbled the Lion, who waved off my offer of food, taking his own plate and assembling a PB&J from the bread basket and jars in the center of the table, put there for picky eaters.

I ignored him. I finished serving and theatrically dug in. "Mmmm, good stuff. Who thinks it's good stuff?" Heads down, shoveling the food into their mouths, everyone could only muster a shrug, except for the Lion, who just shook his head at the idiocy of the question.

"So, what are your favorite activities?" I said, intent on starting some camaraderie momentum.

The full-mouthed responses came: *archuruff, sairing, phuphographuh.* Then more eating. Reg was the first to finish, passing his plate to me. "Oi, Josh, give me some more of that meat, and more potatoes. Fantastic."

The freckled Rabbit looked at him. "You like it?"

"Love it. What's the matter, Pete, you don't?"

"It's Preston," he said. Good, I wasn't alone in forgetting. "No, I love roast beef. I just didn't know Australians liked it. Do you have it at home?"

Reg looked perplexed as he took back his full plate. "What do you think we eat?"

"I don't know. How do you get it, does America send it to you?"

Reg stared at him, deadpan. "Yes, they do. They send us all our food. We get all the Big Macs that pass their expiration date."

"*Really?* And you don't get sick?" All the kids were looking up now, amazed. The quiet Bear still looked down as he scratched his nose with four fingers, an attempt to mask the fact that he was smiling.

"We get used to it. And we wash it down with warm, flat Coke that you Yanks have left open too long."

"*God,* you guys are so gullible," exhaled our cynical Lion, flopping his head back with irritation. I was enjoying Reg's fib, but having this junior-varsity cynic on our side ruined it.

We all finished our food and a round of seconds, and Jackson weaved away, barely balancing a stack of plates topped with a heaping pyramid of PB&J crusts, roast-beef fat, and barely touched beans. I noticed that we were lagging behind, as all the other tables had already cleaned up and were devouring plates of brownies. "Let's move!" I turned to the Lion. "While our waiter is busy, why don't you go get our dessert."

"No way," he grumbled. "That's the waiter's job."

"And I'm asking you to make it your job. C'mon, it's brownies. The sooner brownies are in all of our mouths, the happier we'll all be."

"Oooh, brownies, what a *treat*," he said, then smirked. "Unless there's something extra baked into them, I don't care."

"Like nuts?" asked the birthmarked Rabbit. His freshfaced, confused look would have made him the perfect cover boy for *Unspoiled Youth Monthly*.

"Yeah, *nuts*," scoffed the Lion. He rolled his eyes at me conspiratorially. Not for a minute did I think that this guy was an aficionado of pot brownies. I guessed that the extent of his drug use involved catching an old Cheech and Chong movie on cable.

"I like nuts," said the other Rabbit.

"Whoa-ho!" crowed Reg. "Bradley likes to get *crazy* with nuts."

"Bradford," grunted the Lion.

"*Bradford*," he corrected himself. "Sorry, Big B."

Bradford looked up. "Big B? What's that?"

"It's a nickname, mate," said Reg. "You're Big B. Big B and his big-ass brownies. Getting *crazy* with Big B, choco-style!"

Bradford furrowed his brow, attempting to figure out whether he liked his nickname. Usually kids warmed right up to one. It was flattering, making them feel like they had an alter ego used only by those people in the know. You could put it on the back of a sports jersey and people would always ask questions about you. *Why do they call him The Frizz? I must know!* I always wanted a nickname, but never got one. Occasionally someone would call me "Big Guy," but that wasn't a nickname, it was a physical description. Try putting that on a jersey and see who asks a follow-up question. "Big B" had all the trappings of a party-boy moniker, which was cool, but Bradford was suspicious of Reg's sincerity. He slumped out of his seat and slowly made his way to get some brownies. He returned and let the plate fall on the table with a loud clack.

"Be careful with the brownies, Big B!" yelled Jackson.

Bradford glared at him, still convinced there was a downside to "Big B" that he hadn't found yet. As grating as he was, I didn't want to start the summer with him feeling picked on. "That's right, he's Big B," I said to the table. "I like it. It's strong, punchy. Shows leadership. A 'Big B' may get cocky, but he'll always come through. Oh, sure, at first he *says* he won't get the brownies, but five minutes later you've got a mouthful of Duncan Hines, and without your ever asking, he's handing you a cold glass of milk. How does Big B do it? Does he keep a carton up his sleeve? Does he have his own cow? Don't ask. It's Big B. He just gets it done."

He still scowled. I turned to the table. "Now Big B's got a nickname. Where does that leave the rest of us?" They all looked at me, confused. "Reg, what's cooler than a nickname?"

"Nothing."

"Right. So what if our table was the first to have nicknames? Not even at camp twenty-four hours yet, and they've got a supercool alias. Imagine the jealousy, imagine the respect. So let's come up with some. If they don't seem to make sense, don't worry. The more obscure the better. Let's start with you, Jeff."

"Jackson."

"Doesn't matter. You're not Jackson anymore. You're 'Action.'"

Jackson's head cocked to the side. He looked perplexed. "Why 'Action'?"

"There was a movie a while back, *Action Jackson*. Good. Glad you don't know. That means none of the other kids will know, and that'll make you more mysterious. So when Big B says, 'What up, Action?', someone will say, 'Why'd Big B call you Action?' and that's your cue to shake your head knowingly, wave them off, and walk away. You're gonna have so much mystique they'll start calling you 'Mystique.' And then you'll say, 'Don't call me Mystique. I'm Action.' And the whole thing will start all over again. Reg, let's trade off for the next few. I'm exhausted by all this creativity."

By the end of the meal, the Rabbit who defended America from Big B was named Patrioticus, his cabinmate was arbitrarily dubbed Rattler (after "Leopardo" was deemed too obvious a reference to his freckle spots), and the quiet Bear was, after much debate ("Whispers"? "Quiet Menace"? "Shushtastic Sam"?), simply dubbed "the Fog." As in, "He's the Fog. He looks harmless and creeps up silently, but once he's around you . . . *you're in his power.*" They all mentally tried them on like new sweaters and liked how they felt, using them in every conversation until the end of dinner. "Gimme your plate, Patrioticus!" "Comin' your way, Action!" The Rattler got more enthusiastic when we suggested that he punctuate all of his comments by waggling his finger like a rattlesnake tail and making a *flflflflflfl* sound effect. Even the reticent Fog smiled freely after our repeated cries of, "The Fog . . . he mists, *he kills!*"

Our table got so carried away that I looked around and noticed that once again we were the last table to clear. "Let's get this place cleaned up! Come on, plates, glasses, send it all up to Action!" I turned to Bradford. "Can you help him, please?"

He stood up. "Big B is on the case," he said, leaning forward to grab the milk carton and water jug.

"Hey, he called himself Big B!" said Rattler.

Big B snorted. "Whatever. I was the first one to get a nickname." He looked at me and rolled his eyes in collusion against these Johnny-named-latelys, and then slouched off to the slide.

CHAPTER NINE

I RETURNED TO THE CABIN AFTER DINNER WHEN ALL THE BOYS HAD RECON-vened. Action and the Fog and two others were playing Hearts, sitting on two adjacent beds, tossing their discards on the area floor between them. I was on a conviviality roll and wanted to keep it going, so I sauntered over. "What's up, Action. Fog."

Action barely looked up, but held out a hand for a high five as I stepped toward him. His shirt had slid backward so his distended collar now drooped behind him, revealing a circle of pale back. The Fog looked up, blinked a hello, then went back to his cards. "The Fog?" said one of the other kids.

The Fog shrugged and muttered, "I mist, I kill."

"Hearts, eh?" I said. "Is it too late to be dealt in? But it kinda depends if you like having your asses kicked, face-card style. 'Cause I'll do it."

They snorted and Action shifted over on a bed to make room for me. A hand had just ended and I was dealt in. Magically, my entrée with Action and the Fog lifted the nervous silence of the afternoon, and the foursome happily chatted around me. Soon, other boys came by and jumped in and out of conversation. It only took two hands to get a clear picture of them all, assigning them nicknames that I never used out loud, but which seemed completely apt.

Trumps: Overweight, with a completely spherical head, he may not have looked like an athlete, but that didn't mean he lacked the cutthroat gene. He was single-mindedly intense at cards. Between rounds he'd joke around, but once he had his hand he dropped into a quiet, win-focused zone, and a loss sent him into a muttering fugue state. He was clearly going to be as competitive as a noncompetitive camp would allow.

Captain Marquee: A small, Chinese drama nerd, he was the shortest kid in the cabin, with a compressed neck that made him seem even shorter, yet he had the hearty personality of an extroverted, giant, fat man. He'd been a regular in the camp's monthly musicals since he was an Otter, and he had the brash, overconfident personality of a big star in a small repertory company.

Lefty: His military-style crewcut gave him a look of timeless innocence, an image undercut by the fact that he often walked around with his left hand jammed down his shorts, clutching onto his own balls like worry beads. He never gave the sense he had anything to worry about, though. He radiated a serene confidence, and though his cabinmates returned his crap when he trash-talked them, you could tell that they all looked to him for behavioral cues.

Dewey: Named after the Dewey decimal system, this chubby bookhound unpacked a bulky collection of novels before any clothing. He gave his library the shelf right next to his head, so his books would have the shortest possible distance to travel to get in front of his eyes, adding valuable microseconds to his reading time. While we played cards, he lay on his bed, ankles crossed, his dark, knitted eyebrows the only thing visible over the extravagant dragon-vs.-knight battle on his current book's cover.

Mensa: Tall and sunken-chested, he was clearly brilliant and clearly uncomfortable with the thought that somebody wouldn't notice. Conversations with him consisted of a series of passive-aggressive reminders to others of his mental prowess. He wandered from conversation to conversation, dropping bits of knowledge that he hoped would get him recognized by his cabinmates for the genius that he was. Unfortunately, he was usually ignored or sighed at, leaving him to meander over to give another group a chance to appreciate his intellect. He wasn't in the Hearts game, but he stayed on the periphery, wondering aloud things like, "That's an odd card to lead with, Trumps. I only say that because I remember Lefty was all out of clubs, but who knows, maybe it *will* turn out to be a good play."

Mudge: Short for "curmudgeon." Unrelentingly patronizing, he deemed everything I said to him idiotic, and his universal response was a heavy-lidded glare of condescension followed by a verbal retort sarcastic enough to make my testicles shrink two sizes. When I lost the first hand of Hearts, his response was, "Have you ever *played* this game before?" He had wavy, blond, pro-surfer hair and a precociously muscular physique. Unlike Action, he'd made the connection that his good looks entitled him to a bad attitude.

Wind-Up: So named because he reminded me of a wind-up duck toy I had as a kid; when you cranked it up, its feet would flap and its mouth would open and close, emitting a repetitive quacking. If I held its feet steady and mouth closed, I could feel the bill straining against me, and when I let go, it would quack extra quickly, making up for lost time and catching up to where its inner gears had turned. I think the same fairy who turned Pinocchio into a real boy turned my duck into Wind-Up. With chaotically frizzy hair and gangly rubber bones, he bounced around the cabin, filibustering on the merits of his beloved Phillies (which he'd do while awkwardly throwing imaginary pitches or swinging imaginary bats) or just narrating his entire life: "Oh boy, time to make the bed. This is a tough blanket since it's a little short and hard to get over the edge, but there I go. . . ." If anyone tried to shush him, he'd stay quiet just as long as it took for them to yell, "Will you shut up?" and then jabber extra fast to catch up to where he would have been if he hadn't been temporarily silenced. Despite the potential annoyance, he was also irrepressibly upbeat, which made him impossible to dislike. Usually his chatter was delivered through an open-mouthed smile, and when he looked at you with his goofy, permanently euphoric expression, it was impossible not to smile back.

Afty: A truncation of "After-School Special," because even before he arrived I had him cast in my own personal educational video starring me.

I had been alerted that this long-time camper could be withdrawn and de-bilitatingly self-critical, though he had made definite progress over his time at camp. I took this as a personal challenge: some of my proudest counselor memories involved winning over a troubled camper. Even be-fore I met Afty, I was already flash-forwarding to the last day of camp, when he would inevitably shake my hand, looking down at the ground, unable to express just how much my guidance meant to him; when he left he'd go on to become President or First Man on Mars or something that would involve public speeches thanking me as a formative figure in his life. On this first night, my mission was to validate his interests; I knew he was obsessive about his pet fish, having heard him grill his departing mother to make sure she understood her tank duties while he was away. Between hands I asked him what kind of fish he had. He was portly, with long, limp black hair that drooped over his shoulders, a do seemingly ordered out of the Allman Brothers Roadie Toupee Catalog, and his shaded eyes guarded him against too many questions. He hunched forward over his cards and listed his fish rotely without looking at me. But this stone face was soon freed when he lost the next hand. "Man, I *suck* at this!" he hooted in a strangely upbeat tone. He tossed his cards down and looked around at his fellow players for affirmation of his suckiness. "No one has to worry about me being the cabin champ!" The one thing he took pride in was his utter lack of pride. If I wanted to make him the First Man on Mars, I had a lot of work to do.

Meeting the Bears filled me with a sense of déjà vu. While the lumpy Trumps didn't look at all familiar physically, I recognized his dark seizures of competitiveness from campers I'd known in the past. And every few years the camp got a new Captain Marquee, who would return from re-hearsals annoyed at the lack of professionalism of his fellow castmates, convinced that if they'd just let him play every role, this version of *You're a Good Man, Charlie Brown* just might have a chance on Broadway.

It was like being given a new model of my old Apple computer: I might not recognize the fresh look, but if I worked off my knowledge of the old operating system, I could circumvent some problems. For example, I knew if you teased Trumps too much during a losing streak, it would end with him throwing the cards at you and storming out of the cabin. It was reassuring that while I might not know enough to fix my kids' hardwiring, I knew enough to avoid some error messages.

The door swung open, and in strode Mitch, with Trevor right behind him. "Let's go, boys, we got Campfire Ceremony." Mitch always gave the word "boys" a playful emphasis, making it clear that he had purposefully chosen it instead of "men." I was startled and tossed down my cards. My first instinct was to obediently scurry to my own area to get ready, until I remembered that I, too, was in charge. Waving all the Bears to hurry up, I went to my area to grab my blanket and a small, rolled-up paper bag that I had picked up at my parents' house. It had been exactly where I'd left it for years, in a pristinely packed plastic tub that kept all my Eastwind memorabilia. Inside the bag was a fifteen-year-old piece of charcoal that had patiently waited to be returned to the camp's fire.

Eastwind didn't have a thousand ritual songs and fake-Indian traditions like other camps, but we did have Campfire Ceremony. It was a first-night ritual in which every camper draped himself in a blanket and quietly marched out at dusk through camp and into the woods, down to a path that followed the coastline. Reaching a clearing, everyone sat in cabin groups up a slight incline, looking down to where Frank stacked kindling in a fire pit. Behind him the trees parted, revealing a postcard view of the lake. The sun had nearly vanished behind the mountain across the lake, and a glorious explosion of reds, yellows, and oranges still flared through the clouds.

When the last boy sat down on the carpet of pine needles, Frank stood up and began the annual explanation of the Campfire Ceremony fire. It represented Eastwind and its summer life. Once it was lit, returning campers would first come down and feed a piece of charcoal they'd been given from the remnants of last year's fire, then all the new boys would add a fresh stick. In this way—with old faces and new coming together—we would keep Eastwind alive for the summer, just as we would keep it alive in the off-season by safeguarding our souvenir lumps of charcoal until we returned.

Group rituals like this usually did nothing for me. They felt artificial, and I was suspicious of anyone who became visibly moved by performing them. These were the kind of people who liked prayer circles and group hugs and holding hands to send someone good vibes. If they were really that sensitive, they should be able to send vibes alone without making it a spectator sport. I put them in the class of people who loudly harmonized while singing "Happy Birthday."

But I totally bought the Campfire Ceremony. As a kid, at the end of every summer I carefully stored my charcoal exactly where I knew I could find it the next year. During the ceremonies themselves, I might nudge a friend and mutter a joke, but this was only to present an adolescent sense of aloofness. I truly cherished the ritual, and quietly judged harshly any friend who had misplaced his charcoal over the winter and had to accept a substitute twig.

After describing the ceremony, Frank stood back from his pile of twigs and, as tradition demanded, called down the oldest camper in the Lions to light the fire. I had been the lighter in 1985, an honor that couldn't have filled me with more warmth if I'd been thrown into the flames. I heard a rustling behind me as this year's honoree nudged his way past toward the fire. He looked calm from the back, at least. Frank handed him a match, and he leaned forward and lit the dry, spark-ready brush, which flared and quickly caught. Frank thanked him and the Lion intently navigated his way back through the sitting campers, his facial expression frozen midway between three different impulses: ebullience at the honor; mature gravitas to illustrate his stature as eldest camper and appreciation of his task on levels that the more youthful among the group couldn't begin to understand; and teenage nonchalance to prove to his fellow Lions, that, well, it was lighting a fire, whatever.

The rest of the returning Lions were asked down to add their old charcoal, and then we Bears. I waved my boys down—all returnees—and waited my turn behind them, turning over my small bag in my hand. My turn came and I stepped forward, proudly holding up my souvenir. Frank smiled and waved me toward the fire, and I felt a wave of satisfaction for proving to him with this keepsake just how dedicated I was to Eastwind. Frank was only nine years older than I, but as director and keeper of the campfire, I automatically awarded him my full subservience and eagerness to please. For a moment, I felt like all was as it should be at camp, and I knew my role. I made a pledge to once again represent all that was East-wind, and my cynicism vanished into the flames. It would likely return by the time I tried to wedge myself back into my cot to sleep, but for now I lingered by the flames for an extra moment, feeling the warmth before moving aside for the next old-timer.

CHAPTER TEN

YOUTH ENDS AT AGE THIRTY-FOUR. YOU CAN BE A SCREWUP IN YOUR TWEN-ties and early thirties, but once past that, you're expected to have your act together. And your midthirties begin at thirty-four. You can go to bed on the eve of your thirty-fourth birthday ironically wearing a yellowed, twelve-year-old GO PEROT T-shirt and scratching at your spotty goatee, but when you wake up, you'd better be in patterned boxers and have a full-time job with benefits.

There's a symbolic science to that demarcation. Thirty-three is a palindrome, which gives the number an insouciant, free-love vibe that thirty-four just doesn't have: "Hey, dude, read me forward, read me backward, don't matter to me, it's all good." But the fun stops at thirty-four; the fact that the three and the four are sequential symbolizes a plodding necessity to follow the rules. *When you have three, it must be followed by four. Do not even think of going back to two, much as you must arrive for work at nine, not ten.*

The second day of camp was my thirty-fourth birthday.

I had no great blowout planned to celebrate my last night at thirty-three. I had cabin duty, which entailed making sure the guys got to bed at around ten P.M. The kids fell asleep quickly, worn out from summer's

69

opening salvo, and I twisted my clip-on lamp nearly against the wall, so its tiny ring of light ended just around my book. The only problem with this setup was that late June is the buggiest time at camp. At night, any light in the dark woods attracts jittery bugs of all species, from moths to bizarre, huge, mutant insects that look like they are waiting to audition for another remake of *The Fly*. Though the cabins had screens, some made it inside and came right for my lamp. Since it was dark all around me, I didn't see any of them coming; I'd be in the middle of a chapter when a moth suddenly landed right on my sentence, and with a jolt I'd shake the book to make it flit off. I made it through about six pages and four regulation-sized moths when the most enormous mother moth appeared on my pages. In the 0.0003 seconds before I suppressed a scream and tossed the book on the floor, I think I saw it drag one of its legs across its own throat and then point at me. I snapped off the light and lay in the dark, breathing heavily. Finally I calmed down, convincing myself that the moth had only wanted my book and had likely already flown away with it and was discussing it in its Giant Fucking Mutant Bug Book Club. I closed my eyes, and focused on the cool, clean air blowing in through my screen and on the rhythmic *floosh* of the small waves breaking on the Senior Cove beach below us. Just as I was about to descend into a deep, forest-enhanced sleep, a horrified scream rang through the cabin.

"*Nooooooo!*"

I might have leapt out of bed were my legs not manacled in by the footboard. I lunged for my flashlight and ran it around the cabin. Flicking the light past Action's bed, I saw him sitting up, bleary-eyed and groggily rubbing his face. He didn't look like a person who had just been bitten by a bear. And then he flopped back onto his cot and went right back to sleep. Bad dream. The rest of the boys just grumbled and rolled over; none of them seemed as shaken as I was. When you're a regular at camp, you get used to the occasional piercing night terror.

And that's how I bid adieu to my days of frivolity. Being dive-bombed by a sci-fi beasty and heebie-jeebied by a screeching kid.

The next morning I woke up a thirty-four-year-old, at a confusing place to do it. This age marked my deadline for growing up, and yet all I wanted right now was to be embraced by people around me in their twenties who still had plenty of time before going into maturity lockdown. Though I wanted to be celebrated, I didn't want to have to tell anyone it was my birthday. Experiencing a day of unsolicited well-wishing is divine, but it's off-putting to ask for it yourself.

I repressed my birthday neediness in the morning by concentrating on my first day of real work. At the end of breakfast, Frank clanged the bell and pointed to a giant wipe board on which he'd written all the available activities for the morning. "We have swimming, sailing, kayaking, tennis, ropes course, wakeboarding, archery, arts and crafts, canoeing, photography, windsurfing, wood shop, leather, pottery, fishing, nature, music, and basketball," he bellowed. Eastwind has always worked on a free-choice philosophy. At other camps, kids are assigned their activities, or they pick their schedule by the week. But here, they picked fresh every breakfast (for first and second periods) and lunch (for third and fourth). As Frank called off each activity, the responsible counselors stood and announced their plans for the morning, and kids raised their hands to get picked. As a mandatory activity, swimming was always announced first. If you didn't catch kids before they realized just how much better their options were, they would never remember to save room for a lesson.

Anne stood up and yelled, "We're doing level fives first period, and level fours second period, who wants to come down?" She had asked me if I wanted to make the announcement, and I quickly passed. Dining-hall announcements were an art that I took very seriously as a teenager, and I didn't feel ready to get back onstage yet. For the in-demand activities like archery, you could stand up covered in your own blood and kids would still beg to come down. But for swimming, you had to put on a show to work up any enthusiasm. This morning Anne got a fair number of hands raised, and she sat down with nine each period, a respectable number for three counselors. We could attribute that to general first-day exuberance: Kids were so happy to be there that they would have raised their hands for ditchdigging.

As the rest of the counselors stood and picked their campers, I marveled at just how little the process had changed, right down to the campers' tastes. From September to June, these kids likely spent their free time playing ornate, blinding video games, searching the world on the Internet, surfing through two hundred TV channels, and avoiding any moments of introspective silence by constant text messaging. But now they were back wildly waving their arms in a desperate need to make a wallet in leather shop. At home they had probably begged their parents to buy them a cell phone that could take pictures, play music, and make tiny pizzas, and yet now they were begging for someone to let them make a birdhouse. And it was done with no apprehension or self-consciousness. When kids really wanted an activity, they still gave hand raising their all, leaning forward with their right arm out, fingers extended, their left hand clutching their right tricep and pushing forward, as if hoping to extend their arm the few precious inches longer it would take to make them unignorable.

As water-ski counselor, Reg had the most popular activity. Lake sharks would not keep kids from raising their hand. In Australia, he favored wakeboarding, which is to waterskiing what snowboarding is to snow skiing, and so when he stood, clomping around the Dining Hall in his heavy black sneakers, he didn't even mention waterskiing as an option. He had slight stage fright and mumbled a rambling, syntax-deficient pitch. Add his Aussie patois and thick accent and he could have been offering skydiving for all the campers understood. "Royt, for period one, I'm looking for blokes who know the board, love the board, maybe even done a toe-side goofy. Some instruction, some fun, possibly jumping wake, good chop." Around the dining hall, kids turned to their tables' counselors and whispered, "What's he saying?" and the staffers replied, "Don't worry, it's just wakeboarding." Hands shot up and Reg counted them off. Just as he was sitting down, he remembered something and stood up, "It's a bit nippy out theah, so bring your jumpahs."

The Dining Hall murmured in confusion. I leaned across the table to him. "Jumpers?"

He grabbed his sweatshirt and showed it to me. "Yeah. Jumpahs."

"A jumper is a sweatshirt?"

He looked at me as if I'd said, "A kitty is a cat?"

I whispered, "You should clarify that."

He stood up and yelled, "Jumpahs are hoodies!"

The hubbub only halved. "If you're going to waterskiing, bring your sweatshirts," interpreted Frank. The hubbub turned to *ahhh ohhhhs*.

I brought all my energy to my first two swimming lessons. As the boys begrudgingly slumped onto the swimming bench to kick off their shoes, I joked, cajoled, chirped, and cheered them into enthusiasm. Anne and Helen looked startled by my energy. "Settle a bet, Anne," I yelled over to her, while plopping myself down amidst a few boys who were trying to spend the entire hour-and-a-quarter extricating their feet from their sandals. "I think that swimming is the best activity at camp, but these guys here totally disagree. They insist it's the best activity in the entire history of the world. Past, present, *and* future."

The boys around me groaned. "We didn't say that!" one yelled.

I ignored them. "Don't get me wrong, I appreciate their enthusiasm, I think we all do. But really, the best in the whole history of time? Let's take the past first. Are they trying to tell me that swimming lessons are better than dinosaur rodeos? No way. Wait, what's that you say?" I leaned into the boy on my left who wasn't saying anything. "Swimming is better than dinosaur rodeo because the caveman rodeo clowns aren't as funny as they think they are? Point for you, my little friend in the lake. So I'll give you the past." I mimed etching a point on an imaginary chalkboard. "But that still leaves the future. I can't believe you're telling me there will never be anything better."

The boys all howled "Noooo!" in unison. One leaned over and tried to put his hand over my mouth to shut me up, laughing while he did it. I kept going. "I mean, what about robot horseback riding? It's coming in the year 2254, and that'll be *way* better! Who's with me?" I leaned to my right, pretending as if the boy who was clutching his ears mock-dramatically had just vehemently disagreed. "Robot horseback riding is overrated? You can't enjoy it because you're constantly worried about the day when the robohorses are going to rise up and kill us all?"

"Like *The Terminator*," the boy said, removing his hands. "*I'll be baack*," growled another.

"Exactly. So you'll have to wait around for someone to come back in time to kill the guy who built the first robohorse. Whereas with swimming you just have to wait until someone says, 'Everybody into the water.' Fine! You all win!" I threw up my arms in exasperation. "What's their prize, Helen?"

"A swimming lesson!" she yelled, waving her arms. "Everybody into the water!"

We three counselors divided up the kids, and I jumped into the shallow water at the end of the swim dock, resisting every urge to scream that it was goddamn freezing, and waved for my group of three to follow me out to the crib. Through this and my second-period class, I kept up a frenetic line of patter and instruction, demonstrating every stroke and giving careful tweaking, smothered in positive reinforcement. I picked the number of laps I assigned them carefully: just enough for the kids to feel a sense of accomplishment, but not enough for me to be looked upon as a lap-happy martinet. I was aiming for that delicate balance of doing the duties of an instructor while also being the kid at heart who hadn't lost touch with what sucked. And it was working. At the end of second period, I had my class celebrate the end of the lesson with a few rides down the slide, and after we swam back to the main dock and the boys got their towels, one of the younger ones exclaimed, "I love swimming lessons!" I didn't remember slipping him a twenty, but I must have, because nobody in the history of this swim dock had ever uttered those words unprovoked by remuneration or threat of bodily harm.

After lessons, I went up to the Office to check on the mail and found a large box from Christine. Back at the cabin, I sliced open the box with my Swiss Army knife. Afty was alone in the cabin, and he lay on the bed next to mine, strands of his long, dark hair splayed outward over his pillow like his head was leaking motor oil. He had a book resting on his chest, and he self-consciously kept one hand gripped to the bottom of his T-shirt so it wouldn't ride up over his padded belly.

"What's that?" he asked, careful not to seem too interested.

"Some presents from my fiancée, Christine," I said. Sharing my special day with Afty was good, all part of the bonding process. "It's my birthday."

"Oh. Happy birthday," he said with the same emotion you'd hear in the sentence "You just sneezed on me."

The box was filled with many small, individually wrapped presents. I knew to expect something delightful. The same reflex that made Christine terrified of a generic wedding made her a wonderfully personal gift-giver. For an architect friend's potluck-present holiday party, she made a prefab gingerbread house kit based on an obscure style of Frank Lloyd Wright. And when a good talk show producer friend gave birth, she created a six-pack of onesies with famous hosts' pictures ironed on and their names embroidered in florid script. Every child should spend his earliest years in Regiswear.

I began tearing my presents open, unveiling an assortment of goodies determined to enhance my camping experience. There was a body float, for those lazy days on the lake. A tiny clip-on fan for next to my bed, which was probably a gift more for the Bears than me; Christine knew what a whiner I became when I couldn't sleep on hot nights. I was aware of Afty glancing up at me as I laughed at each gift.

"Your girlfriend's a good wrapper," he said. He sounded disappointed by her ability, like she had robbed him of something to criticize.

"I'll tell her you said that," I said, opening one of my favorite pictures of us, now framed. It was from a wedding, at which she had worn an aqua coat that used to belong to her late grandmother, and her hair was twisted into an elegant bun that looked clipped from a '60s *Vogue* cover. Since her outfit already looked from an earlier time, when I looked at it I could easily imagine someday showing it to our grandchildren to illustrate just how gorgeous their grandmother was.

Then came a small gift with "Your other two great loves" written on the paper. It was a leather, folded double-frame: on one side was a picture of the cast of *Cheers*. It was my favorite sitcom, which I had watched so religiously in college that when a rerun popped up on TV now, I'd gaze at it as mistily as if it was old home movies. "Awwww, Joshie misses Cliff Clavin," she'd tease me. On the other side of the frame was a picture of Mr. Hankey, a talking piece of poo on *South Park*. I couldn't attribute my love of scatalogical humor to nostalgia: I was just immature. As I looked at these two symbols of all I held precious, I glowed . . . not for the love of all things Norm and poo, but because Christine knew just what made me smile.

The last gift was a large box, and as I pulled it out, Afty sat upright and pointed, his round face finally erupting in a smile. "Look!" he said, seemingly anxious to finally join in my birthday joy. "She screwed up the back!"

I flipped it over and saw that when she had wrapped it, her swath of paper hadn't been long enough to go all the way around the box. There was a narrow uncovered stripe down the middle, which she had covered with a separate rectangular scrap of paper. This imperfection gave Afty great joy. "Guess she's not such a great wrapper after all," he said, resting back with his book, a cheery smile on his face. Afty's birthday had come early, and his present was that somebody else screwed up. As I opened the box to reveal a new giant towel (the old ones I insisted on bringing were worn and nubby), I wondered just how you bonded with a boy who is happy only when there's failure in the air.

CHAPTER ELEVEN

AT LUNCH I WAS STILL SMILING OVER CHRISTINE'S GIFTS, AND MY SWIMMING feedback had been an unsolicited bonus birthday present. I felt like the same great counselor I'd always been, and I held out hope that thirty-four wasn't so different after all. I even knew enough not to call myself "thirty-four years *young*," because that was the kind of expression only old people used.

Lunch was tuna sandwiches, and as soon as Patrioticus sped off to get them, I got a tap on my shoulder from a tennis counselor; there was a phone call for me. I dashed to the phone extension kept in a box bolted to the back outside wall of the dining hall. "Happy birthday, counselor!" sang Christine on the other end.

"Awwww, ain't that nice," I said. "I got your presents. I love them. Every night I'm going to kiss that picture before I go to bed. Oh, and I'll look at yours, too."

"Oh, my poo-loving honey, you say the nicest things," she said. "Glad you like them. How's your special day going?"

"Tuna-salad special. In other words, best birthday ever."

"So what's the big plans for your big night? Anyone throwing you a party?"

I toed the ground. "No. Nobody really knows it's my birthday. I don't want to make a big deal of it."

"No," she corrected. "You don't want to *ask* anyone to make a big deal out of it. But I'll bet it would make you happy if someone made a big deal out of it on their own volition."

I'd heard many grooms talk about how their brides knew exactly what they were really thinking, and they portrayed it as a good thing. How was that good? Going along with my false modesty routine would have been preferable to Christine seeing me as the passive-aggressive narcissist I really was.

"I don't want a celebration motivated only by guilt. I can see the card now: 'Dear Josh, Happy birthday! Signed, Our collective sense of obligation.'"

She sighed. "I love you, and I wish I was there to tell everybody. But I'm not, so go back in there and tell someone for me. I hate being the lone keeper of such a deep, dark secret."

When I sat back down at the table, Reg said, "Saved you some potato chips. Tougher than you'd think with these animals. Good phone call?"

"Yeah." I grabbed the basket and dumped the lingering crushed chip shrapnel on my plate, then reached for the bowl of tuna. "Christine." She was right. I was having a great day, why not share the news beyond Afty? He'd only get excited if I lit my hair on fire with my own birthday candles. "Wishing me a happy birthday."

"What? Big secret at the table!" exclaimed Reg, raising his eyebrows. "Happy birthday! Why the surprise?"

"I didn't want to take anything away from Patroticus's special day as waiter."

"Happy birthday," said Action, punching me on the arm. He was wearing a hideous puce polo shirt with pink stripes around the sleeves, and I happily punched him back. There was something about Action being a good-looking kid and so indifferent to his own awful wardrobe that made me optimistic for humanity. Whenever I'd see him at the dock happily wearing a bathing suit that just covered his upper thigh while every other boy was covered down to the knee, I knew that all was not lost for the youth of today.

"This is big, boys, very big," said Reg. "What'd everybody get the old man?"

"But . . . we didn't know," said Rattler. "And we don't have any money here." His panicky look indicated that his mother had ingrained in him a strict sense of duty. His freckles seemed to glow redder with embarrassment.

"Didn't anyone ever tell you that the best gifts are the ones you make yourself?" I said. "Here's my wish list. Action and the Fog: By dinner, make me a DVD player out of leaves and pine cones. Patrioticus, nothing special. Maybe use some Senior Cove sand and some fishing line and fashion me a Playstation. Big B and Rattler, use your best judgment. Just don't knit me a stereo. I've already got one of those."

"How old are you?" asked the Rattler.

"Thirty-four," I said.

"Wow," said Big B, a bit of mayo stuck to his sneering lip. "That's pretty old. That's like my dad's age."

"Your dad isn't thirty-four," I snapped. "You're fourteen so, what, he had you when he was nineteen?"

"Maybe he's not thirty-four, but he's old, you're old, so what's the difference?"

I glared at him. "I am this close to downgrading you to Little B, wiseass," I said, snatching a chip off his plate and taking a bite. "He who giveth the nickname can taketh away."

"And you smelleth like old dude," cracked Big B.

Reg cackled. "Point for Big B on Grampa Wolk's birthday!"

Dessert arrived, chocolate-chip cookies. The boys clamored for the milk, which emptied quickly, and we sent Patrioticus to get more. Since half of us had Patrioticus' cold milk straight from the fridge and the other half were drinking the lukewarm milk that had been sitting on our table the entire meal, an impassioned debate began over whether cookies were noticeably worse in warm milk. I delighted in this inconsequential quarrel, which underscored what a wonderfully frivolous world I was a part of. Perhaps tomorrow tighty-whiteys vs. boxers would be the roundtable topic of the day, but until then, we had milk.

It reminded me of the summer after sophomore year of college, when

I was living at home and working as a waiter at a Pizzeria Uno. My good friend Chris was painting houses. Both were the kind of jobs that had only one benefit: As soon as we were done for the day, they ceased to exist in our minds. When I clocked out, I was done; no going home and worrying about the big pepperoni presentation I had coming up the next day.

This was the summer that Burger King announced "Burger Buddies," which were two tiny burgers served in a rectangular paper coffin, and the sales pitch was that you could eat each one in only three bites. (It was a short-lived campaign, as Burger King had overestimated the target audience of People Who Are Sick of All That Biting.) The commercials were incessant, so one night after work Chris picked me up and we bought three orders of Burger Buddies to test their sales promise. We drove to the parking lot of a community swimming pool near his house, where we opened our cartons and each selected a miniburger. After my third bite, I saw that I still had a sliver left. Chris had the same. We tried different angles on the second and the third, but both times found that the arc of the human jawline meant that, geometrically, three bites would always leave a small shred of Buddy in your fingers. We sat in the car, feet up on the dashboard, idly finishing off our fries and pondering what this all meant. Was Burger King a big liar? If we turned this smoking gun over to McDonald's, would it end the rivalry for good? We talked for an hour about this turn of events, the car filled with an odor of greasy meat and chlorine wafting in from the nearby pool; if someone had squirted suntan lotion into the window it would have made the perfect summer hybrid odor. For years after, I remembered that as the last moment that my mind was entirely uncluttered with worry. It was summer, I was with one of my best friends, and the most important thing we had on our minds at that moment was fact-checking a Burger King commercial.

The cookie discussion was similarly relaxing. I sat back and listened to the various theses and rebuttals fly back and forth, the boys fervently dunking chunks of cookie into their glass to further their point. I leaned toward Rattler, who had his hand in his milk glass up to his palm. "Hey, be careful there! I like warm milk, too, but you can't directly dunk a cookie into it."

He looked at me. "Why not?"

My aim was to play off the old urban legend about how Mikey from the Life cereal commercial had died mixing Pop Rocks and Coke. "It's an explosive combination. You could blow us all up."

Big B snorted at me. He loved to be the first to snort.

"You don't believe me? You know who it happened to, don't you?" I was ready to deliver the punch line: Some young, just-forgotten child star had dunked a chocolate-chip cookie into warm milk and had died in the explosion. But I hadn't thought it through yet, and I had no name. No problem, one would come to me, I wrote about pop culture for a living. Who was the 2003 equivalent of Mikey? I needed a famous kid who would have been big about three years before, the way the Life cereal kid had just vanished when his death became a nationwide rumor. As the kids stared at me, I rifled through my mental pop-culture Rolodex. Olsen Twins? No, they were still too famous. The girl from the show *Blossom*? No, before their time. Were there any popular commercials with kids? Dammit, ever since I got TiVo I hadn't watched a commercial.

The longer I paused, the more quickly my joke was becoming moot. My mind finally lit on the only movie kid's face I could think of: Dakota Fanning. In the next couple of years she would go on to become a ubiquitous child star in huge movies like *War of the Worlds*, but at the time she had only been noticed in *I Am Sam*. I couldn't even remember her name at the time, but I hated to leave my joke unfinished. "The girl from *I Am Sam*," I said, still trying to sell it. "She went dunking and *kablooey!* Killed her instantly."

There was a moment of silence.

"Who?" said Patrioticus.

"Wait, what?" said Action.

"What's *I Am Sam*?" asked Rattler. "Is that like *Green Eggs and Ham*?"

Reg just laughed at me. "The girl from *I Am Sam*?"

"Yeah, her. You know, like the Mikey thing?" I looked back at Reg for support. He just kept laughing. Didn't they have urban legends in Australia?

The Fog said quietly, "Who's Mikey?" His hand fluttered nervously over his mouth when he spoke.

"The kid who mixed Pop Rocks and Coke!" I said impatiently.

They looked at me as if I had just quoted an old Burns and Allen routine.

"What's Pop Rocks?" asked the Fog, his hand dropping to his lap in confusion.

I was three layers out of touch. I might still be able to convince myself that thirty-four wasn't a one-step-closer-to-death sentence, but it was hard to rationalize that I was still just another kid.

That evening I found myself at a bar, drinking a Bass ale and giggling sycophantically at stories being traded by counselors, which I didn't entirely get. Earlier that afternoon I had told Helen about my birthday, and she said that I shared it with biter-turned-counselor Jim; she had plans with him and a few others to go into town that night to celebrate and told me I should come along. I had mixed feelings about the invite. I pictured Helen nominating me to come along, and everyone shrugging, "Well, we were going to sing 'Happy Birthday' anyway, so I suppose we can just add his name into the song." I may have been bonding easily with the campers, but I was still having trouble with the staff.

Sean bought me my first beer, and everyone gave me and Jim a hearty birthday toast, but before the *ting*s of the clinked glasses had faded, they were all immersed in a rousing dissection of all the campers: who had changed, who had grown, who was more or less a pain in the ass. I was lost. I wondered if this would be easier for me if I'd never been to Eastwind before and therefore wasn't so acutely aware of how good it was to know the camper shorthand.

Three beers later, however, things started to get more comfortable, as things always do after three beers. The dart tossers next to us finished their game and wandered off, and Sean hopped up to initiate a game. Even better. What could be an easier bonding exercise than darts? The conversational parameters were "Crappy shot!" to "Sweet shot!", so you couldn't go wrong as long as you didn't hit anyone in the head. The more beer we drank, the louder our game got; the back had emptied out, so we started experimenting by venturing to the farthest corners of the room and heaving the darts twenty feet, seeing how close we could come to the board. Fun with sharp objects! We celebrated every nondeath with another toast. *Ting!*

After practically smashing a jukebox by attempting to stand on one leg, lean to the side, and toss a dart sidearm around a wood post, I realized I was done and plunked down on a chair next to Benny, a twenty-four-year-old first-time hiking counselor with a hippie's imperturbable smile and a long ponytail that might have come free with a VW bus. We chatted about our lives; I told him about New York, he told me about his winters as a ski instructor/short-order cook. At this point I was one beer away from hugging him. He held out his glass for an umpteenth birthday toast. *Ting.* "Hey, man," he said. "So how old are you?"

"You tell me," I said. "How old do you think I am?" I had my hair, I had the ability to recklessly throw darts. He had to land close.

He looked deeply in my eyes, taking in all my life force. Then he nodded, happy with the answer that had come to him. "Forty-two."

It had taken thirty-four years, but I finally did my first authentic spit-take. "*Forty-two?*" I groaned, wiping beer foam off my chin. "I'm thirty-four. What's with forty-two?"

"No offense, bro," he said, shaking his head, making his ponytail lazily peek up over each shoulder. "It's not a looks thing. It's an attitude. It's like, you're pretty set in your career and you've got your life planned, getting married and all that."

"And that's a forty-two-year-old thing?"

"Yeah. Well, no. Kind of. It's your generation. You guys were more intense on getting your career on track early. My generation takes their time a little bit more. Like me. I got out of college and just headed out west to be a ski bum. And I'll do it a while until I can figure out what I really want to do."

I was only ten years older than he was; how did that make us different generations? In my mind, you're only in different generations if you're old enough to be someone's father. Plus, I was "Gen X," or so all the news reports had told me; we were supposed to be the slackers. Had we already been replaced by an even slackier youth? Because the way he was talking about me and my peers' humorless career craziness, you'd think we were the Greatest Generation. Did he think I had gotten my swim-instructor certification on the G. I. Bill?

"No offense, man," he said, flinching as a dart Sean tossed behind his back whizzed dangerously close. "I meant it as a good thing. Someday I hope to have my shit together like that, but until then, hey, it's all good." Up went his glass for an umpteenth-plus-one toast. I tried to muddle through what this interaction all meant: I seemed forty-two, but in a good way? He saw me as career-oriented, even as a camp counselor? He thought I had my shit together? It all made my head hurt, but there would be plenty of time for that tomorrow morning, so I let the buzz settle me on his reassuring take-home lesson: It's all good.

Ting.

CHAPTER TWELVE

CAMP PEOPLE SHARE A SPECIAL BOND, EVEN WHEN THEY HAVEN'T ATTENDED the same one. I could tell I'd met a fellow ex-camper as soon as I mentioned how much I loved Eastwind. I saw the dewy flash of fraternity in his eyes, as if he'd been wandering the land for years, searching for a fellow member of the Brotherhood of Bunk-Beds, and only now had finally found someone who would understand him. And from there we'd effortlessly fall into a trade-off of reminiscences, both drunk in the mutual exuberance of remembering our summer places where everything went right.

My sister's husband, David, spent a total of fourteen years as a camper and counselor, and that was all the reference I needed to know he should be part of the family. We grew closer with every memory we swapped, until one day when we were sharing stories about camp trips we'd taken. His old camp was in New Hampshire, so we'd gone to many of the same mountains, rivers, and beaches. We had both lugged similar backpacks and camping gear, scarfed equitable fistfuls of gorp, left beaches with similar amounts of sand stuck in our bathing suits from poorly ended body surfs. And in the midst of our "Did you have . . . ?" "Of course we did!" exchanges, he said, "And then there was the make-out bus."

"Excuse me?"

"The make-out bus." His alma mater had a sister camp, and they did everything together. "When we had all-camp trips, the 'couples' got to ride on one bus, each sharing a seat, and on the ride home they'd all be totally making out."

"No, we definitely didn't have that." I laughed. "Eastwind was all boys."

"All boys?" he said. "But you had a sister camp, right?"

"Nope. It was just us."

He stared at me for a moment of disbelief. "Then what was the point?" It was as if we'd been talking for hours about our love of fine restaurants, and I'd just revealed that I never ate anything, I just liked to go lick the napkins.

Coed veterans couldn't understand an all-boys camp. When I hit thirteen, none of my friends at home could understand why I went to Eastwind, either. Especially when my other friends who had gone coed came home with bodice-ripping tales of first French kisses behind the arts and crafts shack. I came home with a certificate for scoring at least thirty points on ten targets at riflery. I could have made the argument that a hickey faded, but the title of Marksman 1st Class would last forever, but it was tough to work up any enthusiasm for it.

When anyone asked why I went to boys' camp, my long-standing explanation was that when I started, I was eleven and didn't yet care if girls were around, and by the time I did, I was too in love with Eastwind to switch to coed. Which was partly true. But there was also relief in spending a month sequestered from girls; it was as if you'd spent the entire school year sucking in your gut, and for one glorious summer you could finally exhale and let it droop over your bathing suit. You didn't have to look or smell good; you could be muddy, sticky, or mysteriously moist. School was a hotbed of teasing and snobbery because everyone was consumed with the need to attract (or at least not disgust) the opposite sex, and the easiest way to make yourself appear bigger was to tear down the guy next to you.

When I was a camper, we had one dance a month with a neighboring girls' camp, and it was enough. Only thirteen-year-olds and up were invited, and for the seven days leading up to the dance, we were obsessed. Big talk of inevitable conquests filled the three eldest cabins, though many of us silently dreaded the day. A female counselor usually took an activity period to offer dancing and tutor us in the Eastwind shuffle: for fast songs, step to the right, bring left foot to meet it, then step to the left, bring right foot to meet it. Repeat for entire evening, augmenting with hand claps and chin bobs as confidence builds. For slow songs, do the same, only at half the speed and with hands placed on the girl's waist.

When the girls first arrived, we began with a "getting to know you" event. Some boys were assigned girls to take out in a boat. The rest of us landlubbers went to the Sports Lawn—a large field next to Senior Cove—for an allegedly fun sporting event: tossing Frisbees, playing New Games, etc. One year a counselor from the girls' camp told all the boys to throw a shoe into the center of the field, after which the girls would each pick one and have to chat with its owner. Already wearing a size-13 shoe at age fourteen, I knew this would not end well. If you were a girl and playing the odds with an anonymous shoe pile, would you go with the average-sized Nike, or the gargantuan Air Yeti?

After a barbecue dinner, we all went up to the Theater, a wide building just above the Bears where Saturday-night entertainment like camp plays and talent shows were held. At these get-togethers, a counselor played music, while nobody danced for an hour. Counselors encouraged us to ask someone to dance, but it was less with an eye toward gettin' the party started than with the gleeful hope to embarrass us. "That girl seems cute, and you should ask her to dance. Here, I'll help," they'd say and purposefully wander over to the girl while you begged, "No no no no no, please don't, no no no no." At the last second before reaching the girl they would veer away, winking back at you. We hated it, but of course couldn't wait until we were counselors so we could take up the torture mantle.

But when I was still a camper, by the second hour enough boys had worked up courage so that the middle of the Theater actually looked like a dance floor. A respectable jumble of side-stepping boys and girls stretched across the floor, occasionally backing away to make room for a breakdancing exhibition by an unstreetwise suburban Jew who had worn out his

VHS copy of the movie *Beat Street*. The night ended with either "Stair-way to Heaven" or "Free Bird": Both anthems started slow, paced per-fectly for deep embraces and gentle rocking, but escalated at the end, forcing couples to wrest their grips to fast-dance so when the final notes played it was easier for the girls'-camp counselors to separate their wards and herd them back on their bus.

There were always a few success stories, guys who managed to squirrel their "dates" out into the woods for some blind groping amongst the leaves. My friend Peter was a dance legend, each year getting one base further than any of us thought possible. With his Izod collar turned up and his hair perfectly gelled, he stood at the front of the crowd when the girls first descended from their bus. Like Babe Ruth pointing over the wall to predict where he'd hit his home run, Peter waited through the parade and then, with a mighty finger, pointed out his chosen conquest. And the rest of us stood behind him, solemnly bearing witness to his ability to see the future.

When we returned to the cabin, we bragged about anything we could qualify as successful. It could be for dancing twice with the same girl, it could be for dancing once. It could be for deciding *not* to ask a girl to dance who was clearly eyeing us but wasn't deemed pretty enough. It could even be for having a retort when rejected: A cabinmate who got turned down took great pride in his reply, "That's all right, I had to take a shit anyway." He told the story so many times you'd think he'd discovered the cure for acne on the walk back to the boys' side. But the fact was, none of us had very much tactile experience to brag about. So we'd gather awestruck around Peter's bunk as he took us through every piece of un-derwear he broached. One year there was even a ceremonial smelling of his fingers.

My last mixer as a dancer and not a dance enforcer was in 1985, as a sixteen-year-old CIT. I was an extremely late bloomer compared to my friends, with plenty of female friends but no girlfriend yet. But I was half a counselor that summer, so I had accrued 50 percent more self-confidence, and I mustered the nerve to ask a quiet, long-haired Argentin-ian girl to dance. Her name was Katarina, and we Eastwind-strutted to

Huey Lewis, Duran Duran, and Simple Minds. When the DJ cued up Phil Collins' "One More Night"—a slow song—and she made no move to thank me and back away slowly, I thought that I finally might end a dance with a story to tell. After Phil's last plaintive cry for an additional night, I asked her if she wanted to take a walk. She shrugged and said, "OK."

Where should we go? The woods seemed too forward. The woods were for guys who knew they were going to score and assumed the girls knew, too; I might as well bring her to a motel. Instead I suggested we head down to Senior Cove to look out on the lake. Her English was good but hesitant. My English was great, but more hesitant. We sat at a picnic table and stared out over the water, the moon reflecting down onto it perfectly. From everything I'd learned about romance through movies and TV, this was the most ideal spot you could get. After a discussion of how she liked tennis and I liked tennis, I stopped, took a deep breath, and leaned in for a kiss.

If our tongues were dancers, hers was definitely leading. She swatted mine around her mouth like a cat playing with a dead mouse. It may not have had style, but it was certainly all right with me, since I didn't know what I was doing, and as I thought of where I was—on the beach cookout table, by the lake, my tongue taking a ride on a Tilt-A-Whirl—I knew that once again Eastwind proved itself to be the greatest place on Earth.

As the tumble cycle of her mouth continued for a while, I thought, What would Peter do? Perhaps it was time to go a little further. I moved my hand on her back a little forward, to clutch her bicep. No signs of fleeing. I moved it to the front of her arm. All was still well. And then, slowly, I moved my hand over her right breast.

And with that, it was all over.

It didn't end with a yelp, or a curse, or a slap. It was as if I had been making out with a robot and had accidentally bumped against the reset button. She just abruptly turned away and stared out onto the lake, stone-faced.

"Uhhhhh," I said. "Sorry?"

She said nothing, just looked forward, her arms crossed against her chest.

"I'm *really* sorry." Was there some way I could salvage this? Was there some maneuver, some explanation, some smooth wordplay or gesture I should know how to make at this point to get my tongue back into the game? We sat in silence for another few moments. Finally I said, "I guess we should go back to the dance."

We walked back up the road, me one step behind, muttering a series of apologies, each one incrementally more pathetic than the last. I'd have preferred that she'd yelled at me. Her complete silence implied that my grope had been so egregious that I had shocked her dumb. In the Theater, she joined her friends while I blushed among mine.

Afterward I gathered with my fellow CITs for debriefings. Peter, as usual, had an outrageous tale involving the most attractive girl there. I stayed quiet about mine. I still felt both angry and penitent about the way it had ended, but at the same time thrilled by the fact that something had happened at all. For the next three days I ran the evening over in my head. It had been exhilarating, confusing, arousing, and a part of me wanted to relive it and redo it. But an even bigger part of me was relieved that it was over, and I could go back to letting my gut hang out.

Frank had since phased out dances. He saw how it turned the older campers into nerve-wracked, hormone-inflamed monsters during the lead-ups and decided that wasn't what camp was supposed to be about. But just because there weren't girls around didn't mean the older boys could put them out of their mind. The absence of females only made the boys talk more about what they'd do if girls were there, because there was no danger of having to back it up. We all know the cliché of the lonely boy lying to his friends about his girlfriend in Canada; at camp, everybody had a girlfriend in Canada, and if you went by camper stories, Canada was home to the horniest ladies on Earth.

This summer's collective hormone level was significantly elevated by the presence of Katia, a Latvian kitchen girl. Katia, nineteen, had a round face and apple cheeks, but she radiated pure naughtiness, reminding me of every sexy foreign-exchange student from an '80s sex comedy. Between meals she headed down to the waterfront in a red bikini, asking to go on a sailboat or playfully splashing around our swimming lessons. Her broken

English made everything sound like a come-on. One day I was teaching boys how to dive off the Raft, and when the period ended and I sent them back to shore, she suddenly splashed up onto the Raft next to me, standing a little too close, and said, "Josh, you can please show me to dive, too?" She sauntered over to the Raft's edge. She seemed to always be moving in slow motion, like Phoebe Cates in *Fast Times at Ridgemont High*. "I stand, and bend over . . . like thees?" She stuck her shiny butt out and looked at me with an arched eyebrow. Even in the middle of nature, I swore I heard the sound *boinnnnnng!*

I couldn't take this perceived flirtation as a personal compliment, as every single other counselor thought she was coming on to him. One day I stood on the beach talking to Jousting Chas and Richard—the placid forty-year-old head of the waterfront who spent most of his spare time reading up on Eastern religions—and Katia skipped up happily, having just finished her first kayak ride. After shaking her long brown hair, she leaned into us, her bikini doing exactly what it was made to do, and ex-claimed, "I just did my wet exit!", the term for flipping over in a kayak and sliding out of the boat underwater. She turned and bounced off in slow motion.

After a moment of watching her leave, the Zen-like Richard finally broke the silence. "I think I just had a wet exit."

Katia circulated around camp, giving every activity a sexual overtone it never had before. At leather shop, kids imprinted their names in home-made wallets by using individual letter stamps and bashing them into the soft leather with a hammer. But when she leaned into the activity's coun-selor and said, "So I bang here *real hard*?" wallets and keychains seemed very much beyond the point.

When she walked through the camp, only the youngest kids seemed unphased. Those ages eight to ten just smiled and giggled when she came by and hugged them. But her presence hip-checked all the ten- to twelve-year-olds into puberty, and they lapsed into a confused silence in her presence. She had an emboldening effect on the teenagers. It took only three days for her to be all that the older campers talked about. I walked into my cabin after second period and found a bunch of my campers and some visiting Lions playing cards, bragging about who saw Katia bend over, or who saw that her nipples were hard under her bikini top. This was followed by endless arguments over whom she was clearly in love with.

"She is so totally into me."

"Are you kidding? Today at lunch I went up to get seconds and she was *so* into me!"

"Right," said a Lion sarcastically. "She felt bad for you. I was up there and she was crazy flirting with me. She said, 'What do you want?' I said, 'Give me some of your *mashed potatoes*.' " He accentuated this by fondling imaginary breasts. They all laughed as if witness to a double entendre of Wildeian proportions. Adolescents were able to come up with an endless supply of nonsensical dirty euphemisms because their creativity wasn't hindered by an actual familiarity with breasts or vaginas.

The next day, Thursday, was our cabin trip, an old tradition of bonding. Mitch had assured Trevor and me that he would take care of everything. He had led so many trips over the years that he could throw together any excursion on autopilot, ordering the lunch food from the kitchen, reserving a van, and plotting our itinerary. I offered to help but was just waved away. "I got it, don't worry about it," he said, and then walked away before I could even ask where we were going.

After breakfast, the Bears assembled around two vans, swinging their knapsacks at each other as we waited for Mitch to come back with the lunch fixings.

"Come on, knock it off," I said as Mudge just missed Wind-Up's head.

"I didn't hit him," said Mudge, gazing at me with annoyed eyes.

"That's true, but he did come pret-ty darn close, pretty darn close indeed!" said Wind-Up, holding up two fingers to show just how nearly he was missed. "Felt the wind, too, whoa! It was just a little breeze on the ear, and I kind of jumped to the side. I think—and I'm not sure—but I think I felt the very tip of his backpack zipper graze my earlobe, just a graze, but it was there, wow, it was there!"

"Shut up," said Mudge, and Wind-Up didn't. Mudge just rolled his eyes and checked himself out in a van's side-view mirror.

Trumps stood on the rear fender of the green van, bouncing up and down. His extra weight made it rock dramatically. "Where we going?" he asked me as I waved him off.

I had no idea. I was just as much a guest on Mitch's trip as they were. But the key to looking like a good leader was never admitting you were clueless. "It's a surprise."

"There's no plan, is there," said Mudge.

The kitchen door at the side of the Dining Hall banged open, and Mitch came out clutching a big metal tin of food. "Why aren't you punks in the vans? Don't you want to go on this trip?" he barked.

"Yeah, everybody in the vans!" I echoed. They all piled in, with shouts of, "No, I need the window!" "I get carsick!" "Why do I have to be on the hump?" "Wind-Up, you go in the back."

Mitch threw the food in the back of the white van. "You guys want to follow me?" I had the keys so I drove the green van, and Trevor got in next to me. Lefty, Action, the Fog, and Mudge—who I'd learned were the cabin's tightest quartet of old friends—piled in along with us. Captain Marquee also scrambled aboard, his healthy ego allowing him to join any group and assume he was their leader. As I pulled our van out of the driveway, Katia came out of the Dining Hall. Lefty opened his window and leaned out. "Heeeeeey, Katia." He swept his hand through his bristly, immovable crewcut; it was a testament to his confidence that even though his hair wouldn't move if you placed it at the business end of a leaf blower, the move still looked smooth on him.

"Oh, hello Lefty!" she cooed, waving. For all of everyone's private smut talk, he had been the only one to actually engage her in conversation. Jousting Chas had told me that she wandered down to sailing on the first day of camp, asking to go in a boat, and Lefty had boldly walked up to her, introduced himself, and shook her hand. Everyone else had just stared, unclear that that was even an option. "He didn't drool, he didn't stare at her breasts, he didn't say the word 'gazongas,' he just introduced himself like a man," Chas told me later. "You've *got* to reward that." So he put her in Lefty's boat so he could show off his sailing ability. Now the rest of the boys soaked in her attention by proxy, grinning dopily out the window. "Where are you to go?" she asked.

"Off on a cabin trip," Lefty yelled. "Wanna come? There's room in the van!"

She giggled coyly. At age thirty-four, I admired his self-confidence. At fourteen, I would have considered him a God. "No, I must help make the lunch!"

We pulled farther away, following Mitch and the other boys. "Awww, too bad," yelled Lefty behind him. "We'll bring you a souvenir!" He retracted his head back into the van and was showered with high fives and head rubs, as if by human contact the other Bears could absorb some of his raw courage.

I blindly followed Mitch, gaining speed as we hit the interstate. Ninety minutes later, we pulled off the highway to a spot I recognized from my very first cabin trip: It was a set of falls where mountain runoff water surged between rocks, creating flume chutes that ended in deep icy pools. It was a popular spot, crowded with families and other camp groups. "We're here for an hour," Mitch said to the guys. "So get swimming." He jumped from rock to rock toward the water. The other guys dropped their stuff and ran after him.

I stood watch over their clothes. On the next rock over, a couple of middle-aged women sat on towels, handing out sandwiches to some teenage girls. None of the Bears had noticed them in their rush to the water. "Uh-oh, are you guys a boys' camp?" said one of the women.

"Yeah, Camp Eastwind," I said. "Are you from a girls' camp?"

"No," she said. "We're a mothers group. We plan activities for our daughters over the summer so we can do things together and get them out of town where they just talk about boys all day long." She laughed. "Looks like we took them to the wrong place!"

I looked out at the predatory Bears she was worried about. They had lined up in bobsled formation and launched themselves down a water chute. At the end, the water split into two different directions around a giant rock. As lead man on the train, Trumps went right for the rock and smacked into it. I could see his eyes bulge as the pressure of nine boys pushed behind him. The last man, Dewey, peeled off the line and was swept down to the left, screaming wildly; in front of him, Afty swung right. In turn the rest of them gradually broke away from their entanglement, giggling and yelping, until finally a flattened Trumps slowly slid around the rock, like a hurled egg oozing down a wall.

Giggling madly as they met in the basin, they scurried up the sides of the rock to try it again. I turned to the woman. "I think your daughters are safe."

CHAPTER THIRTEEN

MITCH WHISTLED AND WAVED THE BOYS OUT OF THE WATER. THEY EMERGED with raspberry scrapes patchworking their limbs from caroming against the rocks, but seemed no less entertained for it. When they scrambled into the vans, I asked Mitch, "So . . . where to next?"

"A rope swing I know," he said. "It oughta keep them happy. Then we'll go to one other great jumping spot. Just follow me."

Mitch knew every place in New England where you could leap into water from a great height. Whether it was a bridge or a tree branch or a cliff or a rope swing, Mitch had them all noted on his mental map. Today's rope swing was on a riverbank that we reached by cutting through a suburban backyard and wandering through some woods. The boys needed some coaxing to give it a try. Mitch immediately took the first ride, timing his dismount on the perfect high point of his upswing, eight feet in the air, hovering briefly in a tableau of nature and bravado before plunging into the surprisingly deep water. Hopping back onshore, he sat down on a rock, pulled a music magazine out of his knapsack, and said, "Now which one of you punks is next?" That didn't sound like an enticing invitation to fun and frolic to me, but the boys responded, albeit after an exchange of shoves and "You firsts." While I took Mitch's exaggerated macho jabs as an accusation, the kids took it as a joke.

Action went first, and his wild whoops encouraged Lefty, the Fog, Mudge, and Captain Marquee to get in line. "There's no way I can do that!" said Afty happily, jiggling his belly with his hands. "I'm one hundred and fifty pounds! Trumps, Dewey, and I are fat, we'll never get our legs up high enough!" Trumps and Dewey did not look happy to be involuntarily initiated as members of the Fat Failure Club.

Everyone eventually tried, with mixed success. In keeping with his inability to recognize his own preternatural talents, Action had looked nervous at first, but after his second try he was doing flips off his dismount. Captain Marquee could only muster a short arc because his short size meant he couldn't back too far away from the riverbank and still hold the rope, but he accessorized his truncated swings with a histrionic Tarzan cry. When Wind-Up first tried, he explained his approach with the rope: "Okay, the important thing here is the big leap and to grab as high as you can, and everyone should watch out because there might be quite a splash, quite a splasheroo . . ."

"*Just jump, Wind-Up!*" Mitch yelled impatiently, looking up from his magazine.

"Gotcha, Mitch, here comes a jump." He leapt, and held his body only momentarily before his arms gave out. His gangly legs dragged through the water, which pulled him down into a dramatic face plant. He came to the surface spluttering, with his finger already in the air as if he was a professor who had just proved an undersea point. "That did not go quite as well as planned," he said as soon as the water drained out of his mouth.

"I told you to raise your legs, you goofball," cracked Mitch.

Afty fell similarly short in his attempts, and he seemed jubilant to have more evidence to confirm his low self-esteem. Every time, he sploshed back to the shore with a smile on his face, peeling his long, black hair out of his eyes and shouting, "Boy, *that* sucked!" The other guys whooped and laughed at him, giving him what he wanted. Only Lefty said, "Come on, man, try it again. You can do it." Afty's smile faded into an indeterminate expression of confusion over how to reconcile peer support.

I stood by watching, cheering for the jumps, wincing at the belly flops, and nudging the reticent Fog—who sat on a tree root after one attempt, hugging his knees—to take another turn. I was happy with this role as land-based moral supporter. But then Trevor stepped up and took his swing, spastically waving his arms as he splashed down. Now I was the only dry counselor, which Action noticed as he grabbed the rope as it swung back. "You gonna take a turn?" he asked, holding the rope out to me.

Actually, I hadn't planned to. My goal had been to remain in a supervisory position. Calm. Steadfast. Stationary. Risk-free. Now everyone was looking at me, but their stares wouldn't be enough to curb my sedentary impulses. The problem was, I couldn't see Mitch behind me. What was he doing? Was he oblivious, engrossed in his magazine and indifferent to my participation? Or was he staring at my back, knowing that my answer would once and for all answer the question, "What does Josh Wolk keep in his nutsack: balls or spare tampons?"

I was thirty-four. I should have been perfectly confident in the contents of my own nutsack. But not around Mitch. I'd been in this position before. This leap off the edge of a rope wasn't all that extreme, but I had a deeply ingrained fear of heights and had never seen fit to challenge it until the summer of 1988. I was a counselor, and at age nineteen I was confidently driving the third van in a convoy of six back to Eastwind after a mammoth beach trip. Mitch was driving the first. Back at the beach, when the counselors counted attendance before pulling onto the road home, Mitch had passed by, whispering, "Follow me, we're gonna make one more stop" to all the drivers. And, predictably, that stop turned out to be a river.

Of the many manly arts that Mitch popularized at Eastwind, bridge jumping was the most widely embraced. By 1988, nearly everyone's trip ended with a high-altitude detour. Leaving the beach, forty boys and eight counselors had followed Mitch en masse to a bridge that stood twenty-five feet above a river. There were no rapids, and you couldn't help but extrapolate from the boulders on each shore of the river that similar rocks lay just beneath its dark water. But Mitch swung his legs over the metal rail, pointed out the deep sweet spot in the middle of the river, and jumped. He seemed to hover in the air for longer than he should before crashing into the water. Back on shore, he yelled up to the rest of the staff that he'd stay below to watch the jumpers.

Out of any forty boys, around 85 percent were going to be fearless. And these thirty-four shoved each other to form a line. I felt calm, however, knowing I would take no part in it. I was a counselor now, with nothing to prove. If I didn't want to jump, I didn't have to explain myself to anybody. Off the boys went like lemmings, with staff taking their turns in between. I found myself the only counselor still on the bridge at one point, and authoritatively gave the jumpers instructions ("Remember to jump out, but don't lean forward") that I had no experience to base on. Soon the thirty-four bravest had gone multiple times, and only the reticent and terrified were left. "Anyone else?" I said.

"What's wrong? You puds don't want to jump?" I heard behind me. Mitch had traded off his shore spot and come back up, and he squinted at the remainders. His verbal jostle knocked some of the nervous boys off their indecisive precipices, and they swung their legs over the rail with slow reticence. Off they dropped, except for one boy. We'll call him Clutchy, for the way his fingers dug into the steel rail. He was a quiet, amiable kid, beefy and slow-moving; even though he was from upper-middle-class Connecticut, the way he ambled around camp you expected his response to everything to be "Ayup" or "I reckon." And now he was agitated in a way I'd never seen him before. His struggle to keep a nonchalant smile on his face lost out to a grimace. "I'll do it . . . I'll do it . . ." he kept repeating.

My friend Todd, who had already jumped, came back up to the bridge. He and I had grown up together and were now both counselors. He had become an avowed outdoorsman, a quiet, fearless sort with a bulletproof physique. "You going, Josh?" It was said with no agenda or judgment, he was simply noting that I was the only staffer who hadn't gone. Had Todd been the only one there, I probably would have just said "Nope."

But there was Mitch. And just then, a timid nine-year-old stepped up. He was tiny even for his age, and could barely get his legs over the rail. And a moment later he was gone, on his second jump. Clutchy groaned and turned even paler. And I knew that, goddammit, now I had to jump, too.

I'd never ranked my shortcomings before, but on that day I learned that my susceptibility to peer pressure had seniority over my fear of heights. Mitch had said nothing, but I took his very presence—standing there, still damp from his inaugural, flinch-free leap—as an accusation. If fetal nine-year-olds were hurling themselves off the bridge, what would it make me if I didn't?

Shakily, I found myself on the lip of the bridge, next to Clutchy, who had made it that far, too. "It's not so hard," I said to him, attempting to forget my own fear by spreading inspiration. I gulped, and leapt. It was farther than I thought. When I expected impact, I kept falling. My lungs overinflated with the extra gasp, and the tension that built for the last interminable microsecond until I hit the water was shocking.

But emerging from the river, I was afire with adrenaline, jittery with pride and exhilaration. I bounded back up to the bridge, where I could see Clutchy still hanging on with wide, terrified eyes, all his limbs stiff like rigor mortis. "Are you gonna do this or not?" Mitch was asking him. When I approached, he looked at me, shrugged, and then walked back toward the van, where the kids were slowly being herded.

"I'm gonna do it, I gotta do it," Clutchy mumbled.

I leaned on the rail. "I know it's scary," I said. "Believe it or not, I was scared. But after it's over, you feel incredible. I think we should just count to three, and then you'll go. OK?"

"Uh . . . OK," he said.

"One, two . . . three!" I yelled. He lurched forward slightly, then yanked himself back. He whimpered and cursed himself.

"Relax, relax, you can do this." I felt compelled to make him do it. His day shouldn't be marred by this memory. I counted again. He didn't jump. Tears rolled down his cheeks. "*Why can't I do this?*" he sobbed.

We were now the only two on the bridge. I could see a counselor rounding up the last few boys swimming around the river's edge.

"*Clutchy!*" Mitch was bellowing from the vans. "*It's now or never. We're leaving.*"

Clutchy swallowed an anguished sob and stared down at the river, quivering. "Push me," he said.

"What?"

"*Push me! You have to push me!*"

I shook my head and put my hand on his back. "I can't do that."

"*Please!*"

I couldn't. But a part of me wanted to for his own good. I was still giddy with the aftershocks of my jump; he could have that sensation, too, instead of walking back to the vans, wearing the only dry bathing suit in the group.

No. I wasn't pushing a kid off a bridge. "Why don't you come on back. We have to go. It's no problem, you'll do it next time." I held him firmly by the arm and helped him ease his legs back over the rail, onto the road. His shoulders slumped, jerking with the occasional irrepressible sob. We walked slowly back to the vans where all the other kids waited for him. I got him inside his van, where he sat miserably, head pressed against the window. I was driving a different one; when I hopped in, everyone was talking about their leaps. "Hey, Josh, wasn't that awesome?" someone yelled.

"Pretty kick-ass," I said, glad I did it, even gladder that it was over, and wishing most of all that we had never stopped there.

Fifteen years later I looked at the rope swing being handed to me by Trumps. This dismount wouldn't be nearly as high as the beach trip bridge, but as it had been years since I'd done anything remotely physically daring, it took very little to make me nervous. "Okay, my turn I guess," I said, stepping back onto the launching rock, balancing awkwardly while I cinched my hands up the rope. As a figure of seniority, it was my obligation to look cool; if I took a face plant like Wind-Up, it would be like seeing your dad get pantsed by the captain of your high-school football team: No wisdom he could ever impart would erase the suspicion that when it came to negotiating the important stuff in life, he was no smarter than you.

Letting fly, I pulled up my knees, just clearing the water with my long legs. I released perfectly, savoring that split-second moment between rising and falling before crashing down with a splash. I tried not to seem too ecstatic as I swam in. As I groped my way up onto shore out of the muddy riverbed, I looked up with forced nonchalance. Mitch was still deeply immersed in his magazine. Trevor clapped, though. Him, I didn't need to impress.

"Wow, Josh, you just barely missed the water with those long legs!" yelled Lefty, pointing at me with his free hand.

Wind-Up started in. "Let me ask you this, Josh, were you more bending your knees or pulling up with your arms, because I'm looking to figure out just what I'm doing wrong. I feel like there's just one change to the equation I need and then I'll be flying high." He took the rope again and barely cleared the shore before flailing into the river. I cheered with everyone else as Wind-Up stood again and said, "Ahhh, I think I know what happened there. There's no question that next time I'll have this all put together."

So forget Mitch, I thought. Even if he didn't notice, there was a gleeful jolt in joining the Bears' rope-swinging fraternity.

We loaded into the van, with Mitch muttering that we had one more stop. A half-hour drive found me following Mitch into a very familiar parking lot. "Where are we going now?" grumbled Mudge, his sour delivery unaffected by the fun he'd had that day.

"Not sure," said the ever-chipper Trevor. "But that's part of the fun, right?"

I grimaced at his enthusiasm. I had a feeling where we were going, and it wasn't fun at all. As we all got out of the van and hiked up a road, I saw my instincts were correct. We were back on the same bridge over the same river where Clutchy had begged me to push him.

While childhood landmarks always look smaller when you return to them as an adult, this bridge hadn't shrunk at all. I got very quiet as we followed Mitch, as did the rest of the boys. Unlike in '88, when the boys had run to be first off the bridge, this group of boys all blanched as they peered over the edge.

"So which of you are going to step up and be a man and try this?" Mitch certainly hadn't changed his approach to this activity.

"Are you crazy?" said Mensa, craning his long neck over the edge while stretching a leg behind him to make sure he couldn't possibly fall over. "Clearly, this jump could kill you."

Mitch snorted. "No, it can't, you weenie. Fine, I'll show you." He didn't even bother to swing his legs over the rail, he just climbed up on top of it and jumped from there, adding about three feet to his drop. Madness. The boys went crazy, running in circles of amazement.

"I guess it's now or never, huh, guys?" said Trevor. As a rock climber, he had no fear of heights, and with a big grin, he vanished over the edge. This made the boys even crazier, and they were still flabbergasted when Mitch climbed the hill back to the bridge. He was peppered with questions. "Was it scary?" "What about rocks?" "Does it hurt?" "Is it deep enough?"

"Aw, you Marys!" he yelled. "It's twenty-five feet deep. Now, is anyone gonna get up there or should we just go home?" He flashed a half smile as he scanned the group.

No one moved. Action took a couple of steps toward the rail, purposefully put his hands on them as if about to vault himself over, then looked down and backed away, saying, "No no no no no!"

"Oh, come on, it's safe. I just did it. Let's go, *boys*," said Mitch.

Trevor had stayed below on the shore to lifeguard. He waved and shouted, "It's not bad! Just close your eyes!" Jerk. Eye-closing, "not-bad"-saying jerk. Brave jerk.

Lefty snuck up to the edge and kept staring down. "Why don't you just jump?" said Mudge. "You scared?"

"Me?" said Lefty. "I don't see you up there, you pussy."

"I'll probably go later." He turned to Dewey. "What about you? Scared?"

Dewey snapped, "I don't know! I'll do it, I just don't want to be first. Why don't you go first if you're such a big man?"

A forest fire of derision had spread among the boys, sparked by Mitch's match of machismo. The insults passed counterclockwise: When accused of being chicken, the accusee would deny this and prove it by calling the person to his left a wimp. And round the cabin it went, perpetually looping back on itself, a Möbius strip of attempted emasculation.

I moved to the rail myself, feeling dizzy. There had been no quiet internal evolution on that front, no stealth outgrowing of my fear of heights.

But I had jumped before. Could I do it again? I remembered the post-jump adrenaline as a good thing, so maybe it would be worth it. Prove myself to Mitch, elevate myself in front of the boys . . .

And maybe I would kill a bear with my own hands, build a rocket ship out of its bones, fly to the fucking moon, and jump off a bridge into the Sea of Tranquility.

There was no way I was jumping. A rope swing was one thing, this bridge another. I felt myself thumbing through a mental Rolodex of excuses to find one that I could cling to like the bridge rail and actually convince myself was valid and not flimsy. Bad back? Didn't have the right "jumping shoes"? Uh . . . I had it! I was getting married after this, and Christine would *kill* me if I did anything that might result in me walking down the aisle either on crutches or in a sling. Women! And within five seconds I firmly believed that were it not for my worrywart of a fiancée, I'd be in that river right now.

Armed with my new rationalization, I relaxed and began to enjoy the panicky bickering. I wandered over to Mitch and rolled my eyes. I wasn't worried about him judging me anymore because I couldn't jump if I wanted to. "Think any of them will go?" I asked.

"Probably not. Unless we see some serious sack-growing in the next five minutes," he replied, and we laughed together. Boy, this whole emasculation thing was an excellent way to male-bond.

Action cautiously lifted his legs over the rail. He had proved to be the most fearless on the rope swing, having eventually climbed the rope's tree and jumped off an upper branch.

"Oh God, he's gonna do it!" yelled Afty, stepping back in disbelief.

"About time someone did!" I cheered.

"Holy shit, this is high," stammered Action from the edge. His legs shook. "You sure this is deep enough?"

"Don't chicken out now," said Mitch. "You can be the first guy *not* to be a weenie."

Action vanished over the edge, screaming all the way down. The remaining Bears rushed to the edge in disbelief. "HOW WAS IT!" they yelled down.

"AWESOME! AWESOME!" he hollered back, swimming over to Trevor.

Next thing I knew, the Fog was delicately removing his shirt and stepping over the rail. Still waters jumped deep, I thought. All I heard out of him was a quiet, "Oh, shit," before he vanished over the edge. "It's now or never!" yelled Mensa, who then let out a quick "Eek!" and followed him into the river. A few of the other guys echoed his enthusiasm, moving closer to the edge. But nobody got any farther than that. They'd walk to the rail, lift up one foot toward it, and then quickly put it back down and retreat. Finally, Mitch said to me, "Looks like nobody else grew a pair. We should go home."

I snorted. "You got that right," then I yelled to everyone, "All right, that's it. No one else is gonna go, so if you're lucky Action, the Fog, and Mensa will carve out a little slice of reflected glory for all of you. Get to the vans!"

"Maybe next month we'll get some real men," said Mitch loudly to me as we walked back. "Instead of *boys*." The guys weren't offended; they reacted the way they always did to Mitch's crap, by smiling sheepishly. They were more relieved than anything else that they were getting farther from the bridge.

"Hopefully by next month both their balls will have dropped," I replied. Mitch laughed as he jumped shirtless into his driver's seat, and I felt a frisson of kinship. Mitch and I could become good friends, just as long as we kept ourselves surrounded by chickenshits.

As I drove home in my van, listening to the guys talk about how brave the Fog was, Mudge asked me, "So why didn't *you* jump, Josh? Mitch did."

I shot back, "I've done it before, years ago. I didn't need to do it again. Plus, Christine would kill me if I hurt myself."

This seemed to satisfy him and the rest. I had it all. The freedom to chicken out, and the ability to bond with Mitch over the foolishness of chickens. Hypocritical? Maybe. And if I had Clutchy weeping in the back of my van right now, my feeble, contradictory house of cards would likely crumble with shame.

CHAPTER FOURTEEN

I STOOD ON THE END OF THE DOCK NEXT TO HELEN ON FRIDAY MORNING, watching eight boys play water Ultimate Frisbee in front of us. It was the end of fourth period, and after a day of hearing, "Are we done yet?" we'd acquiesced and turned the end of our last lesson into a free-for-all. I was eager for the day to finally end. My old friend Rocco, whom I'd met my first day of camp in 1980 and grown up with to be counselors together, was driving up to visit. My familiar surroundings would seem far more complete with him around. Though the Staff Lounge both looked and smelled the same, it never felt complete without Rocco acting as player/ referee for yet another drinking game he learned from his high school buddies on Long Island.

The fact that Rocco had "buddies" and not "friends" summed up his personality. He was a lug in the best sense of the word; he talked rapidly with a deep New York accent and wore a baseball cap with a perfectly curved brim yanked over his short, bristly hair. When we first met, he went by his given name, Rich, and was as scrawny as me and hyper, with thick glasses and slightly crossed eyes. Upon reaching high school, he got contact lenses that straightened out his eyes, bulked himself up, and joined the wrestling team. His teammates gave him the nickname "Rocco," which we camp friends immediately adopted, since it suited his bellowing voice and physical nature. All it took was the slightest physical contact to activate his rassling reflex. If you only brushed up against him, he'd turn and wrestle you into a friendly headlock or club you with a fusillade of affectionate punches.

Since we both left camp, Rocco and I sometimes went a long time without speaking, but he was the kind of friend whom I could reconnect with after two years and fall right back into the same interplay we had when we were seventeen. That was the summer Rocco introduced me to the world of teenage drunkenness. At seventeen, we weren't supposed to drink, but the directors usually looked the other way. Drugs were an instantly fireable offense, but underage drinking was a self-policing rule, and as policemen, we were always willing to let ourselves off with a warning. Rocco dragged me up to the Staff Lounge, where he had asked a twenty-one-year-old staffer to get him a case of the cheapest beer available. He made someone give up their seat at the Quarters table for me and passed me beers until I achieved my first inebriation. It ended, predictably, with me throwing up an effluvium of Busch and stale-potato-chip bolus all over the Staff Lounge bathroom. The next morning, suffering from My First Hangover, I looked back fondly on the night before. Eastwind had once again proved itself my safe haven for trying new things: Drinking until puking may not be as noble a triumph as, say, facing my fears by jumping off a bridge, but it was still a momentous step.

When Rocco and I spoke, we'd exchange the necessary updates on our careers, girlfriends, lives, etc., and, with those adult rituals out of the way, dive into reminiscing over our teenage exploits. Within seconds we'd be effortlessly joking with each other, and that was what I was looking for tonight. When I was surrounded by campers now, I felt at home, but as soon as I found myself among younger counselors, I instantly became an outsider. Many of them still seemed uncomfortable around me, and vice versa, and this was dragging down my whole summer. Rocco's presence might help me loosen up even more and show them that underneath my souvenir T-shirt from a friend's chiropractic office beat a very young heart.

"So remember I told you about how as counselors we learned a technique called the Ten Steps of Discipline? We used to say Rocco had the One Step of Discipline. When a kid mouthed off, Rocco'd go, '*What* did you say? Because if I hear it again I'm gonna knock your head off,' and it worked a lot better than anything psychological we tried."

"Yeh, yeh," said Helen, absentmindedly tapping the plastic splash-proof sheet covering her clipboard with a chewed-up pen. "You told me that this mornin'. Man, you've been talkin' about this bloke all day."

"What can I say, I'm excited," I said.

A younger camper in the deep water started coughing loudly. "You all right they-ah, sluggah?" Helen yelled in her thick Aussie accent. She was a slow learner of names. After a few last hacks, the kid gave a thumbs-up and swam back into the game.

"Seriously, learn a name or two," I said. "Just for fun."

"He answered, didn't he?" she said. "I'm learning the kids in my cabin's names first. Then working my way out."

"I guess I should just be glad you didn't call him 'Drowny.'" She punched me in the arm.

"You gonna bring Rocco up to the Staff Lounge for the party?" she asked.

Party?

"Yeh, everybody's going up there tonight who doesn't have cabin." She said it like "kibbin." "Jim's been taking orders from people for a beer run after dinner. He didn't talk to you?"

No, he hadn't. Because when you're envisioning the perfect party, no-body wonders if there will be enough old quiet guys in the mix. Huh. Maybe it was bad for Rocco to come; it would give me one night of feeling like the old days, and then he'd leave and I'd feel all the more lost in time from the recent taste of what things used to be.

I was shooing the last of the campers off the dock after Free Swim when I heard Rocco's voice boom from somewhere along the wooded path.

"Hey, I need a buddy, can I still go in? I want to go down the slide!" Rocco burst out onto the dock, grinning wildly. He was thirty-four, too, but he still loped like a high-school wrestler, arms held slightly out from his body as if always on the alert for someone trying to take him down. He came forward and threw his arms around me, pulling me down to his height and crushing my sternum with his mighty welcome. "This is weird, man, this is so weird seeing you down here. I mean, it's wild, right? Wild! I feel like I must be back here to work, man. You want me to open the wood shop? Want to make a birdhouse? Ha!" From my close vantage point—Rocco refused to release me from his crippling embrace—I could see his eyes vibrating in their sockets with happiness. I was worried this flashback would knock them back into their childhood crossed position. "Seriously, you need a birdhouse? Bring it back to NY, get a couple of nice pigeons in there. Rev me up the bandsaw, we'll get that birdhouse." I could tell he was getting overexcited: whenever he did, he repeated his punchlines.

"Yeah, it's weird all right." I coughed, trying to free myself from his hug of death.

"Man, I keep expecting to see Tom over there at sailing with Funky and Randall, and Todd over there doing canoeing with Smitty doing waterskiing . . ." He manically continued his roll call of everybody who used to work on the waterfront, finally letting go of me so he could survey the whole area. I worried that he was slipping into the fantasy that everyone *was* back again, the same fantasy I'd had painfully dashed my first day here when I saw so many unfamiliar faces.

I hated to be the one to interrupt his imaginary time-travel. Ten years before, at a time when I was working at a particularly crappy job, I once had the most lucid dream that I had won the lottery, and just as the possibility of quitting work started to seem real, the sound of a local DJ yammering about the traffic report blared out of my clock radio and woke me up. As I slipped back into consciousness, I realized that instead of telling my boss to fuck off through a solid-gold megaphone that morning, I would be laughing at my boss's stupid jokes from a solid-mauve desk chair. For the rest of the day, I felt an irrational hatred for that DJ, and I didn't want Rocco to feel the same way about me. But I had to be honest.

"Well, they're not here, Rocco, it's just you and me. Oh, and Mitch. But it's not really the same."

He was only half listening. "Mitch is here? Oh, shit! Damn, where is that guy?"

His enthusiasm was infectious and, more important, familiar. My joy in seeing him slowly blurred over my discomfort from learning about the staff party. "He'll be at dinner, which is any minute. It's good to see you, Rocco." I patted him on the shoulder, triggering his headlock reflex, and I quickly found myself trapped in his familiar armpit, struggling to breathe, just like those asphyxiating days of old. "Good to see you, man! I almost didn't recognize you, but now that I've got you down there, I do! Ha!" As I slipped into my low-oxygen reverie, the first bugle for dinner blew, and Rocco cocked his head up. "Dinner! Let's go, man, I can't wait!" he yelled, and dashed off the dock toward the Dining Hall, thankfully letting go of my head first.

As a treat, Reg and I let Rocco serve the food. He was touched by the honor, like Hank Aaron being asked to come out of retirement and bat during the World Series. Throughout the meal, he tried to stuff an entire summer of dining-hall fun into an hour; he deputized Rattler to refill our food tray, learned all the kids' names, teased them, and lied to them. Rocco and I used to share a table—in the exact spot where Reg and I now sat, actually—and back then we spent most of every meal trying to dupe gullible kids. Kids love to be lied to, as long as you're not targeting just one of them. An entire table will feel a sense of unity over learning that they were *all* wrong in thinking, for example, that I was descended from Maine royalty, and that my great-great-great-grandfather commissioned the digging of this lake as a playground for his collection of rare leeches.

Rocco was tossing out lies faster than he could scoop chicken tetrazzini onto our plates. "This stuff looks familiar. Hey, Josh, remember how the cook got sick of making chicken tetrazzini back in '86, so he made up a four-hundred-pound batch of it and froze it? I snuck in and carved my name in some of the noodles, and I think I just saw one. Hey, this guy Action's looking at me like I'm crazy, but it's true, four hundred pounds, kept it in an underground freezer by the Leather Shack. Go ahead, next time you're at Leather go out back and take a deep breath; you can smell the Shepherd's Pie—he made about a half a ton of that, too. Isn't that right, Josh, a half a ton!" He punched me in the arm. "Half a ton of Shepherd's

Pie, right behind the Leather Shack. Make yourself a wallet, then get some lunch. Why not?" The kids just stared at him, accepting their plates. "I used to sit right there, Reg. Hey, Reggo, does that end of the table still have the secret compartment where they keep the candy? Oh, damn, was I not supposed to tell the kids? Never mind, tell me later. Although Big B looks like the kind of guy who'd kill his mother for an M&M."

Big B opened his mouth for a sarcastic remark, but Rocco had no time to listen to retorts. He leaned in close. "Hey, any of you guys do any acting? Because I'm actually a talent scout from Hollywood, and I come out here every summer to look for new kids to put in movies and TV shows. You know that *Malcolm in the Middle* kid? Found him about five years ago down at Waterskiing. Remember that, Josh? He was doing slalom, and I said, 'That guy's gonna be in a TV show.'"

"But Josh wasn't here six years ago," muttered the Fog.

Rocco didn't hear him; he was too busy trying to get me into another headlock. "This guy was like, 'No way,' and I was like, 'Yes, way, I can totally see him in a TV show where he's in the middle of something. Down at Waterskiing! The kid was at Waterskiing! Rattler, we're outta bread. . . !"

Mudge, Lefty, and Trumps were playing Hearts on Lefty's disheveled bed when we entered the cabin after dinner, and Rocco took an instant air of intimacy with them. "So these are the badass Bears. I don't know, Josh, they don't look as tough as you said."

"*Everybody* looks tough to *Josh*." Mudge sneered.

"Ha ha! This one got you good, Wolk!" roared Rocco, parking himself on the bed next to Mudge, unleashing another laundry list of camp touchstones. "So tell me what's up with the Bears. Is the big man over there treating you all right? Taking you on cabin dips? Hey, whose Frisbee is that?" He yanked Lefty's Frisbee down from the nail it hung on over his head and twirled the disc on his finger. "You into Frisbee golf? Once I only took two throws for the third hole; who can take *that* on?"

Mudge and Lefty looked confused, while Trumps, trying to ignore Rocco, continued to stare at his cards, absentmindedly scratching at the mosquito bites on his legs. His ankles were spotted with scabs from obsessive itching. If he ever made it down to the bone, I was sending him to the nurse. "Guys," I said. "This is Rocco; he and I were campers and counselors together."

"Oh, so you're like a million years old, too?" cracked Lefty, discarding a seven of spades.

"So you got a cabin of wise guys, Josh?" Rocco adopted a mock-fuming tone. "I'll take care of that." He leapt up over Lefty, pushing him down on the bed, dealing him a series of pulled punches to the arm. "Would an old guy do this, huh? Huh?" Lefty cackled and tried to push him off, and then Trumps, who clearly had a winning hand and didn't like it interrupted, grabbed Rocco's arm. "C'mon, quit it, we're playing."

Rocco, still sitting on Lefty, whirled on Trumps. "Oh, we're playing something different now," and lifted him off the bed, shaking him from side to side. Heavy kids like Trumps weren't often lifted in the air, and I could see the glee in his face that he was now part of the fraternity of roughhousing. Within seconds Rocco somehow managed to get all three in headlocks with only two arms. They struggled and giggled through their collapsed tracheas.

How did Rocco get this friendly with my campers in two minutes? I was comfortable with them now, but it had taken time. The first day I had met these guys, it was with the deep suspicion that they wanted me to leave them alone. Rocco's hair was flecked with gray, too, and he had wasted no time in acting like a teenager.

"All right, time to go," I said to Rocco, heading for the door. "Let's get out of here before I have to explain to their parents how some counselor from 1988 hopped in a time machine to kick their sons' asses."

He dropped his prisoners and followed me, but as soon as they fell to the ground, they rebounded and jumped on his back. "Oh, it is on, it is on!" he yelled, swiping backward at them. I sighed. "We gotta go, can you guys get off of him?" They regretfully released him and we walked down the stairs.

"Hey, Josh!" yelled Lefty. I turned and looked back to see their faces pressed against the screen door. "Is Rocco coming back?"

Rocco grinned as we walked away. "I wish I *was* back. Man, I envy you."

Rocco and I escaped to a bar in town, and over two foaming pints of Sam Adams in Bass Ale–decaled glasses he peppered me with questions, pushing his baseball cap back on his head. "So tell me, man, is it the best? It's the best, right? I am so goddamn jealous of you."

"It's okay," I said. "Well, that's not entirely true. It's rough. If you and the rest of the old guard were here, that'd be something else. But it just feels weird without anyone around that I remember."

"Yeah, but *come on*." He snorted. "You're back at camp! We always used to talk about coming back, but you did it. Man, if I didn't have a family right now, I'd be back here in an instant. Would you rather be back in New York City, sweating your balls off on the subway? Gee, the lake . . . or the A train. Tough choice, man, tough choice." He laughed. "Plus, Reg seems like a good dude."

"He is."

"And what about Mitch? He's still here." Rocco had always gotten along well with Mitch, because he got along with everybody. Also, after becoming sick of running the wood shop after his first year as staff, Rocco had switched to hiking. He took to the mountains like it was crystal meth, and from then on he felt more comfortable among outdoorsmen. "I think you're crazy, man. I'd jump at this in a second. Beats the A train, man. Beats the A train."

I changed the subject, and we caught up on our outside lives. As he told me about his peaceful, picket-fence life with his wife and daughter, I was struck silent. He told me the story of how they'd met: They were both working on the senatorial campaign for an Arizona senator, he in the D.C. office, she in Phoenix. First of all, what was Rocco, King of the Beer Can Pyramid, doing on a campaign? A write-in campaign to bring back Spuds MacKenzie, sure, but for the U.S. Senate? And now he was a successful software salesman with a daughter. And, he was telling me, he just bought a new house.

"Wow," I said. "I've been in the same rental for twelve years now. Christine and I are talking about buying a place after the wedding, but it seems daunting."

"Oh, you know it, bro," said Rocco, and then went on to detail the specifics of the mortgage he had negotiated, and how the taxes were killing him, but the school district was good, and . . .

The same man who on a road trip once announced from the backseat, "Drinking in the car is a *lot* of fun," then peed in an empty bottle and passed out, was more savvy in the ways of the adult world than I was.

On the drive home, I told him about the party at the Staff Lounge. "The Stiff Lounge!" he boomed, using the shack's nickname. "Awesome, man, awesome. I brought some brews in the cooler in the back, so I can share those." He started tapping on the steering wheel with excitement.

"Remember, your old pals aren't going to be there," I warned.

"Whatever, man, it's cool, it's cool."

The Lounge was packed when we arrived, and as I looked back at Rocco, who had dragged in his own cooler of beer, I saw his eyes bulge in joy. As I looked around for someone to introduce him to, he pushed past me and plunged into the crowd, patting people on the shoulder. I saw him reach Jim, who shyly introduced himself the same way he had to me when I first arrived, unclear on how to treat this authority figure from the past.

"Hey, Rocco, I'm not sure if you remember me, my name's Jim, you were my counselor."

"*Holy shit!*" Rocco's arms shot around him like a Venus Flytrap catching a bug. "Wolk, do you remember this kid? Oh, what a pain in the ass! Didn't you bite someone? He did! Chomped right down on his arm, like a little beaver! Chomped his arm! Remember, Josh, he bit some kid? And now he's staff. Fuck me, he's staff! What's up there, Jimbo, you're not gonna bite me, are ya?" I watched Jim's face change from sheepishness to surprise, then to embarrassment, and then, like everyone powerless to Rocco's gregariousness, to amusement and glee.

Rocco continued through the Staff Lounge, ingratiating himself with everyone at the same rate I seemed to have made them indifferent. When confronting a long-unseen ex-camper, he won him over with rabbit punches and funny stories from his childhood. And everyone else he won over by loudly announcing that the "brews in the red cooler are for everyone," and then pointing at everyone individually and tossing them bottles of Miller. "You, bro? Yeah, thought so. Howboutchoo? C'mon, they're frosty! All right, man, they're there if you change your mind." A warm crowd gathered around him, and in just one flurry of circulated beers he knew everyone's name, and they knew his. It was this easy? Really? Had I rolled in the first day of camp with a keg strapped to my back and an open bag of Fritos hanging around my neck, would I have instantly been hailed as King Eastwind?

Helen entered the Lounge, went to the fridge, and got herself a Coke. She never complained about the strict drinking age here, but as an Aussie used to washing down a six-pack of beer with two six-packs of beer, it tormented her. "So that's your famous Rocco," she said, looking over at him as he loaved and fished beers to the masses. I waved him over, and he pushed through the crowd, six beers jammed between his fingers, like a gunslinger who never left without a full holster. I introduced them.

"Hey, hey, Helen! Another Aussie, just like Reg. Hold on . . ." He turned around and shouted across the room to where Reg stood talking to Katia. "Reg buddy, you need a beer, or you cool?" Reg held up his own beer and winked. "All right then, bro, you just let me know." He waved his dangling Miller wind chimes and turned back to us. "Sorry, Helen. Hey, what's with the Coke! Take one, take one."

She shrugged, holding up her soda, and I explained. "Times have changed, Rocco. No more underage drinking. She's only twenty."

"Yeah, but *we* weren't supposed to drink at seventeen, and we did. Remember?" He kept his hands outstretched.

"Yeah, but now you really can't. She'll be fired."

"Rough times, rough times," Rocco said empathetically, meaning it from his soul. He took a swig of his one open bottle to wash away the pain. "So you're Australian, huh? Tell me this." He pretended to get serious. "Is there ever a moment where you say, 'You know what, there's *enough* shrimp on the barbie.'" Cracking himself up, he collapsed into me. "Oh shit! Oh shit! 'Put another shrimp on the barbie.' 'There's no room, and I'm sick of shrimp! Pass the cold chicken!'" In spite of her unavoidable fatigue with Americans thinking such jokes were funny, Helen had to laugh. Rocco threw his arm around her, narrowly avoiding knocking her unconscious with his dangling bottles. "You ever hear that before?" And just then, Jim and a friend ran up behind Rocco and tried to wrestle him to the ground. I grabbed the beers out of his hand before he could drop them, and watched the scrum collapse to the filthy floor. "He's really something," said Helen, still chuckling.

"He's not acting any differently than he used to when we'd party up here fifteen years ago."

She laughed. "You never partied up here."

I squinted at her. "What do you think I was telling you about all day?"

"I believe *he* did. But you're not a partier, mate. You're always in bed by eleven."

"I did so party. Just ask Rocco. Rocco!" I leaned down to shout, but he couldn't hear me over his own monologue of, "You're dead, Jimbo, *dead!*" as he tussled on the floor. "Whatever. He'll confirm it once he tosses Jim into the rafters. But I can so party, I'm just getting acclimated."

"*Acclimated?*" she said. "There's a party word."

I snorted, put Rocco's beers on the windowsill, keeping one for myself, twisted off the cap, and took a deep swig. Good Lord, Miller was bad. But I channeled my teenage palate, which only cared that it was fizzy, alcoholic, and cheap.

I started out strong, and after the third beer, I felt a familiar buzz, a pleasant dulling around the edges. No slurring, just an indifference to whether I did slur. I moved around the room with ease, not caring which conversation I swooped into. Mitch arrived, and after Rocco tackled him, I even went up and joined their conversation. Mitch and Rocco had a lot in common, in that both were the kind of guy who, after telling an anecdote or joke, retold the entire story in reverse order while everybody laughed. For example, if they told the old why-did-the-chicken-cross-the-road gag, when it was over, they'd say, clutching onto the arm of an audience member, "Can you believe that! Just to get to the other side! He crossed it! And he was a chicken!" Someday, when Rocco had his greatest anecdote ever, it would end with him retracing the steps of his entire life until he was back in his mother's womb.

Mitch and Rocco raucously compared hiking trails, and even though I had no interest, I threw my arm around Rocco and listened in. Mitch told about our cabin trip, and how our campers were "soft" this year: In past years he had kids doing backflips off the bridge, he said, and these guys wouldn't even jump straight. So ebullient was I with this feeling of brotherhood that I sold out all the Bears again, echoing Mitch's diagnosis of "pussy." It was just talk, anyway.

And then, in the middle of my fourth beer, I got full. And tired. I felt every hour I'd stood up on that dock today. This was the point I always had to push through in college; a weak man succumbed to the fatigue and bloat and went home, but if you finished that beer, something magical awaited: drunkenness. And with that came deadened senses, which rendered discomfort moot. But, I realized, I had no desire to take it to the next level of mushmouthedness. This had been a great evening. Looking around the room at my fellow staff smiling and laughing—even the underage, teetotaling counselors were so caught up in the good cheer that they looked flush with good times, right along with the sots—I felt a part of things. But I also felt no compulsion to prove anything to them.

I put down my half-empty beer and went over to Rocco to tell him I was heading out. "Come on, Wolk!" he bellowed, waving vaguely over at his cooler. "Get another brew, take off that dress!"

There was a time when that all-purpose insult would have had me grab for another beer, but no longer. "Rocco, I'd douche and stick a tampon up my ass if it would get me into bed quicker right now," I said. One beer ago I would have regretted making that joke around Mitch. "I'm wiped. I'll see you in the morning. See if you can make it to Assembly."

"All right, cool," he said, then smiled and we exchanged a buddy hug.

"It's really great to see you," I said. "I wish you could stay. But I'm glad you came. It really made my summer." I turned on my flashlight and left, and as I walked down the trail I faintly heard the clatter and thud of someone being tackled.

CHAPTER FIFTEEN

THOUGH CAMP'S ROSTER OF ACTIVITIES WAS MOSTLY UNCHANGED FROM MY last stint, riflery was conspicuously absent. It used to be one of Eastwind's most popular offerings. Campers shot their hands up during activity picking, begging for the chance to come to the open-walled riflery shack, located between the Lions cabin and the Theater, lie down on a dirty mattress, and aim a .22 at a paper target, hoping to accrue enough points to earn the next ranking. Each one came with an NRA-administered patch, which I'd beg my mother to sew onto my sweatshirt sleeve as soon as I got home. Every summer I'd add another one. The better I got, the more intimidating—and less flexible—my patch arm became. But at least the thick, stiff patches were sturdy enough to serve as body armor in case some other NRA-approved shooter came after me.

The sound of riflery was an omnipresent backdrop on the Bears' side of camp during the activity periods. You could hear a faint volley of cracks and pings of bullets fired and stopped by a metal backstop, and then ten minutes of silence as the campers—their guns now empty—ran down the range to get their targets and compare bull's-eyes. And then the next round of shooters would start. As a treat, occasionally the riflery counselor rolled an orange out onto the range and shot it himself to illustrate how a bullet tears though flesh, satisfying our lust for spilt pulp.

Riflery had vanished almost accidentally. Frank shuttered the activity in the summer of 1997 when he couldn't find a qualified teacher. He was relieved for the excuse; he had been noticing what he called an "unhealthy preoccupation with violence" among the kids, and he saw no reason to encourage it by arming them. At the end of the summer, he and the camp's Board of Directors decided to close up the range permanently. They sold the guns, threw away all the targets, and ate all the oranges. The Columbine shootings happened two years later, reinforcing the belief that turning boys into marksmen was unnecessary at best, foolhardy at worst.

Enough time had passed since Frank did away with riflery that none of the current campers ever knew an Eastwind with it. Riflery existed only as myth, in a faraway time when people used wood tennis rackets and turned cubes made by a man named Rubik. During Rest Hour, while playing Hearts with a few of the Bears, I casually mentioned that riflery used to be one of my favorite activities. When they discovered I was there in the "gun era," they responded as if I'd just been chipped out of ice and could tell them firsthand what it was like to ride a brontosaurus.

You were here when they had riflery? How big were the guns? How many bullets did you get? Were you allowed to stand up while shooting them? Did anyone ever get shot? The reaction was instantaneous, the game immediately forgotten. This confirmed to me that today's kids were firearm-crazy. If Frank ever reopened riflery, within fifteen minutes this place would be crawling with snipers.

I responsibly played down my enjoyment of the sport. "It was fun, I guess, but it kind of ruined camp," I said. "Wherever you went, you heard guns going off. It was annoying."

Nobody bought this. A little sound pollution was acceptable collateral damage in exchange for firepower. I changed the subject again. "Besides, it was a different time. A lot of stuff went on then that wouldn't be cool today. There was a counselor who used to lead the trip up Mount Washington, and on the way home he'd buy the kids dinner at McDonald's. When's the last time you had fast food here?" Outsider food was forbidden; kids were kept on a strict cold cut/PB&J diet when outside the boundaries of camp.

As soon as it came out of my mouth, I knew it was a pathetic comparison. *We got to have Chicken McNuggets, it was a lawless time!* I looked at Mudge, steeling for the inevitable sarcastic reply. Instead, I only heard awed silence.

Then came a disbelieving cry, nearly delivered in perfect unison. "Whaaaaaaa? McDonald's! No way!" They bounced on their cots in disbelief, and then fired another fusillade of questions. *What did they eat? Could they get a shake? Did they have to share fries?*

They probably ate fast food all the time at home, but the fact that it was out of their lives now made it utterly tantalizing. Just like riflery. It was the fascination of the taboo, whether it was something they'd never had a chance to do in their life or something that they had and was taken away. If we had forbidden them to brush their teeth, I could have kept them mesmerized for hours with tales of half-squeezed Crest tubes. *With—get this—tartar control!*

This made me think: When we were campers, guns weren't taboo at all. Firing rifles was as everyday an activity as making a pot out of clay. "What'd you do today?" "I was gonna go sailing, but the wind died, so I spent the afternoon mastering a deadly weapon." In that light, maybe *we* had been the gun nuts.

I had driven up to camp this year with the smug theory that everybody comes to in middle age: that the next generation is inferior in every way. But the longer I was here, the more contradictory evidence I collected. For example, I'd expected the boys to be intellectually lazy and bookphobic. I'd read many alarmist newspaper articles about how children were so distracted by the Internet, e-mail, and instant-messaging that libraries were slowly biodegrading from inaction because otherwise-distracted youths never came in. (Never mind that those same articles were written when I was a kid and the first Ataris came out.) However, when the fifth Harry Potter book came out this summer, the Office was filled with Amazon deliveries of the hardback ordered by their parents. The kids got so engrossed in it that we had to knock the eight-hundred-plus-page books out of their hands at the end of Rest Hours and swat the boys out of the cabin into the fresh air with brooms like they were bats.

And as for all the warnings of a childhood obesity epidemic? Maybe en masse the camp body was a little heavier than it used to be. We had three heavy kids in the Bears, and during all-camp shirts-versus-skins match-ups in evening sports, there was a fair amount of jiggling to be seen in all age groups. One morning when I did a demonstration of CPR down by the docks, one particularly hefty boy volunteered to play the drowning victim, and probing through his neck folds to find a pulse felt like trying to find spare change that fell behind a sofa cushion. But it wasn't like East-wind had turned to fat camp; there were overweight kids, yes, but there were also plenty of skinny, metabolism-jacked boys who could ingest eighteen pounds of potatoes au gratin during dinner but burn it all off during one frantic game of soccer.

To my relief, the familiar archetypes I'd first noticed in my cabin could be found all over camp. The kids' shorts were longer, and they wore dif-ferent logos on their T-shirts, but underneath they were the same kids that I grew up with. It even extended to the younger staffers. One night I passed Dwight, the gangly, rubber-boned, seventeen-year-old pottery counselor, playing Frisbee Golf through camp with a couple of boys. Dwight had a shaggy head of hair and a bouncy gait as yet unflattened by college worries. I often saw him in the Dining Hall at night playing Dun-geons & Dragons. As he was preparing to hurl his disc toward the rack of canoes (hole 5), I overheard him quoting Bill Murray's character from *Caddyshack* to himself. "*This crowd has gone deadly silent,*" he muttered, aping Murray's mushmouthed drawl. "*A Cinderella story outta nowhere. Former greenskeeper and now about to become the Masters champion . . .*" The movie was released in 1980, but every summer since, there had prob-ably been a stringy, goofy, D&D-happy comedy nerd standing on this very spot quoting that very same movie.

The rules of boy behavior at camp were also timeless. New develop-ments were nothing but revamped versions of old ones. One afternoon I witnessed a game being played called "Get Down, Mr. President." The rules were simple, and the game could be played anywhere in a small group. Someone initiated it by casually pressing their finger to their ear, as if listening to a Secret Service intercom. When the others noticed, they, too, put their fingers to their ears, until only one oblivious player was left with his hands down. Then, in unison, the "Secret Service" all yelled, "Get down, Mr. President!" and pushed the loser on the ground, piling on top of him as if protecting his life. Bruises were suffered, laughs were had. At its core, this game was simply a variation on the age-old pig pile. There was no new pain to cause, just new executions. Some enterprising kid would soon find a way to cross-pollinate the Purple Nurple with the game of Punchbuggy and come up with the most popular and painful driving game ever.

Cynicism rarely made it down the camp road. Kids showed an untainted glee over camp life, no matter how uncool such glee might be in school. Even Mudge, for all his surface sarcasm, never mocked the activities or traditions of camp, just the people doing them. I watched the campers get the same joy out of the same innocent games and traditions. After the tables were sponged down at the end of every meal, the waiter still lunged for the salt shaker. The reward for his duties was to play the Salt Game with whoever sat across from him. I'm not sure when the Salt Game was invented, but I think it was the day after they invented salt. The rules, which I learned my very first night of camp in 1980, were simple. Two players slid the salt shaker back and forth across the table, attempting to get it to land with any part of it hanging over the edge. Nobody ever passed up their opportunity to play, though it was the counselors' prerogative to commandeer the salt from the campers and play down the length of the table. The campers moaned a bit, but they liked seeing their staff play. It was like getting front row seats to the Senior PGA Tour of Salt Gamers.

At dinners, the game ended when Frank rang the bell and began announcements, where counselors stood to single out kids who had accomplished something special at their activity. For the first few days this summer, I clapped along with everyone else as the daily huzzahs were proclaimed.

"Today down at archery, Peter Zwecki earned his Silver Archer!"

Hurray!

"Let's hear it for Trevor Upkirk, who passed out of level four down at the swimming dock today!"

Yippee!

"Big day at fishing this afternoon, when Rob Stilson caught a three-pound bass!"

Yay for humans! Boo for the fish!

Evening announcements had always been the positive-reinforcement portion of the day, when kids would beam as they heard their name trumpeted and the entire camp applaud them. As a camper, I loved the unapologetic peer recognition. These were people who understood what was important. I certainly didn't get anything like it in school. I wasn't an athlete, so my accomplishments were all academic, and in junior high the quickest way to be identified as a "gaywad" is to show that you studied for something. If handed a test with an A on it, you had to feign surprise, shake your head, and whisper "I *totally* guessed on most of these" to those around you for cover. If you had to be smart, it was imperative that you were accidentally smart.

Over my first week at camp in 2003, however, I noticed that the parameters for an accomplishment to be considered noteworthy had widened a bit over the years. I was all for whooping for a passed swimming level or a new sailing rating, but many staffers stood to single out campers for far smaller achievements.

"Today at canoeing, Terry Daggle made his first solo trip halfway across the lake!"

Um . . . okay, yay!

"At kayaking, Doug Goodwin nearly rolled his kayak for the first time!"

Nearly? So he didn't do it yet? Well, I guess you have to applaud the effort, so, uh, hoorah?

"A rare feat down at Frisbee Golf today when Ben Ward got his Frisbee stuck up on the Cheetahs' roof not once, not twice, but three times today!"

Hip, hip, hoo . . . now wait a goddamn second!

Now you didn't just get rewarded for accomplishing something, but for every step along the way, and even for failing especially miserably. It was as if you handed out medals every half-mile of a marathon. Not only did this dilute the effect of the applause, but I worried that after a summer of this, we'd be throwing these kids back into the real world with unrealistic expectations of what constituted an achievement; come September, I wouldn't want them to feel hugely let down if they didn't receive standing ovations for tying their shoes in the morning.

I feared that this kind of overenthusiastic praise could give kids an inflated sense of confidence, the kind that made them lazy. Wouldn't they be more likely to give up on any quest that didn't result in constant praise along the way? Perhaps I now did have proof that my generation was different, and by different I meant *better*.

And then, one afternoon, the Rabbit Patrioticus seemed unable to pick a third-period activity. He went to Wood Shop nearly every day, but today the carpentry counselor refused to pick him, saying, "Try something new this afternoon." Patrioticus was a hyper but nervous kid, conversationally outgoing but reluctant to attempt anything he didn't already know he was good at. When each new activity was announced, Reg and I leaned in and tried to cajole him into raising his hand, but he frantically shook his head and crossed his arms in front of him lest they attempt to volunteer for something without his brain's consent. Finally, when kayaking was announced, Reg grabbed Patrioticus' arm and forced it up in the air. He looked up at it with panic, angry at its betrayal as the counselor pointed at him. "Hey, Patrioticus! Awesome! See you down there." Reg let go of his arm, which slammed back down onto the table upon release. He glared at Reg but had forgiven him by dinner, when he regaled us all with the intricacies of paddling a kayak. To a camp full of kayakers, this was like listening to someone extol the glories of a hot new trend called "breathing," but everyone politely listened. Except Big B, of course, who just muttered, "Ooooh, a kayak! Where did you find one of *those*?"

After dinner, the kayaking counselor stood up, and I could see Patrioticus shift in his seat. "Today we had a new face come down to kayaking," bellowed the counselor. "Never been in a kayak before, but you'd never know it. By the end of the period, Patrioticus paddled all the way out to the sailboat moorings!" He didn't pass a rating, he didn't roll the kayak

360 degrees. He just paddled in what probably was not even that straight a line for about fifteen yards. But the Dining Hall erupted, and the Rattler and Action grabbed Patrioticus' shoulders and shook him in a congratulatory mauling. Unlike with Reg, he didn't make an attempt to break free; he just grinned and took in the applause, no doubt wondering when he could get down to kayaking next. All right, I thought, as I clapped loudly. So maybe it won't kill these kids to get a little extra applause.

On a cool Monday night, I sat in the Staff Lounge while Reg slumped down on the couch across from me, tinkering with his omnipresent computer. Katia pressed up against him, *oohing* and *aahing* at his technological know-how.

"How big *your* hard drive?" she asked, quoting either her Russian-to-English phrase book or *Debbie Does Dell Computers*.

The radio was tuned to one of northern New England's many classic-rock stations. A rigid canoeing counselor with short, accountant-like hair bobbed his head stiffly to the Grateful Dead's "Casey Jones." When the song ended, the disc jockey broke in. "Yeah, Casey Jones better watch his speed, and you better watch *your* speed, and hope it's fast, because the third caller's gonna win tickets for our Summer Rocks jackpot! You'll be going to all the biggest concerts coming through town, seeing Boston, Pat Benatar, KISS, and Aerosmith! So if you want to see this kick-ass collection of shows, you'd better start *takin' care of business!*" . . . providing a seamless segue into the egregiously overplayed Bachman Turner Overdrive anthem.

Wow. I could not imagine a bigger punishment masquerading as a prize. Most of these has-been bands had been has-beens since I was last at camp. I was just about to share my sarcasm when a nineteen-year-old photography counselor spoke first: "That'd be *awesome*."

He wasn't the only one excited. Other young voices piped up with their agreement that, yes, this tour package *was* awesome. The group that was most excited were the youngest counselors, all high school and college aged. The age that I was when I was addicted to classic rock . . . except that was fifteen years ago.

With my social standing at the Lounge still precarious, I didn't want to alienate the young staffers by scoffing at their musical taste en masse. I quietly endured the soundtrack until I was finally driven out by a double-shot of the high priests of generic rock, Bad Company. Twenty-plus years later and nobody had realized this band was the rock-and-roll equivalent of a Mad Lib, cranking out tunes with the same structure as every other song you'd ever liked, only with a few different guitar-solo adjectives. I finally staged a passive protest by leaving the Lounge, and I stopped at the empty Office to call Christine. The machine picked up, and I began rambling. "Sorry I missed you. Or maybe you're asleep. I was just checking in, it's been a weird day. Turns out—"

"Hello?" her bleary voice cut in.

"Oops. I woke you up, didn't I."

"Uh . . . yeah. Whatime izzit?"

"Around eleven thirty."

"Oh." There was a pause as she weighed the pros and cons of talking to the love of her life versus going back to sleep and hoping he popped up in a dream. "Whazzup?"

I had beat out unconsciousness. "Today was kind of wild. I've been expecting all the kids to be so different, but the more I'm around them, the more I think they're no different than I was at that age."

"Do they go to bed earlier? Because that's what we do at *this* age." She must have been waking up; sarcasm is usually the first faculty to return after a deep sleep.

"Ha. No, they just act exactly like I did," I said, and prattled on about the announcements, the pig piles, the classic rock. "It's weird, but it's also really refreshing."

I heard the sheets rustling as she rolled onto her back to a more conversational position. "That's nice, I guess. But what'd you expect? Jet packs?"

"I just think it's nice to know that kids aren't jaded. That they can still be thrilled by the same things that we were twenty years ago. I like that idea. What's not to like?"

She sighed. "No, it's good, I guess. I can definitely see why it gets *you* all excited."

When she stressed the word "you" like that, I knew I was about to be analyzed. It implied, "you and just you, for the clear reasons that I will now pluck out of your psyche and hold up to a bright light." I quickly switched from wistful to defensive.

She continued. "You like things to remain the same. Seeing evidence that kids are having the exact same experience that you did makes you happy."

True. And obvious. I was back *at* camp because I thought it was the perfect experience for kids, so why wouldn't I want it to be the same as it ever was? "You make that sound like a bad thing," I grumbled.

"It's not," she said. "I just worry that you're gonna do the same thing with our life. Are you gonna make us duplicate your parents' life, so you can give our future kids the same exact childhood you had? What if I want to do things differently?"

"What exactly do you have in mind? You want us to be bank robbers? Circus performers? Swingers?"

"You know what I mean," she said. "Maybe we'll move abroad for a few years. Maybe our child will turn out to be a Goth, not clean-cut. I don't know what will happen. I just don't want you to be disappointed if our life doesn't follow the same exact path that your family's did."

"I think you're overreacting . . ."

"Josh." She sounded scared. "I'm serious about this. This is the kind of thing that really worries me. I don't want our life together to be compared to what you've imagined since you were ten."

"OK, OK," I said. I just wanted to get off the phone. "Just because I take solace in kids listening to Lynyrd Skynyrd doesn't mean I'm not open to a whole new world. Now go back to sleep; I'm sorry I woke you."

She was quiet for a moment. "OK. I'll talk to you tomorrow. I love you."

We hung up. I felt drained and misunderstood. I had wanted this to be an optimistic call, telling her that we would be OK because we wouldn't be starting a family in an alien world we wouldn't understand. And she had to turn it into a referendum on whether I would freak out if we ended up living in a Bangkok slum with a mopey, black-mascara'd son.

I was open to change. Within reason. It had to make sense. No reason to do something crazy just for the sake of proving you're different. What did she have in mind, exactly? Changes were not a problem, but surprises were. Why did she do this to me right before I went to sleep? Yes, technically I woke *her* up, but was that an excuse for her to say things that would have me muttering in my bed in the dark for two hours? Why did this have to be so complicated?

I shut out the lights and walked out on the porch. I'd forgotten my flashlight. When I was last at camp, I rarely carried one, because I knew every root and turn on the path and could make it home by sense memory without tripping over anything or wandering into the woods. But I remembered it being lighter then. At the bottom of the porch's stairs I let go of the rail and slowly inched down the hill, lifting my legs comically high with each step to avoid my feet catching on phantom tree roots. I flinched wildly when my head grazed a low branch.

I inched along like this until I passed the Possums cabin, and my eyes adjusted slightly. I could now make out the shadow of the Raccoons in front of me, and if I looked straight up, I could stay on the path by using the sky in the break between the tops of the trees on either side of me as my guide. My springy steps lowered, as the latent instinctual memory of the obstacles on this route came back to me. And after only one close call with a tetherball pole, I was at the Bears steps. When I climbed into bed, I was noticeably calmer than after hanging up with Christine. The fact that I made it home without walking into a tree proved it: There was nothing wrong with familiarity.

CHAPTER SIXTEEN

SATURDAY NIGHT WAS SHOWTIME. ALL THE BOYS WERE BACK IN CAMP, AND everyone gathered in the Theater for the evening's extravaganza. This summer's entertainment would kick off with Staff Talent Night, the hope being that by making fools of themselves on stage right away, the staff would encourage the kids by example to do it themselves on future Saturdays.

Organizational duties for all Theater events fell to Brooke, the perpetually chipper drama counselor, of which there is no other kind. Through the first week of camp, she spent most meals circulating around the Dining Hall, cajoling counselors into participating. Now, at Saturday's breakfast, there were twelve hours left before the house lights dimmed, and she was determined to pack her bill. Armed with a clipboard, her bushy brown hair tied into adamantly perky pigtails, she was an unstoppable mixture of cheerleader enthusiasm and budding-starlet extroversion. I tried to look busy with a bottle of ketchup or a sponge whenever she headed my way.

As a kid I had stage fright, but participating in cabin skits was mandatory; for the first couple of summers I volunteered to write them just to make sure I had a silent role. But after years of hearing my fellow campers applaud piano solos whether they were the intricately mastered display of an obvious prodigy or the one-fingered key-poking of the tone deaf, I began to feel more open to putting myself in front of the crowd. I'd write myself a line or two, and then three, and by the time I was a counselor, I embraced every opportunity to get on stage, the more embarrassing the better. Yet now I found the idea of getting on the Eastwind stage unnerving again. While you couldn't find a less discriminating audience for entertainment, I still worried about appearances.

Brooke bounced up to my table. "So, Josh, what's it gonna be? Come on, you'd be so goooooood!" she peeped. "You want to play an instrument? I heard you had a guitar."

Christine had given me an acoustic guitar for my previous birthday, since I was constantly musing on how I should learn how to play. I took just eight lessons, then let my rock-star dream lapse. But I'd brought the guitar with me because I assumed that at camp I'd have plenty of time to practice. I hadn't yet taken it out of its case. "I do have a guitar," I told Brooke. "But I'm not good enough to perform."

"Come on, I bet you're not that bad!" Brooke was used to dealing with campers, whom you could cajole into doing anything by just saying "you can do anything!" with enough conviction.

"Brooke, I only know the G chord," I said. "Not the E chord, not the D chord, not the C chord. The G chord. I think you need to play a little more than that to qualify as a performance."

"Oh my God! I just thought of something!" Brooke's eyes widened until I thought her eyelids were going to roll up over her hairline. She waved jazz hands out by her sides to emphasize the excitement of her brainstorm. "You write about TV, you could totally do a hilarious skit on *Survivor* or something! It'd be *soooo* funny! You could call it *Eastwind Survivor*! Or *Survivor, Eastwind Style*! Or . . . *Sur-Eastwind-vivor*! I'll bet Reg would be in it!" She was suddenly standing with her arm around Reg, leaning her head on his. I think she teleported.

"Whatevah you say, Brooke, I'll be there," he chirped helpfully. "C'mon, Josh, write us a skit."

I glared at him. Kiss-ass. "All right, sign me up. Won't be *Survivor*, but I'll come up with something."

"Yay!" Brooke teleported back next to me and scribbled on her clipboard. "I'll write, 'Josh surprise!' Awesome!" She dashed off to harass another counselor.

Reg grinned at me. "I'm already doing some skit with Anne, so I'm out. But I'd love to hear that G chord a few times. Who's with me? Big B?"

The Theater steps were abuzz with opening-night excitement as the kids gathered in wait for the signal to enter. I wandered backstage—otherwise known as the small clearing behind the building, next to the basketball court—and found Brooke nervously dashing about, wearing a white Marilyn Monroe dress and a platinum wig. Because there's nothing the youth of today appreciate more than references to *The Seven Year Itch*.

"Josh! Thank God you've made it!" She brought her hands to her chest theatrically. "What do you have for us tonight?"

"Just put down 'Nicknames,'" I said. Expanding on my rechristening of the boys in my cabin and at my dining-hall table, I was going to assign every single camper a nickname.

"Ooooh! Sounds intriguing!" she squealed. "All right, you're going on second, so *don't go anywhere, dahling!*"

More staffers came behind the Theater, conferring about their sketches and comedy acts. Rehearsal hadn't been a high priority for anyone, and so they raided the costume box to distract from their lack of preparation. I could hear a thunder of footsteps rush inside the Theater as the kids were let in.

"Whaddya think?" asked Reg, who wore a thick orange wig and a giant polka-dotted tie.

"I don't know. Maybe too subtle. What are you doing with Anne, anyway?"

He straightened his tie. "I don't really get it, but I'm supposed to walk across the stage and pretend to throw up. Not sure why, but, whatevah."

"Sounds like a scene from *Uncle Vanya*. Oh, wait . . . is Anne also gonna stuff a pie down your pants? 'Cause then it's *The Cherry Orchard*."

Anne approached wearing a Hawaiian skirt over her jeans and an Indian-chief headdress. "Am I Uncle Vanya?" Reg asked her.

"No, you're 'guy who throws up.' You remember your lines?" she asked.

"Think so. *Rrrrretch.*"

She laughed. "Sounds about right. What are you doing, Josh?"

"Nothing special, just a nickname thing."

"Oh, cool," she said, then paused. "There's some old football pads and a helmet in there if you want to wear them."

I wandered back around the building to watch the show through the screen door. Brooke was giving her introduction in a breathy voice punctuated by giggles and much knee-bending and skirt-smoothing. The kids squirmed in their seats, impatient for pratfalls and poop jokes. There was a reason you didn't get a lot of celebrity impersonators at a ten-year-old's birthday party.

She first brought out Sean with his electric guitar. He kept a childhood dream of being a rock star buried beneath his surface, but it was buried only about a centimeter deep. When you visited him in his cabin, he was always strumming his guitar and asking his campers to yell out tunes to see if he could play them. Now, onstage, armed with an amp, he was crooning the Rolling Stones' "You Can't Always Get What You Want" and imagining that there were twenty-year-old girls out there admiring him in the front row, and not just preteen boys.

As he wound up, I jogged backstage to where Brooke was waving. As she went out for my introduction, Sean walked back past me with his guitar. "Hot crowd, hot crowd," he said.

Standing offstage, I still felt jittery. I kept running over and over in my head, They are just a bunch of kids. And the most ridiculous mental argument began: But the staff aren't. YOU HONESTLY THINK COUNSELORS ARE GOING TO JUDGE YOU AT STAFF NIGHT? CAMERON IS GOING TO VOMIT WHILE WEARING AN ORANGE WIG. But if this nickname thing tanks right away, I'll still have a hundred names to get through. AGAIN: VOMIT. ORANGE WIG. Yeah, but that's just silly fun. This is my attempt at being clever. VOMIT. I know, but . . . ORANGE. WIG.

And with that, Brooke finished a befuddling song parody called "Campers Are a Girl's Best Friend" that would have been creepy had it not sailed right over the audience's tiny heads. "Thank you, boys, thank you so much! I love you all! And now, here's Josh Wolk with 'Nicknames'!"

I strode out onstage, looking out on all the boys sitting on benches, some staffers scattered between them, others leaning up against the back wall. They all looked on with big smiles. I delivered the same spiel I'd given my dining-hall table: that the coolest thing they could leave camp with at the end of the summer was a nickname, but since everyone might not have time to get one organically in just eight weeks, I'd taken the liberty of assigning one to all of them. "So listen up, we've got a lot of names to get through," I bellowed. "And as soon as this show is done, start calling each other by your new names to get used to them. The sooner you learn how to answer to it, the sooner it'll stick." Holding my cabin list in front of me, I rapidly read each camper's name and then their nickname. *Ridgie, Cheddar, Iron Fist, Bubbler.* The boys giggled as I gained momentum. *Blacktop, Frenzy, Timebomb, Honey Nut Frankie.* I could see them all nudging each other when their names came up. *Sweet-Talk Pete, Sharky, Slick, Slick 2: The Slickening.* Laughter started to build. *Cheech, Umlautski, The Mighty Clam, Kid Kidney!* I had to yell the last names to be heard over the collective chanting of their new names to each other. *MEMBRANE, ONE-HIT JUDDSY, PINKY THE MAGNIFICENT, DR. PERFIDIOUS.* "You now have your nicknames!" I bellowed. "Now go forth and nick and be nicked!"

Brooke passed me at stage left as I walked out. She squealed her approval, then dashed out to introduce the next skit. I felt foolish for the relief I felt in scoring at Talent Night, and yet I was no less relieved for it. I ambled back into the audience to watch the rest of the show stress-free.

There were serious musical interludes and an unintentionally hilarious karate demonstration by one intense nature counselor, but it mostly came back to randomly costumed silliness. Anne's skit had no discernible point or punchline, but it featured Reg and other counselors miming throwing up, peeing, and nose picking, which was more than enough for the audience. Jim, Zach, and Dwight brought out the old "fake hands at a restaurant" chestnut, in which Zach sat behind a small table, draped in a sheet tied around his neck. He had sneakers on his hands, and Jim crouched down behind him under the sheet, reaching around him on both sides to serve as Zach's arms. Thus, when Dwight—playing a waiter—served him a series of increasingly messy foods, Zach sat helplessly while Jim blindly tried to stuff them into his mouth. Soon Zach's face was covered with the day's leftovers. It didn't matter how old the skit was. It was already old when I first saw it here in 1980. It still killed.

It was all so unapologetically foolish that I roared along with the kids. To think I had had stage fright. I could have gone onstage and soiled myself and it would have been okay. Hell, it would have gotten an encore.

When it was over, Brooke thanked everyone and sent them back to their cabins. I exited in the throng with Reg. A couple of Caribou ran to catch up with us. "Hey, Josh, what were our names again?"

I looked at my list. "You were Wedge, and you were the Grifter."

"That's what I thought you said," said Wedge. "I don't get it." But his dissatisfaction quickly turned to glee as he turned to Reg. "That was so funny when you threw up! That was like the best thing all night!"

CHAPTER SEVENTEEN

I HAD STOPPED SHAVING AS SOON AS CAMP BEGAN AND WAS QUICKLY ON THE road to a beard. When I was a teenage counselor, I tried to grow one every summer. Though I never made it to what anyone would call a full-grown beard, I could create a dark enough shadow to fake one. After I left camp in 1988, I never again attempted the full hairy. I always wondered what I'd look like, but I couldn't confront that kind of change. After all, I was the guy who never altered his hairstyle. The day I was born, I think the doctor drew a line down the left side of my scalp and declared it my hair part forever, and since then I had let no hair stylist veer from the diagram.

This summer was my opportunity to finally finish a beard. I didn't care what I looked like here, nor did anyone else. When I was a teenager trying to grow one, I worried about facing girls on my day off. This year I didn't even care about that. I understood why so many guys got fat after they were married. Husbandhood was the death of vanity, because it was just too exhausting to pursue unless you had to.

I loved to scratch my beard. It was a tactile symbol of the carefree life I was living. Every rub was an itchy reminder that I was one step away from not getting out of bed to pee. At home, I was ritualistic about my morning showers. But here, two or three days went by between them.

The lake did the trick, I thought, and even if it didn't, I couldn't possibly smell worse than the kids or some of my coworkers. Jousting Chas seemed to take perverse pleasure in rarely washing his clothes or himself. One pair of khakis that he wore every day must have had its own sweat glands, because one man couldn't possibly generate that much body odor by himself. When he stood up in the Dining Hall to pick for sailing, he left a vapor trail.

I was now fully embracing the low-impact camp life. Three meals a day were brought to me by campers. The weather was delightful, and all job pressure had slowly faded away. I no longer felt the omnipresent tension of career worries that I had been carrying around in my shoulders for the last twelve years. At camp I didn't worry about the cost of a restaurant or whether I should switch phone companies or whether I needed new clothes. I just worried if some kid out there was drowning, and some kid never was. One morning I left lunch and was halfway back to my cabin when I looked down at my sandals and noticed I had a large glob of jelly stuck to the top of my big toe. What better indicator could I have asked for that my life was at its simplest? I crouched down, wiped the quivering purple mass off with my thumb, flicked it into the woods, and then licked my thumb clean. That's right, I licked toe jelly. And if anyone had seen me, they wouldn't have cared, either.

In an all-boy environment with no parents to noodge them or girls to impress, many of the campers would go a whole summer without touching soap if their hands weren't forced. I always thought the real reason we had a barbecue dinner outside every Saturday night was because by that point of the week, the collective stink of the camp was too strong to risk being brought indoors. This was why on Sunday mornings every camper had to take a mandatory shower.

There was no reveille bugle on Sundays; campers could sleep as late as they wanted, provided they went for a buffet breakfast, took a shower, visited the nurse for a once-over, and changed their bed sheets before eleven A.M. While most of the staff could luxuriate in their cots all morning, three unfortunate counselors were assigned to the showering areas around camp to check off campers as they scrubbed clean the collected grease, grime, and unidentified muck that had resisted the rinsing waters of Free Swim.

On shower morning, these three counselors dragged folding chairs in front of the doors into the three shower rooms spread around camp, and a line of boys with towels slung over their shoulder and toiletry bags in their hands formed behind him. These counselors' job was to check off each camper as he entered, and to yell "Knock it off!" when they heard the crack of a rat tail from within. As dull as this job seemed, it was infinitely better than when I was last here. Back then, the shower counselor also had to check every camper for butt rash.

I'm not sure what the medical term for butt rash even is; I've never had it or personally seen it. It announced itself with a spray of red bumps and was often caused by sitting for too long in a wet bathing suit. Though it was one of the more innocuous of ailments, Eastwind treated it like Lyme disease, where early detection was all that stood between you and a hobbled life. So those staffers on shower duty spent up to three hours staring at a screen door as it swung open to display a cosmos of white moons, marking down any trouble spots for the nurse. The task was far more traumatic for the counselor than the flashers. For campers, it was a rare thing to be *asked* to moon somebody. Every so often a camper would try to shock the counselor by giving a "red eye"—in which he pulled his own buttocks apart with his hands and peered at the grouchy counselor with an unblinking sphincter—but that was just gilding the lily. Thankfully, those days were gone, Eastwind having finally realized butt rash was not the insidious plague that tradition had declared it.

This Sunday I had no reason to get up early, but it was impossible for me to sleep late as the Bears' idea of being quiet involved yelling to each other in raspy voices, a loophole that they hoped qualified as whispering. At the Dining Hall I grabbed myself a couple of over-easy eggs and muffins from trays left out on the slide. Every kid there had come straight from the shower, and they all looked fresh out of the box. Lefty, Action, and Mudge soon came through the door, all wearing bathrobes. Action's robe was of a piece with the rest of his comically ugly wardrobe, bright yellow with SCRUB A DUB DUB! stiched on the lapel, no doubt picked from the JCPenney "Lonely Stud" line. They joined me at my table.

"Well, look who's less smelly!" I said.

"Not you," grumbled Mudge through a mouthful of Cheerios.

I brought up the butt checks of yore, and they looked at me as if I said we'd had our pinkeye cured with leeches. I could not convince them I wasn't lying. The other night I had told them there used to be a roller coaster in the assembly grounds that went right through the Cheetah cabin; *that* they believed, but not that we used to have to get our asses checked. Zach, veteran of eighteen summers, walked by, and I grabbed him. "Zach can vouch for me. Did we or did we not used to get butt rash checks?" I asked him.

"Yep," he said, scratching his goatee. I could see black under his fingernails. No showering for that counselor. "We also had to dip our testicles in rabbit blood, just to keep the evil spirits away," he added as he headed for the door.

"Oh, come on, now they'll never believe me," I yelled after him.

"Whatever, Mr. Butt," razzed Action.

"Just 'cause you showed your ass to all the counselors doesn't mean they asked to see it," added Lefty, jabbing a spit-soaked finger—a wet willie—into my ear.

At eleven A.M. the bugle summoned everyone to the Birch Grove for the weekly secular service. This quiet, peaceful clearing among a stretch of towering birch trees is tucked up on a hill behind the Sports Lawn and has an inspiring view of the lake. Counselors sat on wood benches that circled the area, while most of the campers sat cross-legged on the ground or rocks, building tiny houses with twigs and chunks of bark while ostensibly listening.

The services were built around themes that all came back to what was important about camp, and after the speakers finished talking, anyone who wanted to add something could stand up and speak, Quaker-meeting style. When I was a camper and a counselor, I heard the same life lessons week after week, year after year. But they always moved me, because I felt the same things. It was like being in a political convention for your party, where every speech confirmed your worldview: *I totally know what you mean about a canoe being like life, sometimes you need someone behind you steering, and sometimes you need to steer! And in pottery, we can make something out of a lump of clay, just like in life we have to make our own opportunities! And I will vote yes on mountain climbing being a metaphor for man's need to respect nature!*

I sat on a bench next to Jeannie, the tennis counselor, and the wooden plank sagged underneath us. Kids were scattered on the browning needles in front of us, madly hoarding twigs and bark for their architecture projects. Frank stood up in front of the group, and talked about the symbolism of this place, and the camp's history. Zen Richard then took his place to describe his "living in the now" philosophy, to encourage kids to try every opportunity camp offered. Zach explained that Eastwind was one of the few places in the world where he could really feel that he mattered, that it needed him as much as he needed it. Campers started to volunteer, talking about how they looked forward to camp from the moment they got home the previous summer, or they described why their Eastwind friendships were so much deeper than their ones at home. Often the speeches rambled, as kids tried to articulate an intense feeling of community for the first time. In their eyes was a pleading look of "Don't you get it?" as they circumnavigated the emotion they felt determined to describe.

I considered going up, but I wasn't sure what I wanted to say. I knew how strongly I'd felt all those years at camp; those tenacious emotions were what had me wanting to return for so long. But now that I was here, were they still accurate? I didn't want to just parrot some greatest-hits material that no longer held. Things had been more complicated since I got back; perhaps those old feelings could no longer be summed up in the same gushing way. The summer was getting better, and I was more comfortable, but still . . .

Then a long, ropy Lion shuffled up front next to where Frank was sitting. He wore his bangs long in a skater style, and his hands were plunged deep into the pockets of his ripped cargo shorts, pushing them farther down his butt. He looked like he had been pulled by Central Casting to play "Disaffected Teen #12" in a very special episode of *Dawson's Creek*.

In a shaky voice, he began, "I haven't been here in like three years. And I was sent here this year as punishment." He dragged his flip-flop through the dirt. "I got in trouble this year at school, and my dad said he didn't want me just hanging around with my friends all summer. I was really bummed, because I had this great plan to just skate for, like, ten weeks straight. So when I got here I was pissed, I was like, what the hell . . . sorry, Frank . . . heck, am I gonna do here all summer? This place is for little kids.

"But then I saw that I knew a bunch of guys in my cabin from when I was here last time, and they were kind of cool." He threw a smirking glance at his fellow Lions. "And then I started doing activities, and going rock climbing, which I never did before, and that was cool, too."

He paused for a minute, then shrugged. "I don't know. I guess I just forgot how much fun this place is." Then he shuffled back to his spot on a bench.

Wow, I thought, wondering what was wrong with me that I could make camp feel complicated.

CHAPTER EIGHTEEN

"REALLY, TRUMPS? REALLY? YOU *REALLY* THINK YOU CAN BEAT ME?" I STARED at him intently over the backgammon board, fascinated by his delusion. We sat on different ends of my bed, leaning over the board, which barely stayed level as my flimsy mattress shifted under our weight. Some of the other Bears hovered around us as spectators.

"Shut up, I'm thinking," Trumps grumbled. He rubbed the top of his ear with his thick ring finger, the tell that he knew he was losing and was desperately trying not to lose his mind over it.

"Oh, I see that. It's impressive to watch, really it is." I leaned in toward him with mock respect. "But maybe—just maybe—you could put all that brainpower to work on something you had a better chance at pulling off. Like, I don't know, learning how to fly? Or solving the meaning of life? But backgammon . . . this may be a bit beyond you."

"Oh, shit!" yelled Lefty, leaning into Trumps' face. "You gonna take that from this big dope?"

"I got next game against Josh," yelled Dewey from his bed.

"I kinda hoped for a better challenge than that," I groaned, and saw Dewey's eyes peep over his book at me. "Like from Mudge's dirty underpants. Sure, they smell like crap, but at least they know what to do with double sixes."

Mudge sneered at me. "Gee, *Josh*, it's *so* impressive that you can beat someone at backgammon."

Not looking up from the board, I said, "By 'someone,' do you mean 'everyone'? Because not one of you maroons has beaten me yet. Maybe after this, you should all eat the pieces. Then you can actually get something out of this game other than a series of punishing losses. Bam!" I leaned sideways and flicked Mudge and then Lefty on their foreheads.

Trumps slowly moved his pieces, then withdrew his hand carefully. I snatched up the dice, rolled them, got a three and a two. The perfect numbers to let my straggling pieces take out one of his and then double up in safety. "I'm trying to think of a word to describe my playing," I said, clacking my pieces into place. " 'Godlike' comes to mind, but it makes me seem cocky. How about 'otherworldly'? 'Awe-inspiring'?"

"How about 'douchebaggy,' " cracked Lefty.

"Oooh!" I squealed. "Someone got a thesaurus and his name is Lefty!" I lunged out to grab him and he stepped backward, stumbling over the scattered sneakers in my area. I went back to finishing my victory against Trumps. "All right, Dewey," I yelled when it was over, and Trumps moved over to sit with the spectators on Afty's bed, his fists clenched. "Your turn. I promise to use at least three percent of my mighty brain to beat you." I leaned forward and flicked Mudge's forehead again. He glared at me. "I'm sure you'll deserve that in a minute," I said. "So I figured I'd get a stockpile going before I get distracted by the game."

I returned to the cabin for most Rest Hours to get to know the kids better. And Rocco's visit reminded me that to become a favored counselor, you had to get down to their level. Sure, I saw how a thirty-four-year-old attempting to look like a god by beating kids twenty years younger at backgammon might seem pathetic. But it was necessary: All-male environments speak the language of trash talk. The important thing was not the victory but the accompanying lighthearted browbeating. To be gracious would just be weird. That kind of good-job, never-mind-the-loss-I-can-tell-you're-getting-better boosting was great for the Dining Hall and activities, but the cabin was like a frat-house training camp. This was where young men learned how to bond through giving each other crap. The only important rule was to make sure it didn't go too far, so no one's feelings got hurt.

The more I trounced the Bears at backgammon, the quicker they came back to play again. Everyone wanted to be the one to finally topple me, and others gathered to watch, and we all grew tighter through these skirmishes via the bonding powers of abuse.

Dewey got some good early rolls in our backgammon game, giving him false hope of a victory. He even made some shrewd strategic moves, blocking off my reentry early after bouncing me off the board. Hearing Lefty and Mudge's cheers, the other members of the cabin congregated around my bed to watch what could be my monumental loss.

"Things look good for Dewey, don't they?" I said, surveying the board. "You all *think* this could be the moment where Josh goes down."

"Not think, dopey. *Know*," said Lefty, who was rocking from foot to foot in my area, limbering up for a vicarious victory dance. "He's gonna kick your ass."

I blew on the dice. "One of you will kick my ass the day Lefty gets a girlfriend. And your left hand doesn't count, no matter how much lipstick you draw onto it."

"Hey, her name is Palm-ela and you don't talk about her that way," snapped Lefty, who then began gently kissing his hand. He then swung it in front of my face and began opening it and closing it like a puppet, saying, "You're going down!"

"If he was any good, he'd be a professional," mumbled Afty, who lay down on his bed, which doubled as a bleacher for Trumps, Mensa, and Action. He didn't acknowledge their presence, just spread out his legs and nudged them to the precipice of the cot.

"That would be difficult," said Mensa primly. "As there *are* no professional backgammon players."

"How would you know?" asked Afty. Actually, neither knew, but in an argument among fourteen-year-olds, evidence was immaterial.

As this side debate continued, I broke out of my slump, taking advantage of Dewey's occasional abandoned discs, knocking them into the dead zone. Lefty and Mudge got quieter the more I rebounded and soon were hissing at Dewey, who was powerless to his weak dice rolls. "A three and a one?" howled Lefty, stumbling out into the cabin's main aisle and pacing the floor while holding his bristly head. "What the fuck is wrong with you, Dewey?"

After I won, I said, with exaggerated gravity, "Good game, really good game." Then I paused a moment. "Wait, that's not the word I was looking for. What is it, what is it . . ." I tapped my forehead with my finger. "Oh! 'Bad'! *Bad* game, that's what I meant to say. Man, playing with dumb guys is really wreaking havoc on my vocabulary. Now, who is gonna clean up this board? It's too depressing. Too many memories of too many spanked opponents."

"Yeah, you'd like to spank Dewey, you perv," said Lefty.

"Oooh, well played, Mr. Witty. I'm surprised you held back from your usual knockout punch, calling me a 'doodyhead.' "

The sound of the bugle call signaling third period wafted in, and everyone got up to run to their activities, dodging damp towels draped over the rafters like slalom flags. As he walked away, Mudge muttered, "I get to play you after Free Swim. You're not as good as you think you are."

"Do I need to flick you all the way down to tennis?" I said, raising my finger to his forehead. He ducked and stumbled over to his area to pick up his racket. "That's what I thought. You go win yourself a match to get your ego up, and then come by here after dinner and I'll beat it back down for you."

That night when I talked to Christine I told her how I was bonding with the Bears. I recounted my backgammon dominance, as well as my favorite verbal jabs. Just a month earlier, our conversations had been about office politics and arguments with our insurance company. Now I gleefully reconstructed the elaborate production I had gone through before beating the Fog the day before: After setting up the board, I asked for silence then went into a fake psychic trance; snapping out of it, I scribbled a note on a piece of paper, then sealed it in an envelope. After beating him, I had the Fog open the envelope and read aloud the note, YOU DIDN'T HAVE TO BE PSYCHIC TO KNOW THAT THE FOG WAS GOING TO EAT IT.

She laughed and then said, "So that's what you do all day? Beat kids at games and then rub their noses in it?"

"*No.* I teach swimming. Oh, speaking of which . . ." I then recounted something that had happened that day on the dock. Helen and I had offered water baseball in place of swimming lessons. The water was the outfield, while the at-bat team swung a tennis racket at a Nerf ball from the end of the dock. I warned everyone repeatedly to take a step back from the end of the dock before swinging, but one kid didn't. He stepped into his swing right off the edge, which led to one of the most spectacularly spastic tumbles I'd ever seen. In the millisecond before plunging into the water, he did a split, his arms tied and untied themselves into a square knot, and he bent so far forward in trying to regain his balance that he ended up with one of his toes up his own nostril.

"Oh my God!" Christine gasped. "Was he all right?"

Was he all right? That wasn't the point of this story. Of course he was all right, I wouldn't be telling the story if he had sunk down to the bottom of the lake. He was more than all right, he was hilarious. It was the kind of fall that *America's Funniest Home Videos* was invented for, only improvable if my pitch had hit him in the balls midflail. As soon as he surfaced, and I saw that he was okay, I couldn't stop laughing. When I swam up to him, I could only muster, "Are you all . . . *pffffffff* . . . sorry. Are you all righhhhh . . . HA! No, seriously, can you feel everyth . . . B-HA! I'm soooo sorry, but HOOO HEEE HA HA HA!"

Now just recalling the water-baseball tumble made me laugh all over again. Reg sat behind me, at the Office table. That night at dinner the water-baseball tumbler had stopped by our table and feigned a slip on the floor, which sent me into a guffawing retelling for the rest of the meal. "Are you thinking about that kid's fall again?" Reg asked, which only made me laugh harder, and he joined in.

Christine listened in silence on the other end. When I finally calmed down, she said, "I'm not sure I like the way boys relate to each other."

I glanced over at Reg and rolled my eyes, pointing to the receiver. *Women.* Thank God for boys' camps, where we could have a good time the manly way without them dragging us down.

CHAPTER NINETEEN

WHEN I ENTERED THE CABIN AND MADE MY WAY DOWN THE CENTER AISLE, IT felt like I was passing through a museum of goofy adolescent behavior. Each area housed a different exhibit: The Fog and Mudge comparing pimple medicines, Wind-Up summarizing the plot of *American Pie* to himself, Mensa and Dewey debating whether the X-Men could actually exist, and then Lefty, lying on his bed with his legs thrown back over his head, his neck craning his head forward toward his crotch. "So . . . close . . ." he grunted.

All of the Bears got along beautifully, confirming the Eastwind Utopian ideal. Even when an argument sparked, it was too laughably foolish to take seriously. As I was reading one Rest Hour, I heard Dewey and Afty's voices rising in anger from where they sat on Dewey's bed across the cabin. The night before, when Mitch had come back to the cabin late at night, he had bumped into something and woken the boys up with his loud clatter. But what he had collided with remained in doubt. Dewey said it was the card table set up in the aisle; Afty took the contrary position that it was the Fog's bunk-bed post.

"It was the *table*, I heard it scrape."

"I'm right next to the bunk bed, I think I would know. And he was right there!"

"Why would he hit the bunk bed, you retard? It's lined up with all the other beds, but the card table is right in the middle of everything!"

"Ask Fog, he would have felt it."

"I already did, and he slept through it, which means he probably didn't get bumped!"

I tried to ignore them until their voices reached the pitch that usually prefaces a shove. I sat up on my bed and barked, "This has got to be the *stupidest* argument I've ever heard in my life."

They stared at me. "He's just wrong," said Dewey. "I was right th—"

"I don't care. Mitch doesn't care. The card table doesn't care and the bunk bed doesn't care. *No one* cares except you. And I promise you, if you spend twenty seconds thinking about something else—*anything* else, mashed potatoes, unicycles—you'll realize that you don't care either."

I lay back on my bed, theatrically harrumphing back to my book. I was actually less annoyed than I was jealous that the worries in their lives were so few that Mitch's stumble could pole-vault to the top of their stack of issues. Moments later, when they were back on their individual beds reading and playing solitaire, the great stubbed-toe debate was forgotten and "to sail or play backgammon after dinner" regained its top spot on their lists of concerns.

The next evening I was walking out of the Office when I heard a distant howl of anger drift over from across camp. With no intrusive urban sounds of highway traffic or large crowds, camp was small enough that if you concentrated you could hear trace sounds from all the activities across its grounds. All the splashing, thwacking, whooping, and yelling combined into the general white noise of summertime. It was the ambient soundtrack to camp that you learned to take for granted. A few minutes later I sauntered past the tennis courts, where I saw the assistant director, Roger, coming toward me. Fit, white-haired, and gregarious, he had been a camper himself in the '50s. Unlike his predecessor as AD, who was a guidance counselor during the year, Roger was a semiretired financial manager with no therapeutic training. He was less a disciplinarian than a fun enforcer, in charge of making sure everyone was having a good, safe time, and keeping parents happy when they visited or called. He'd circulate around camp with a clipboard, stopping at all activities to hobnob with staff and campers, and like a great comedian, he'd always leave on a laugh, even if it wasn't his: When a joke was told, he'd look at the teller with a quick, "Why you *devil*!" expression, then throw his head back with a loud "Ha!", turning to quickly saunter off down the trail, waving behind him in perfect timing. Now he approached me with an eyebrow raised, its default position for when something went down.

"Ahhh, *there* you are," he said. "We had a bit of a situation with Wind-Up and a few of your other campers." He raised his other eyebrow to complete the set, in a way that simultaneously conveyed concern and practiced familiarity with this kind of issue.

He didn't know much of what had happened, as he had arrived only after it had defused. But from what he heard, Wind-Up had thrown an angry fit at Mudge, Action, and the Fog just a few moments earlier, and he had threatened them all with a large stick. I couldn't imagine Wind-Up acting violent. That was energy that could have been better spent describing what kind of sneakers he was wearing.

As wearying as Wind-Up's endless chattering could be, he was so upbeat and eager to be with you—with anybody—that to get angry at him would be like getting angry at a puppy. He was uncoordinated, but that never stopped him from avidly sampling many activities without a single care toward his hopelessness at them. His first love was hiking, a sport that was restrictive only to the legless. He went on every trip he could sign up for, and, though slow, never complained or begged for more rests. The trips counselors appreciated his presence, although many wished there were higher-altitude peaks in New England on which Wind-Up would be forced to conserve his oxygen.

Just that afternoon, Wind-Up had been down to swimming for the first time. He was still in level four while the rest of our cabin had long since passed out of classes. We had only a few campers that day, so I took him for one-on-one instruction. I asked to see his crawl.

"Gotcha, crawl!" he said. "An excellent stroke, sometimes known as the *arm*stroke." He took a deep breath, pushed himself forward off the sandy lake bottom, and promptly began thrashing all of his limbs. It was to the crawl what being hit by a car was to ballet. His wake splashed up over the dock onto my feet, but for all his frenetic movement, he remained in one place. I yelled at him to stop, but he couldn't hear me over his own turbulence. Finally he stood up, rubbed water out of his eyes, and looked up at me with a wide smile that anticipated my holding up a scorecard with a big "10" on it.

I jumped into the water next to him. "OK, that's a start. But let's . . . uh . . . *hone* it. We'll break it down a little bit, just work on your arm motion." I went through every movement of the stroke, holding on to his arms and slowly easing them through the correct range of motion, and at each step Wind-Up echoed my teachings with the awed attention of a daytime talk-show host. "Oh, so the elbow comes out of the water *first*, interesting, interesting. And then you reach forward as if grabbing for your destination? You don't say!" When I finished, he mimed the stroke I'd just worked on with him, narrating each segment. "So the elbow comes up *first*, and *then* I reach forward . . ." He'd actually grasped it.

"OK, are you ready to try it again?"

"Yes, yes, I think I am." And then he took a deep breath, pushed off, and resumed the same epileptic thrashing he'd done before I'd given him any instruction. He created an even bigger froth of angry whitecaps, and I couldn't tell if he was swimming or being attacked by piranhas.

After a minute, he stopped again, rubbed his eyes, and stared at me. "I *really* felt my elbow come out first there," he said.

This was not the behavior of a violent boy. As I headed back to the cabin I saw Wind-Up wandering alone through the woods by the Photo Shack.

Wind-Up usually walked with a jerky bounce to his step, the rubbery spring of the ever-ebullient. Now his walk was like everyone else's, pulled down by gravity and the inkling that the world wasn't perfect.

I jogged up to him. "Hey. Everything all right? I heard there was some problem down by the courts."

He squinted up at me. No rictus of pain or rage on his face, but no goofy grin either, which was as telling as his flat pace. "I exploded, and I shouldn't have. I ought to know better." He was parroting disciplinary directives that he'd been given by other counselors. "I can't let my anger get the better of me."

I put my hands on his shoulders to slow him down. "OK, easy, Wind-Up. Just tell me what happened."

His story took me on a scenic tour, stopping at every side note, extraneous detail, and nugget of self-analysis, with no linear structure. But from what I could gather, he had followed Mudge, Action, and the Fog after dinner. Mudge often used him as a whipping boy and tonight made a joke about Wind-Up being gay. Wind-Up misconstrued it as friendly ribbing and tried to engage Mudge in banter. What followed was a tutorial on the difference between laughing with and laughing at; Mudge contemptuously mocked him, while Wind-Up assumed it was an invitation to stick around. When they reached the tennis courts, Mudge looked directly at him and yelled, "Get out of here, no one wants you around." No joking, no teasing, just straight-out rejection.

Wind-Up didn't know how to process this. He had worked so hard to interpret the situation as amicable that he was trapped in the momentum of the situation. He kept lashing back at Mudge, but now it was 10 percent attempted humor, 90 percent fury. And as the percentages shifted, he slipped into a textbook freak-out. Certain kids were prone to them, and it was a Hulk-like transformation: A well-placed taunt could cause a spastic synapse to fire and the kid turned into a spit-and-expletive-spraying dervish, complete with pinwheeling arms and kicking legs. Once a crazy-person trigger reveals itself, bullies can't resist flicking it like a TV remote on a rainy day.

When Mudge and the others had turned to walk away from him through the tennis courts, Wind-Up screamed some nonsensical insults, then ran to pick up a large stick and throw it at the fence that stood between them. "I was going to throw it at them," he pointed out to me, "but luckily my sense kicked in that it was wrong."

I led him down to the Senior Cove, where we sat down on one of the benches. I explained to him that I was glad that he had realized he shouldn't throw the stick directly at the other campers, but he needed to learn to walk away from situations like this. Wind-Up raced to concur with every bit of advice I could hand him.

"You can't give him the satisfaction of exploding like that, because—"

"No, he just wants that satisfaction, I can't give him that."

"Um, right. He only teases you because he knows he'll get a reaction."

"I'm just playing into his hands, Josh! It seems so silly, I don't know why I do it."

"You need to be able to walk away, be the bigger person."

"The bigger person, exactly! So walking away is definitely the answer."

It was too easy with Wind-Up; he wanted to please me, but I knew that the next time Mudge called him a homo, Wind-Up would chew through a chain-link fence just to get at him.

I sent Wind-Up down to the dock to enjoy the rest of his night, maybe take out a canoe, then I returned to the cabin. It was empty, except for Mudge, who lay on his bed, reading. One of his legs lazily hung over the side, his tennis shoe tapping on the floor. I sat down next to him and asked him what happened. Though I fought to keep my voice from sounding accusatory, Mudge immediately treated my question like an affront. As if he had been rehearsing for this confrontation, he dropped his book in his lap and told his side of the story breathlessly and defensively, starting in the middle of an argument that hadn't actually begun yet. Wind-Up was bugging *them*, he said, and wouldn't stop following them. Mudge had tried to hint that the three of them wanted to hang out by themselves, but Wind-Up didn't get it, and when he was flat-out asked to leave, he went crazy, throwing a stick at them. Mudge glared at me, daring me to disagree with his reality.

"So you didn't say anything else that might have set him off?" I asked.

He scrunched up one side of his face in the international symbol for "Puh-*leeze*." "No!"

"You weren't calling him 'gay'?"

He shrugged. "Maybe once. But I was just kidding."

"So that wasn't really nothing, was it."

"It's not nothing, but it's a lot better than throwing a stick. One is a joke. The other could break my head open."

Like a dog with two bones thrown in opposite directions, I was momentarily confused as to which way to go. Should I make a teaching point out of his homophobia? Or did I address the bigger "don't be a prick" problem? The first was a subset of the second, so I went for the bigger bone. If a kid became kinder, maybe as a side effect the words "queerbait" and "homo" would automatically fade from his vocabulary.

"You've known Wind-Up for years. You know you can't joke around with him the way you joke around with Lefty or Action."

"It's not my fault he freaks out!"

"No, just like it wouldn't be your fault if a diabetic went into a coma after you fed him sugar."

He glared at me. "What are you *talking* about." So much for the power of metaphor.

"He just wants to be your friend."

"I don't want to be his friend."

"Maybe not, but you can't be cruel about it. If you tease him, you know he'll flip out. There are other, nicer ways of dealing with him."

"All I said was, 'Please leave us alone.' "

Perhaps that was what he said. But I knew from experience that Mudge could recite the lyrics to "That's What Friends Are For" to you in such a dismissive manner that it would come out sounding like a hate crime.

After a few more minutes of attempting to show Mudge why Wind-Up's need for better self-control did not excuse Mudge's role in making him lose it, I started repeating myself, so I wrapped up with a feel-good, let's-all-get-along maxim and left the cabin. I had solved nothing tonight. Wind-Up had yessed me, and the second I had stood up from Mudge's bed, I heard his sigh of relief at the interruption being over as he reopened his book. That was not the soundtrack to a lesson learned.

This was not the Eastwind way. Camp was a magical land with no bullying. Isn't that what we all talked about during staff orientation? And wasn't that what everyone reflected on so beatifically at Birch Grove on Sunday? Mudge shouldn't have sneered at Wind-Up, he should have asked him to join him, Action, and the Fog for a game of doubles tennis. And then they'd become pen pals over the winter. And, eventually, be best man at each other's weddings.

Later that night I returned to the cabin when all the boys were there.

Mudge and Wind-Up stayed far apart, but other than that it was like any other night. Trumps played backgammon with Lefty on his bed, and Mensa hovered over them, twirling a flashlight in his palm and second-guessing every move.

"Interesting choice, Trumps," he said, a hand on his chin. "I would have doubled up there instead of knocking him out, because you're leaving yourself wide open on two men, but we'll see, we'll see."

"Yeah, we'll see, and you'll shut up," growled Trumps. Lefty rolled but couldn't make it back onto the board. Trumps rolled and took out yet another of Lefty's chips, then glared up at Mensa. "Gee, looks like that went well after all. So why don't you save your suggestions for when you're playing . . . and losing."

Mensa mumbled a response and then wandered away. I watched as he stopped in front of Dewey, who was reading the new Harry Potter book. "You're still reading that? Are the big words slowing you down?" He chuckled to himself humorlessly as Dewey looked up, confused as to why his reading skills just got sucker punched. It was the food chain of abuse: Trumps mocked Mensa, Mensa mocked Dewey, then, inevitably, Dewey would mock Wind-Up, who would then go mock some plankton.

I recognized Dewey's surprised, hurt eyes from an old friend of mine, and I had been the cause. His name was Kyle, and he and I had been friends until my last year as a camper, when I formed a tight clique with two other friends and our counselor. I never meant to alienate Kyle, but, selfishly, I was having too much fun with my other friends to pay him much mind. I reassured him that we were still buddies, but I was unable to repress the look of annoyance on my face when he'd ask me to hang out and I'd wonder what good times with my other friends it would cause me to miss.

By the end of the summer, Kyle wore the expression that I now saw on Dewey. It was the look of someone betrayed by the promise of summer camp. The same ignoring, teasing, or marginalization that they thought they'd left slammed in their school locker had somehow picked the lock and followed them up to Eastwind. No matter how much the staff may work to block it out, adolescent cruelty will always find a way to sneak in.

A satisfied cheer filled the cabin. Lefty had just beaten Trumps. "Hey, doofus," Lefty yelled over to me. "You ready to take on the champ? I've been letting you off easy, but the time has come to show you how I *really* play."

I sat up. "So you're a genius now? Does this mean you're going to stop counting the triangles out loud every time you move?"

"Sounds like someone's scared!"

"I'm just scared that you're going to roll a six and a five and your head's gonna explode because you'll have to count past the number ten. I don't want to get Lefty brain all over my good T-shirt. Not that it would make much of a mess. It would be like blowing up a blueberry."

"Like I don't see you moving your lips when you read at night. Why don't you move to something easier, 'cause *Hop on Pop*'s a little above your level. Now get over here, dummy, and let me beat you and then you can go back to trying to figure out what C-A-T spells."

All tension was forgotten as we joined together for the pleasure of listening to trash talk. Which, I realized, was a nonsensical solution to the teasing problem: When kids started to turn against each other, should I unite them with the healing power of abuse? My razzing was delivered in a jocular spirit, but did that really make it any better than Mudge's sharp slashes?

"I don't see you coming over here, so I guess this is a forfeit, making me the new cabin champ," crowed Lefty. "Don't worry, maybe you can beat me in something that suits your talents more, like a dork-being competition."

I scrunched up my face. "A 'dork-being competition'?" How could I let that go unanswered? "Wow, the public schools are really letting down the youth of America. Or as you'd say, 'Schools be am down-letting America youth.'" I went over to his bed. "All right, this shouldn't take long. Let's go through the ground rules again: Don't eat the dice. I know they look like candy, but show some restraint." It was just so *natural*, I couldn't stop. And, I rationalized, I knew Lefty could take it. It wouldn't occur to him that anyone would actually think poorly of him.

Was there a happy medium? I didn't know. All I could do was try to find one. "Hey, Wind-Up, you want to come over here and watch me trounce Lefty? It'll only take three minutes."

Mudge had come over to watch the game, and he sighed deeply when I invited Wind-Up. "Oh, this is gonna be great," Wind-Up guffawed, as he leaped off his bed and bounded over, plunking himself down next to me a little too closely. He showed no awkwardness around Mudge as he rambled about the upcoming game. "Lefty will be going doooooown, as they say. Down to the ground! Back to the minors!"

I clapped him on the back, then turned to the cabin. "Dewey, Mensa, you guys want to watch Lefty go down? He might need someone to dry his eyes when he loses, so bring some tissues. All right, let's make this quick."

CHAPTER TWENTY

SWIMMING COUNSELORS HAD A HIGH BURNOUT RATE. IT WAS EXHAUSTING compensating for the fact that most of your students had zero enthusiasm for what you were trying to teach them. At archery, for instance, kids desperately wanted to shoot, so you could show up in a bad mood and no one would notice; all they needed you for was your ability to disseminate arrows, count rings, and give them their damn certificates, thank you very much. But at swimming you had to be at your most inspiring just to convince kids to get into the water.

Anne never confessed to a single frustration. Helen, on the other hand, was a fine ally in weariness. Though her jet lag had long since worn off, she was perpetually tired and therefore often cranky. After postbreakfast cabin cleanups and Rest Hours, she would flop down onto the bench and say, "Do we *have* to do this? Can't we send them all sailing?" And then, after a deep breath to summon strength, she'd try to rally her kids to indulge in the wonders of the scissors kick.

Both Helen and Anne were spectacular athletes. While I spent my off moments reading or playing backgammon, Helen vanished for a ten-mile run. Anne spent her days off rock climbing or mountain biking. I had gotten myself into reasonable shape at the gym before the summer, but though I had brought my bike to camp in anticipation of many invigorating, quiet, prebreakfast rides, it was getting as much use as my guitar. I now resigned myself to spending the summer slowly losing my muscle weight. Hopefully I would get married right before the last muscle evaporated and I started gaining fat-ass weight.

Helen and Anne were also better swimmers than I. I was okay with the strokes. I could break them down into small movements for the kids, helping them pace their side breathing with their arm strokes for the crawl, coordinating their gasps out of the water with their frog kicks for the breaststroke. But occasionally, in the midst of explaining a skill, I realized that I wasn't sure I could demonstrate it myself. Like pike surface dives, often used for rescues: You propelled yourself to the bottom of the lake in the midst of swimming by thrusting your arms downward and lifting your legs straight out of the water. "The key to a pike," I said to three students, just as I realized that I hadn't attempted one in years, "is to keep your legs straight and together. Watch my legs as I do it." My legs were probably surprised to hear this directive. *Watch us? Why? If you want to see us really shine, watch us put ourselves up on an ottoman. For this, maybe you'd better go watch Helen's legs.*

I swam the breaststroke, then took a deep gulp of air and yanked my head downward. Up went my legs, and I willed them to perform a perfect maneuver. As I went under I felt them lift up with the precision of a fire-engine ladder. Today I am a textbook, I thought.

After touching the sandy bottom, I turned around and shot myself out of the water. "OK," I said, wiping the water from my eyes. "Did everybody see how straight my legs were? You all ready to try it?"

"Um . . . your legs bent," said a quiet, eleven-year-old Coyote, sitting at the edge of the raft, making circles in the water with his feet.

"No they didn't," I said, then immediately felt my sureness wane. "Did they?"

He shrugged. "Kinda. And they were far apart." The other two classmates nodded.

"OK . . ." Be a man about it, be a man. "Good eyes, then. I'll try it again." I swam out a few yards, then a few strokes back. Down went my head, up went my legs. I pretended I was clenching a piece of paper between my knees, just like I had instructed them.

I came up. "Legs straight?" I asked.

The Coyote shrugged again, then said. "I guess they were straighter."

"Straighter, or straight?" I asked.

"I thought they were about the same," said a nine-year-old Raccoon.

"I think they were straighter," said the Coyote.

"Well," I said, swimming back to the crib. "They were a lot straighter." I had to take the "Because I said so" approach or I'd lose all credibility. "Now let's see you try it, and I want to see your legs as straight as mine."

"But yours weren't—" began the Raccoon.

"I said get in!" I barked.

More than anything, I lived in fear of teaching the butterfly. It was swimming's most aggressive stroke, a balance of angry lunging and undulating grace. And I had no idea how to do it.

When I grew up learning and teaching swimming, the butterfly wasn't included in any of the basic mandatory levels. I was never taught it, nor did I ever have to teach it. It was a stroke used for racing, so you only learned it from a swim-team coach, if you requested it at all. It was a frill stroke; if someone wanted to be a showboat, pinwheeling his arms dramatically like Mark Spitz, fine, he could do it on his own time, but we purists were happy to stay on the other side of the pool, practicing our calm, rhythmic elementary backstroke with nothing to prove to anybody. But sometime in the years since my swimming heyday, the Red Cross changed its qualifications, and now butterfly was part of the core curriculum. Though only the legwork—known as the dolphin kick—was necessary for level 5, the handful of enterprising kids who kept up with lessons past the mandatory requirement faced the entire stroke in level 6.

You could get by with a mediocre crawl or backstroke; it wouldn't be pretty, but at least you'd get from point A to point B. But it was impossible to be just OK at the butterfly. You had to meld the dolphin kick with a simultaneous two-arm lunge; if you didn't have them perfectly mastered and synchronized, you'd stay splashing spastically in one place, gargling on your own wake. Like a half-gainer off a high dive, it took only one slight error to become an utter disaster.

I decided that it would be better to neither teach nor perform the butter-fly, as long as both Helen and Anne knew it well. I didn't want to reveal my shortcoming to either of them, so I discovered deft ways of avoidance. I taught other strokes with enough vigor to drown out the possibility that the butterfly existed. And if a kid asked, "Can I work on the butterfly?" I quickly and loudly changed the subject to another stroke. If the kid was es-pecially tenacious, I'd substitute a distracting bribe, announcing that it was time for everyone to go down the water slide. Once, I was paired with only one student for the day, an overachiever who wanted to pass all levels; I looked down with horror at his progress sheet and saw that the butterfly was the only skill he had yet to master to pass out of level 6. I tapped Helen, who was about to head to the shallow water with a tiny level-3 Otter, and mum-bled a series of contradictory directives and questions to her that so con-fused her that by the end she didn't notice that I had switched students. She dazedly then took her new level-6 student off to the crib, feeling slightly vi-olated but not sure why. She had fallen for camper three-card monte.

I was living the motto "Those who can't do, teach." I probably wasn't any less accomplished than when I last taught swimming, but back then it didn't occur to me to have doubts. My insecurity only mounted the next Sunday morning at six A.M., when I shuffled down to the motorboat dock. In addition to passing out of level 5, Eastwind had a new requirement for graduation from swimming lessons: Boys had to swim all the way across the lake and back, a journey of about a mile. Much to my disappointment, these trials were held early Sunday mornings to avoid motorboat traffic, thereby robbing me of my only chance to sleep in.

When I got to the dock, seven boys were anxiously waiting with Anne and Helen. We divvied them up into three groups, with each one to follow a different counselor's rowboat. As I gathered up some life vests to toss in my boat, I looked up and saw British Sean coming down the road toward the dock.

"Anne asked me to come and row," he said, eyes half-shut. "She's gonna do the swim with the kids."

I turned around and saw Anne—peppy even at six A.M.—kick off her sandals, strip down to her bathing suit, and gather the boys around for a rallying huddle. This was lunacy. It was bad enough to get up this early, but she was going to willingly hop in the lake as well? This kind of self-sacrifice just made the rest of us look bad. I looked over to Helen to get an "amen," but she was catching a few last moments of standing sleep, her forehead leaning against a pole.

"That's insane," I said. "Isn't one of the benefits of being a counselor that you never have to do that again?"

Sean hopped off the dock into his rowboat, gained his balance, and then unclipped his line and pushed off. "I dunno. I've done it before. I may swim it next week."

I shook Helen awake and got into my boat, tying a floating orange flag to the stern, and then rowed out where the kids were climbing down the rocks at the edge of the dock and into the dark, chilly water.

"All right guys, you're all awesome!" Anne hollered as she splashed in with them. "See you in level six!"

Damn Anne and her showing off. This was a little early in the morning for a passive-aggressive guilt trip, wasn't it? Because now all I could think about was the fact that I needed to do the swim one week. And it was early, and it was cold, and I was an adult, and, most important, I was out of swimming shape and didn't know if I could do it.

Granted, these kids didn't know either. In fact, many of them had aired that worry to me as soon as they'd passed their last level-5 task and realized that all that was left was the lake swim. I had reassured them that they were strong enough to do it, and that they would feel fantastic when it was over. All the while I was thinking, Better you than me.

I rowed around the dock and called for my two boys, a twelve-year-old Antelope and an eleven-year-old Cheetah, to get in the water and follow me. After a lot of howling about the cold water, they both fell into a rhythm, and I made tiny dips into the water with my oars to keep a slow, swimmerly pace so they'd remain two feet behind. The Antelope looked like he was on a sightseeing trip, showing no fatigue whatsoever as he kept up a steady breaststroke, looking around the quiet lake. The Cheetah, on the other hand, soon looked problematic. Which was strange for him: He was a cocky kid from Boston, precociously smart, and he felt his urbane, cultured home put him a step above his suburban cabinmates. Now his sense of superiority was failing him. With every stroke he grimaced.

"You doing all right?" I called to him.

"*Grrmph* . . . no . . . ," he grunted. "Don't think I can make it."

"Sure you can," I said. "It's early, and you're doing great."

"No . . . no . . . can't."

It was early for someone to bow out. Even I could make it past here. We were only one-quarter done.

"If you really think you're done, you can get in the boat, but I bet you can go a bit farther," I said.

"OK . . . OK." He switched over to his side. The Antelope looked over at him bemusedly and kept swimming.

Three minutes later, the Cheetah cried out, "I'm done. Done. Let me in." He took a few strokes toward the back of the boat, more forceful than anything he'd been doing since we left. He clearly had some strength left.

"I don't think you should come back in," I said, dipping my oars into the water a little deeper to nudge the boat just out of his reach.

"What?" he gasped. "But I'm tired, I need to."

"I know you think you're tired, but I know you. You're stronger than this, you can do it. Look, you can see the buoy." A large orange buoy with a red globelike top bobbed near the far shore, marking our turnaround point. "We're getting closer, and you can make it. Just push it a little bit farther and then if you're still tired you can get in."

And he kept swimming. Slowly. While he caught up, the Antelope had to stop and tread water. He didn't seem to care, content to spin around in the water and take in all the shores from his central point. Meanwhile, the Cheetah complained and moaned, while I nudged him on with an endless loop of motivational chatter. "You don't want to get into this boat now. Because at the end you'll think, That wasn't so far, I could have done that. But if you stay in, at the end you'll say, 'I *did* that.'" Every so often he'd lunge at the boat with a clawlike hand, and I'd row forward just enough to stay out of his reach. "Once you grab on to the boat, you're done, and you don't want to be done."

We reached the buoy and I twirled the boat around. "Halfway! Did you ever think you could make it halfway? Now we'll go back, which means everything you do, you've done before." He let out a dramatic wail, and the Antelope bobbed placidly next to him. On the ride back he professed to be on the brink of drowning every three strokes, and I revved up my go-team chatter. "*Comeonyoucandoitonestrokeatatimewiththeverykickyougetclosertotheendyou'reachampyou'reachamp . . .*" I broke for brief moments to cheer on the nonchalant Antelope, but it seemed like my attention was all that was keeping the Cheetah afloat, so I could only veer my voice from him for a second or two.

And then we finally neared the dock, passing within the arc of moored sailboats that formed the outside perimeter of the waterfront. We were the last boat there. Sean was putting his life vests away, having sent his kids back to their cabins to warm up. Anne was hugging and high-fiving her three fellow swimmers while Helen docked her boat. "OK, you can zip ahead if you want," I said to the Antelope, who effortlessly sped past my boat and clambered up the rocks. Over my shoulder, I yelled to him, "And congratulations!" I turned back to the Cheetah. "Look," I said softly. "You're past the sailboats. And there's the raft. And there's your finish line. You did it."

He looked up fiercely, with a strength he hadn't shown since he first jumped into the water. After a last few strokes that were more doggy paddle than crawl, he reached out and touched the rocks.

After I'd docked my boat and put away the life jackets, I walked back down toward the edge of the dock, where he was sitting on a deck chair, wrapped up in a fluffy yellow towel.

"So," I said. "You're here. And you did it."

He looked up at me, his eyes exhausted but alive. "I did. I made it. I can't believe I made it."

I put out my hand. The Eastwind handshake. Welcome to manhood, m'boy. He shook it and smiled, then got up slowly, and gingerly walked over to get his shoes. He was limping with both legs, an impedimentary affectation that would enhance the legend of his mighty accomplishment. Anne's and Helen's boys were just about to leave the dock, and he forgot his hobble as he rushed to catch up to them. "So you guys finished, too, huh? Which strokes did you use? I was all about the backstroke . . ."

I went to get my shoes, next to where Anne stood madly drying her hair with her towel. When she lowered it, her long hair a frantic, tousled bush, she gave me a big grin. "So how'd it go out there?"

"Pretty good," I said, and I told her about how carefree the Antelope had been, but how the Cheetah had been ready to bail out before he even got wet. "I have a feeling that when he retells the story, he'll leave out the part about begging to get into the boat. But that's OK. He did it, I'm proud of him."

"That's awesome. It was a *great* swim this morning. Great! So exhilarating!" Helen sat at the end of the dock, waiting for us. "You guys want to do it next week? I can row and you guys can swim."

Fat chance, I thought. I don't do, I teach, and I'm proud enough of that right now not to push my luck.

CHAPTER TWENTY-ONE

WHEN I FELT A HAND TAP ME ON MY SHOULDER DURING MEALS, I KNEW IT meant one of three things:

1. A camper was about to explain why he couldn't come to swimming lessons.
2. A counselor was about to ask me for a favor.
3. A camper was playing "Made you look" and was standing on the other side.

I could tell the difference just by the force of the touch. The about-to-shirk camper clamped down hard on my shoulder with a force that said, "Look, we're all men here, I'm sure we can come to some sort of a deal." It was the training-wheel version of the hearty handshake that car salesmen give new customers before convincing them to get heated seats. The second was a bit lighter, but radiating with just as much exaggerated camaraderie. And the third was a frenzied series of taps, all hyped up with the excitement of a master con brewing. This one happened about three times a meal from campers who assumed they were the first one to try it.

During Monday's breakfast, I felt a clap on my shoulder that was definitely a number two. Before I could turn, I heard the pop of knees as someone crouched down to ask for something. Shrewd: coming down to my level. It said, *Hey, man, we're all just working men trying to get through the day, so I'm sure you can relate to what I'm about to ask you.* And I knew it was Mitch. I had grown to recognize the sound of his joint pop; I could pick it out of a stadium full of people doing deep knee bends.

"Hey, man," he said, weariness in his voice. "Frank just asked me to go into town to pick up some supplies." He rolled his eyes. Nobody knew the trouble he'd seen. "Think you can cover the cabin for cleanup?"

I smiled weakly. "Sure, no problem." He clapped me again on the shoulder, and then pushed down on it to stand up. I was the granter of favors *and* leverage.

"Thanks, I owe ya." He sauntered back to his table.

"Can I play you in backgammon?" asked Action.

"As long as your area's clean, sure," I said.

He high-fived the Fog, who looked at me and then said in a near-whisper, "How come you're always there?"

I liked spending much of my free time in the cabin, but only when it was of my own volition. Trevor was usually out on trips, so most daytime coverage duties fell to Mitch and me. We divvied it up at the beginning of each week, but I suspected that Mitch, noticing how often I was in the cabin, had extrapolated that if he couldn't make it when he was supposed to, he could always count on me to sub in. The fact that today he actually asked me to cover for him was an anomaly. Increasingly I had been returning to the cabin at free periods and finding no other staff there, so I stuck around. It rankled me, as I loved knowing that I *could* sit on the empty dock for Rest Hour, even if I rarely did.

Mitch didn't seem to know what to make of this month's Bears. When Captain Marquee had strung up white Christmas lights around his area a few days earlier and asked Mitch what he thought, Mitch stared at them as if they were a luminous garland of turds. The only one in the cabin who shared Mitch's outdoorsman passion was Wind-Up, a fact Mitch looked upon as God's cruel joke, since it meant that he received a far greater percentage of Wind-Up's attention. Wind-Up's bed was next to his, and as soon as reveille blew, he was up peppering Mitch with questions about mountains or observations about his own hiking boots. Mitch growled, "I'm barely awake, will you shut yer yap for ten minutes?" but Wind-Up would not be snooze-alarmed, and he segued perfectly into a filibuster on the morning weather.

Mitch didn't dislike the cabin, he just didn't have much to say to them. His interaction with them was limited to occasional smart-ass remarks and tossed epithets such as "chumps" and "girls." Though I found his cutting tone to be a little too sharp—a subjective and self-serving distinction I made from my own cabin mockery—none of the Bears took offense. Mitch was a legend at camp, and his sharp tongue was part of his persona. So when he covered cabin at night and sent them all up to the bathroom by growling, "You weenies better get up there and put your pimple cream on," they just laughed. He confided in me that his bedtime strategy was to read aloud the dullest book imaginable, thereby putting them to sleep. But sometimes he sent them off to slumber with stories from his life, crazy tales involving psychotic friends, wild parties, and terrifying adventures in the wilderness; the next morning I'd hear the boys retelling them to each other, occasionally begging Mitch to repeat them or give more details. One night when I pulled a book out to read, someone said, "Forget that, Josh. Tell us a story about something that happened to you." But I had never been surprised by a grizzly bear or had an insane bartender pull a bowie knife on me. I was a guy who occasionally drank too much in college but never broke anything without paying for it and generally followed the rules. Did they want to hear about the time I interviewed John Ritter in his dressing room, and he turned out to be a very pleasant fellow? Maybe I could graft a horror-story ending to my visit to the set of the sitcom *Scrubs*. ". . . and when I got home, and listened to my interview with Zach Braff, in the background I could hear a ghostly voice whispering, *Joooosh, surreal comedies like this rarely find a mass audience! Run away, run away!*"

As for Trevor, for the first few days, the boys only saw his square, science-teacher personality, which was kryptonite on summer vacation. But on a recent night, Trevor draped a sheet over the door and plugged in a slide projector. They all groaned, expecting a lecture on the periodic table of the elements, but instead he brought out a carousel with pictures of his most extreme rock-climbing trips. He flashed through photos of himself swinging from rocks by a hangnail, standing on top of a rock face that looked unscalable to anyone who wasn't 80 percent glue, and sleeping overnight tied to a ledge no wider than his spinal cord. A few days later, I'd asked the cabin if they'd seen Trevor. "You mean God?" said Lefty.

I looked at him quizzically.

"God," explained the Fog softly. "We gave him that name after we saw his slides."

I, however, had no holy nickname. Just more cabin duty. After breakfast, as I walked back to the Bears, I heard some footsteps scurry up behind me and felt someone's warm palm on my cheek. "Wibble," said Lefty.

I brushed his hand off. He was walking with Mudge, the Fog, and Action, who were all giggling. "What the hell is 'wibble'?" I asked. More giggling.

"Nothing, just wibble." He reached out again, and I smacked his hand away as it grazed my cheek.

"Seriously, what are you doing?"

"You never heard of a wibble before?" asked Mudge.

"No."

"It's when you stick your hand down your own pants and hold onto your own balls, and then you pull it out and put your hand on someone's cheek and say, 'wibble.'"

Mitch called them weenies. Trevor was God. And I got a wibble.

Every morning after cleanup, each cabin was graded on tidiness, and the weekly winners got a rare candy prize. We had won the first week, and the boys received a pack of Skittles each. Unfortunately, this victory taught them that one dose of candy wasn't worth all the energy. Since this epiphany it took serious effort to get them to do even the most minimal cleaning. This morning I moved down the aisle slowly, shouting jovial orders to tidy up. As I made my way through, I left a trail of resigned sighs in my wake as they begrudgingly began to clean. Finally, as I neared my area, I gave one last yell to Afty, who lay on his bed reading a book.

"Let's get moving, Afty. That bed isn't going to make itself under you." He didn't look up. "Did you hear me?" I asked, bending down to make my own bed in a show of "We're all in this together" solidarity. Counselors' areas weren't judged, but Afty might have been willing to follow my example if I showed that no man was above the laws of cleanliness.

"Yes, I heard you." His voice was chilly, and he continued to read. "I'm waiting until I'm finished with this section."

My face grew warm with the heat of a thousand wibbles. I was already feeling prickly from the suspicion that Mitch was taking advantage of me. And now a camper was jabbing at my seniority, too?

"Afty," I adopted a stern tone. "I need you to do it now."

"No." His response wasn't defensive. It was just declarative. The tone said "Fuck you," but the fact that he couldn't even be bothered to waste profanity on me made it even worse.

"Yes."

"No."

Up until now, no camper had so openly flouted my authority. Sure, kids resisted directives like do a lap, make your bed, get us more cereal . . . but only in jokingly rebellious ways that were easy to quash. In fact, they only stood up to me with the expectation that they would be quashed. It was all part of the camper/counselor dance. Even the persistently sarcastic Mudge did what I told him to once his eyes finished their full-circle roll.

The other boys sensed a failure to communicate going on in my corner. The sibilant sounds of broom on wood floor dwindled as they all eavesdropped.

I crossed around my bed to his area and stood over him. "It will take three minutes to make your bed, another five to sweep and clean up your shelves. And then you can go back to reading your book."

"If it'll only take that long, I can do it at the end when I'm done reading."

My head throbbed with frustration and the suppressed urge to grab the book out of his hand. Instead, I wildly grasped at counseling straws. I sat down on my bed. Perhaps getting on his level was the answer, just like Mitch got down to mine. "Everyone else is cleaning now. It's a group project. And when everyone is done, they will go back to their books or their letters or their backgammon, but not until this place is clean."

"I *said* I'll do it when I'm done with this section."

Right. So sitting wasn't the answer. How about squatting? Lying down? Suspending myself by pulleys? Now I was out of options. Oh, wait: was flipping the bed with him on it an option? No. OK, I was out, then. All the other campers were gawking, and this was becoming an ugly showdown. Through clenched jaw, I said, "Afty, please come outside with me. I'd like to talk to you."

"No," he said. "If you have something to say to me, say it here. I don't care if these guys hear." He was still staring at his book, but he wasn't reading; the pages were just a backboard to volley his anger back at himself. Where was this coming from? I thought he had a poor self-image; shouldn't that make him more cowardly? And what an odd line in the sand to draw. Of all the things to push a kid too far, the making of beds should not rank so high.

I looked up at everyone else. "Please go back to cleaning your areas." I then lowered my voice to a clenched whisper. "You do not need to turn this into a huge fight. This is cleanup. This is the time we clean. I am not asking you to do anything . . ."

And with that he slammed his book shut, rolled off his bed with a grunt, and silently made his bed, radiating a tangible fury. His stringy hair cloaked his face as he looked down at his bed, but I could feel the intensity in his glare. I had to sidestep out of his area because he made no effort to acknowledge my presence as he pushed past me. He dug the sheets and blanket under his mattress with stiff fingers as if giving them a karate spike to the windpipe, and slammed the pillow down at the head of his bed. Storming out into the aisle, he grabbed the broom from where it leaned against the Fog's bunk bed and dragged it through his area in angry lunges. When he accrued a small pile of pine needles and sand, he pushed them into the communal pile in the center of the cabin to wait for whoever had dustpan duty. With that he dropped back onto his bed, grabbing his book on the way down. "Gee, that took four whole minutes. I could have done that in the last four minutes of clean-up and it would have been just as clean, and you wouldn't have had to yell at me like that."

"Yell at you?" I splurted, rapidly feeling myself lose the last vestiges of my maturity. "I wasn't asking you to do anything that I wasn't asking everyone else to do. And I was trying to be nice about it. You're the one who turned it into something it didn't need to be."

He then looked up at me slowly with a steady calm that proved he had won the argument. "No, you're speaking in that tone that says you're *trying* to be nice, which means you're not being nice." He delivered his logical knockout punch with such a smug air of "Case closed!" that it stopped me short. Had I just been schooled in an old-fashioned parse-down?

Finally I gave up, stalking away from him into the middle of the cabin, loudly judging the other boys' areas while I pondered what had just happened. How did I let an argument about something so simple escalate so much? And why did it feel like I lost it? I had been so friendly to Afty since he got here; why was he so disrespectful? Was it something in his past? And more important, what the hell could I do about it? I wasn't a child psychologist.

Afty spent the rest of the period with his book pulled down close to his eyes. After ten minutes I could see the tension in his arms relax, and I actually believed he was reading, rather than just using the book as a wall. I, too, calmed down, and when the bugle for first period blew, I thought there was some way I could salvage the moment. Everyone piled out of the cabin, and Afty shuffled out on his own. I came up behind him, and put my hand on his shoulder. Not a "do me a favor" clap, or a practical-joke tap, but a "bygones be bygones" pat. I could feel his shoulders seize up.

"Look, Afty, I'm sorry about what went on in there. It shouldn't have blown that far out of proportion. All I was trying to say was that I had made everyone else clean right away, so I couldn't make an exception for you."

He replied like an automaton. "Yep."

"So you understand I wasn't trying to bully you? But I need to keep things consistent."

"Uh-huh." He stared in front of him, never breaking his stride. He looked like he was praying for a giant vulture to fly by and snatch either him or me away. This was not the détente I was hoping for.

"Um . . . all right. So we cool?" I asked.

"Sure. Yep."

This was going nowhere. I made some more have-a-great-day chatter and broke away down to the dock. We were both relieved at the separation. As I rounded the corner past the kayaks, Lefty popped up next to me. And then, warmth.

"Wibble!" he yelled, then darted away as I lunged at him. "You know you love it!"

CHAPTER TWENTY-TWO

THE NEXT MORNING, I STOOD AT THE ASSEMBLY GROUND WAITING FOR AT-tendance to begin. At seven twenty A.M., you could see a visual timeline of the aging process. The youngest kids darted around, having been awake since before reveille. The older the cabin got, the slower its campers slumped onto the assembly ground. When the final notes of the assembly bugle call faded out, the last straggling Lions were still jogging down past the flagpole, wearing pajamas, sandals, and bedheads.

I moved to the Bears' penultimate row in the cabin lineup, standing on one side while Mitch stood on the other to bracket the kids. Trevor was out on his day off. Lefty threw his arm around my shoulder while Action gave me a fake jab to the stomach. "Good morning, Sunshine," said Lefty, sticking me with a wet willie. Given all the willies I'd been jabbed with in two weeks, it was a wonder I still had functioning eardrums.

I batted his wet finger away. "Get that out of my ear. I know where it's been."

"Ten-*hut!*" yelled Frank.

"Can I say it? Can I say it?" said Action. For a camper, to get to shout "Bears all present, sir!" was considered a brief but shining honor.

"Yeah, sure," I said.

"You should say 'All pheasant, sir,' and we could all flap our arms like they were wings," whispered Dewey.

"Sure, if you want to be *dumb*," Mudge said, groaning.

"Hey, zip it during assembly," I said.

Possums all present, sir. Raccoons all present and accounted for, sir.

"Josh should say, 'All stork, sir,'" said Lefty. "All dorky storks."

I put my arm over his shoulder, reaching around his head to place my hand over his mouth. He stuck out his tongue and licked my palm, making me yank it away.

Antelopes all present, sir.

"Hey, Mr. Stork!" Wind-Up blurted from a couple kids down. "Counselor Stork, are you going to bring a baby down to swimming today?" His mouth hung open with the joy of his joke.

"Shut up, Wind-Up, you killed it," grumbled Mudge.

"That's it, everybody . . ." I began.

"Wind-Up, Mudge." Mitch's voice snapped down the length of boys, lassoing their attention. "Everybody shut yer yaps and pay attention."

They all immediately stepped back into line. "Bears all present, sir!" yelled Action.

After the flag went up, Frank and a couple of counselors went to a pile of clothing dumped next to the Caribou cabin as a Lost and Found. They held up mud-caked socks and crumpled T-shirts for the assembled cabins, searching for nametags inside to identify the owners, most of whom wouldn't recognize their clothing even if it had their own face decaled on the front. This was the moment most kids stopped paying attention, and Mitch sauntered to the middle of our line, planting himself between Mensa and the Fog. "You dudes watching? Because I'd hate for your poop-stained underwear to be up there and you not be able to get it back." They both giggled and stood up straighter, watching Frank.

The last sock claimed, Frank hollered "Dismissed!" and everyone turned to make their way to the Dining Hall. I fell into step next to Marquee and Trumps.

"You so should have hung out at the cabin last night, Josh," said Marquee.

Oh, really. I was thinking I was spending too much time there myself, so the idea of piggybacking on someone else's bedtime duty really didn't appeal to me. "Why?" I asked. "What'd I miss? Keg party? Dance-off? Motorboat races?" Given Marquee's penchant for dramatization, I wasn't expecting much. What, Mitch told them a bedtime story about how he once nailed a Bennigan's waitress? Oooh, and to think I missed it.

"Actually," said Marquee, "you're close. Mitch took us all out on his boat. We were totally zipping all over the lake, and it was all dark and cool."

"It was *awesome*," added Trumps.

Now Mitch was giving them private motorboat rides? How the hell could I compete with that? I was the one there every goddamn day playing backgammon and talking to these kids, but quality time doesn't get you up to 40 mph on the lake.

That night Reg and I sat in the Office, him hovering over his computer, posting digital photos to his Web site for the enjoyment of his friends back in Australia. I was trying to check my e-mail, but the communal computer kept freezing.

"Goddamn this thing," I said, pounding uselessly on the enter key.

Reg came over and started pushing combinations of buttons. "That's my next big project, y'know," he said. "Gonna make me rich. Computer repair service. For people whose computers are hopelessly fucked. Viruses everywhere." He explained that he'd develop a program that would barrel through all that corruption, tearing its damaging tendrils away from the workings like a psychotic gardener ripping at vines.

"But aren't there already tons of tech companies that do that?" I asked.

"Not like mine," he replied. "They dick around, all dainty like, and take forever. Sometimes you don't have time for all that crap, you just want your computer back, and you don't care if you lose a little of your data along the way."

"A little of your data?"

"Yeah, maybe twenty percent. It's gotta be done if you want it back right away."

"What do you do, just pour bleach into the disk drive?"

"No vision, Wolk. You've got no vision at all." He gave up and yanked out the camp computer's plug, then replugged it in.

"Don't even think about ever getting near my computer." I pointed a warning finger at him. "And do me a favor, if I ever start choking at dinner, do the Heimlich. I know it seems easier to just slash my throat open with a butter knife and grab the piece of meat out of my windpipe, but I'll take the more delicate approach."

"You don't want to get results, fine. I get *results*."

I put my head down on the table. "The only result I want now is sleep. I'm wiped. I think I'm gonna head back to the cabin early."

Katia wandered into the Office and leaned over Reg to look at his computer. She was like a pirate's parrot, always perched over his left ear. "What are you to work on now, Reg?" she asked, her breast resting on him like a shoulder pad.

"Usual. E-mail. Web postings. Project the Maine lifestyle back to the homeland," he said, glancing at her with a wry smile. "What are you up to, naughty girl? No big party up in kitchen HQ?"

She sighed dramatically. "No, there is no party." She craned her neck to look him in the eye. "You think there should be party?" Katia's single entendres got even less subtle around Reg. They were only slightly more obtuse than a hardcore porn movie. But Reg had no interest in her flirtation, telling me it was too easy, not his thing. Then he'd launch into a confusing diatribe about how this summer was all about concentration, freeing himself from something or other that I could never understand, but which struck me as a philosophy concocted by mixing a boxing movie, a ninja handbook, and Mormonism.

"Not really a party night," he said. "For a good party there should be food. Maybe some beer. Noisemakers. Josh, you think noisemakers?"

"Not a party without them," I said.

"Oh, Reg, there could still be party—" she began.

"We'll talk tomorrow. Work out the noisemakers thing." Reg slammed shut his laptop. "Josh, you going back to yer cabin? I'm with ya, I need to borrow a magazine. Night, Katia. I'll look for my invitation."

It was around ten as he and I tromped past the Theater, and we saw a hovering light walk toward us. It was Zach, who wore a headband with a halogen light attached at the forehead, a popular accoutrement among the outdoorsy counselors. Whenever someone came at you with one on, the light drowned out the rest of the body behind it, so it looked like you were slowly being approached by an enormous firefly. Zach was OD for our side of camp, which meant he was "on duty" until at least one counselor from each cabin returned at eleven P.M. During a shift, the OD walked loops around the cabins; kids were told to shout for him if they felt sick and needed to go to the nurse. But the more common task was to quiet down kids getting rowdy in the dark.

Apparently tonight was one of those nights for the Bears. Zach said that they'd been loud all night, and he'd had to tell them to shut up at least three times. I thanked him and Reg and I continued on while Zach headed downhill toward the Tigers.

"You want to see a crackdown?" I asked him. Back in the '80s, we reveled in finding new ways to intimidate noisy late-night cabins. The silent approach was best. If the boys were particularly loud, you could get right up to the screen door, wait for the perfect moment, and then bellow in your deepest, most threatening voice, "This will stop *now!*" Then there was the two-man yell-and-sneak maneuver. A counselor stood at one door of a noisy cabin, warning the boys to be quiet. While the kids were distracted, the other counselor slipped silently in through the door on the other side of the cabin and lay down on a counselor's empty corner bed, where it was too dark to be noticed. When the decoy staffer left, the undercover counselor waited around five minutes until the kids inevitably started to giggle and talk again, picked his moment, and then intoned mightily, "I thought you boys were told to be quiet." It was every disciplinary horror story come true: *Oh my God, it's coming from inside the cabin!* You could feel the cabin buckle as all ten boys flinched at once.

When we neared the Bears, I could hear their laughing starting to build again. I waved at Reg to hang back as I slowly tiptoed up the steps. Marquee was telling a dirty joke, and Lefty urged him on, asking about extraneous details that might spark a new, dirtier angle to it. The rest of the boys roared appreciatively.

"*Knock it off,*" I thundered, dropping my voice as low as it could

176

reach. "*Zach has told you three times, and now this is the last time, do you hear me?*"

No one said anything, which was the best indication that they had heard. I smiled and gave the thumbs-up back to Reg, and waved to him to meet me in back of the Bears where I'd give him the magazine. I pushed open the screen and walked sternly through the cabin toward my area.

"Who is that? Josh?" I heard Marquee ask.

"Yes," I said. "No more talking."

The entire cabin let out a unanimous sigh. "Oh God," said Mudge, the derision in his voice just as powerful in the dark. "I thought it was Mitch. I'm scared of *him*."

"Well, maybe you should be scared of me, too, because if I hear another word tonight, you'll all be going to bed at eight tomorrow. You get that?" I heard sheets rustle, probably the sound of twenty shoulders shrugging. Bastards. I grabbed the magazine off a shelf and left again to hand it to Reg.

"I got bad news for ya, mate," he said, having overheard the whole thing. "I think you're the Mummy in this cabin."

Lefty had received a care package earlier in the week from his parents. Since campers weren't allowed to have their own candy or other edible treats, when a package arrived, the boy had to open it in the Office in front of his counselor to make sure there was no contraband inside. Staffers told me you had to be very careful, since some parents were known to hide a layer of candy bars underneath a false bottom. That seemed like quite the cloak-and-dagger endeavor just for the sake of spoiling your son— especially since they were the ones who sent their kid to a camp with these rules in the first place. One mother sent her son a stack of paper plates that had been hollowed out and stuffed with candy, an intact plate resting on top to hide the cache. It was the perfect crime, except for one giveaway: Who the hell would send their kid paper plates as a care package?

Instead of food, Lefty had received a sampling of games. None of them edible: I checked. One quickly captured the interest of the cabin: It was called Snatch. (I knew the Bears were euphemizing at only a ninth-grade level since none of them batted an eye at the unintentional double entendre.) There was no board, just a tube of Scrabble-like letter tiles. Players took turns flipping over one tile each, and as soon as someone could make up a word out of any or all of the exposed letters, they shouted it out, collected the tiles, and brought the word over to their area. It was called Snatch because you could also "snatch" someone else's word by re-arranging it and adding one or more of the exposed center tiles to create a new word. For example, if someone had TIP and an S was flipped over, you could yell SPIT!, take their word and the S, and put it in front of you.

Backgammon was quickly forgotten, and Snatch was brought out at every free moment for an anagramapalooza. I served as the cabin dictionary when squabbles arose, barely looking up from my book as someone yelled, " 'Pattle' is too a word. Josh, is 'pattle' a word?"

"No."

"Oh, what does he know."

I wormed into a game and was instantly even more dominant at this new sport than I was at backgammon. And I took just as much pleasure. Hooray, I, a professional writer, could outspell fourteen-year-olds! Now look out as I form my own math team and singlehandedly trounce the local elementary school's!

The day after Mitch's cabin motorboat ride, I returned to the Bears to see that he had been drafted into a game. There was much hooting and razzing going on around the card table, and as I walked in, he had just swiped a word from Trumps, who was looking glum. Everyone had a roughly even number of words, and I looked down at Mitch's collection: all simple words—CAT, RASH, DIE—and then Lefty pointed out the word I was just now noticing. "Check it out," he laughed. "Mitch got CUM." They all laughed, including Mitch, who looked up at me and smirked.

I laughed too, but for different reasons. Technically, "cum" is a word, but only as a preposition, not a spermy giggle. And next to it Mitch had WIFF. Honestly. I wondered if Mitch's van came with a Speak & Spell built into the dashboard. Dear God, was I smart. I may not be able to shred the gnar, but at least I could spell "shred." Maybe this would be the beginning of a power shift. Every time he asked me to cover cabin, I wouldn't even look up from my enormous book—*the kind with many pages, polysyllabic words, and no pictures at all*—and say, "Tell you what. You spell 'cabin' and I'll cover it." Oh, the Bears would have a new Daddy, all right.

I went over to my area to change clothes, alone in my smug thoughts as the white noise of shouted words filled the cabin. Then the screen door swung open next to me and Dewey walked in. No one would respect my mental dominance more than he. He wandered over to the players and surveyed the game. Surely he would notice the spelling error. And then the emperor would be exposed as clothesless, and I would seamlessly grab the throne in a grammatically correct coup.

"Hey, Mitch," he said.

"What." Mitch didn't look up from the game.

"Can you show me how to roll a kayak?" Dewey asked. "I've been trying, but I can't seem to get all the way around."

"Yeah, come down tomorrow. We'll get you to be a kayak badass."

"Cool," Dewey said, smiling, and then wandered back to his bed.

When I was in high school, grumbling about the unfairness of a world where the smart kids weren't nearly as respected as the jocks, my mother told me to just wait until I was an adult. That would be my moment to shine, and the jocks' moment to fill my gas tank. Here I was, an adult, and a flawlessly spelling one at that. But at camp, it looked like until I got myself a motorboat and an adrenal gland, I was still waiting at the pump for self-serve.

CHAPTER TWENTY-THREE

ONE OF THE BIGGEST INCENTIVES FOR BECOMING A CERTIFIED LIFEGUARD was the ability to surprise your cabin with a "cabin dip," a quick swim in the lake just before bedtime. Offering one was the quickest shortcut to becoming a hero to your wards. During dinner on hot nights, the Dining Hall stuffy and humid, I felt the Bears' eyes on me like I was a Vatican smokestack, and I savored their desperation. Dewey offered to get seconds at his table as an excuse to get up and pass my table, asking, "Cabin d—"

Not looking up from my meal, I interrupted. "Sit down. Haven't decided yet." He slumped away, shaking his head at the cabinmates watching in anticipation. As gloatable governances went, the cabin dip was pretty low rent. But everything was relative at camp. Near the end of dinner I dabbed my mouth with a napkin, stood up, and ambled around the dining hall. Aware of the Bears' hopeful stares, I stopped to chat with a couple of other counselors as misdirects, and then, on the way back to my seat, I leaned over to Lefty and muttered, "Dip tonight. Be ready at the cabin at eight fifteen. Spread the word." And thus did the benevolent lifeguard give joy to the masses.

As godlike a power as a lifeguard might have, Mudge found a way to make me feel very mortal indeed. I returned to the cabin to find everyone running around in their bathing suits, eager for me to set them free in Senior Cove. "All right, guys," I yelled, swinging the door open. "You ready for a cabin dip?"

This question usually got the same hysterical reaction that a rock star got when asking Cleveland if it was ready to rock. And it did from everyone who ran out of the cabin except Mudge, who stopped in front of me and said, a threatening scowl on his face, "Not a cabin dip. A cabin *swim*."

"Excuse me?" I said.

"A dip is short," he said. "This will be a cabin swim."

"I'm sorry," I said. "I didn't realize *you* were in charge." But he was already out the door, having dropped the last word on my feet like a turd and sauntered down to the beach, confident that I would now give him the swim he so deserved.

The heavy-lidded smirk with which Mudge punctuated each sentence was haunting in its very embodiment of disdain. He was the Mona Lisa of contempt. Unlike the trash-talking I exchanged with the campers, his comments were mirthless because he wasn't joking: He seemed to legitimately think everyone else was a disappointment to him and that they should know why. I was twenty years older than he, but his comments still left me speechless, as the effects spread like a rash, offending me on a wider and wider level. After the dip (most definitely not a swim; I sure showed *him* who was boss), as a bedtime story, I told the cabin anecdotes about my college friends from Tufts; I mentioned that my roommate Stu was incredibly smart, and before I could continue, Mudge's voice piped up from the dark: "If he was so smart, why did he go to Tufts?" I was silent as I peeled back all the comment's offensive layers. *Hey, that's not nice to say about my friend.* Pause. *Actually, it's more a slam on my school.* Pause. *Which is, by the transitive property, a slam on me.* If left untreated, one poisonous drop from his mouth would go on to impugn your entire family, living and ancestral, not to mention your town, race, country, and, gradually, everyone else on the planet. Except him.

Reasoning did nothing. A few nights later, apropos of nothing, he asked, "Do you teach swimming because you're not good at anything else?"

I stared at him. "*Wow*, that was rude."

He looked confused. "What do you mean?"

"Seriously? You don't see how that was incredibly rude?"

"I didn't mean it that way." Was it possible that there was an apology coming? No. "I just meant, were you not good at anything else?"

"OK, that's *still* rude." I grimaced with repressed rage. "In fact, you didn't even bother to rephrase it. It was the same exact rudeness twice."

He brushed his hair back slowly with his hand. "I wasn't trying to be."

"That can't be right, it was too rude not to be on purpose," I replied. I needed him to understand this. "Let's break this down. You asked why I taught swimming. Right?"

"Yeah, that's all I wanted to know."

"No, there was a little bit more to it. In asking why I taught swimming, you presented a theory of your own. Do you remember what that was?"

"That you weren't good at anything else?"

"A-ha!" I cried. "So your theory is that I teach swimming because I am untalented in every other possible way. Think about that. Does that seem like a compliment I should tuck away into a locket so it will always be close to my heart? Can you see why that would bother a person?"

He raised his hands helplessly, in the way that people do when arguing with a crazy person. "I'm sorry I hurt your *feelings*, Josh." This, technically, was not an apology at all, but rather a pitying statement about my hypersensitivity. And then he turned away and went back to reading a book.

I stomped up into the Office afterward to check my e-mail. Chas sat at the table, fiddling with his laptop. "You seem a little cranky," he said.

"Mudge is making me crazy," I growled. "He's the rudest kid I've met in my life. I think to myself, You're twenty years older, ignore him, but every time he makes one of his snide remarks I want to rip off my own ears and throw them at him. Except then he'd say, 'Nice *ear*-throwing, Josh,' and I'd get twice as mad and have nothing else to rip off."

"But you wouldn't have any ears so you wouldn't hear him say it."

I plunked down in front of one of the communal computers. "Knowing him, he can sign language sarcastically."

"Why don't you try relating to him on that level?" he said, excitedly jumping out of his chair. Chas loved to come up with creative ways of breaking through to problem kids, and they often involved some complicated combination of reverse psychology, fast patter, and props. "He's really negative, right? So why not be negative back, but so ridiculously that you make a joke out of it? Like, if he's sitting at your table and complaining about the food, you start complaining about really minor things. 'Yeah, the dinner stinks, but you know what else stinks? Salt shakers. Look at them, with their tiny holes. Why do I need that many holes? And check out these bowls. You call these concave?' "

"And what will all this do?"

"In a weird way, I bet he'll feel more bonded to you, even though you're making a joke out of it. And then when you've won him over he might be more willing to listen to your constructive criticism."

"Hmmm. Maybe," I said. Chas was so thrilled with his plan that I didn't want to contradict him, but it was a horrible idea. The goal was to make Mudge more sensitive to others' feelings, and joining him in the world of negativity seemed a pretty roundabout way of doing that. How would Chas suggest trying to get a friend off heroin, getting hooked myself and then hoping to wean ourselves off together? No, I wouldn't be challenging Mudge in a contempt-off. There had to be another way. I just hoped I found it before I gritted my teeth so hard they shattered.

Visiting Day came on the third Saturday and was a day of chaos and exaggerated smiles. The parents—who often missed their sons more than the other way around—started snaking down the camp road right after breakfast. Attempting to teach swimming in the morning was a lost cause. Lessons were constantly interrupted by parents dashing down the dock and screaming and waving to their son, who was in the midst of practicing his crawl. Helen, Anne, and I had to shuffle around lifeguarding responsibilities depending on who was busy telling a beaming mother what wonderful progress her son was making as a swimmer. It would be morbidly ironic if we got too busy gushing about one kid and didn't notice another one slowly sinking to the bottom of the lake.

Most of the parents had arrived by second period, so we made the rest of the day one long Free Swim so moms and dads and sons could swim together. The waterfront was also open for anybody to sign out a boat, even though it became instantly clear that many of our boys did not descend from a long line of seafarers. But since the parents were considered responsible guardians, not to mention they paid the camp bills, Zen Richard and Chas had to stand on the edge of the dock in a perpetual wince as they watched canoes, kayaks, and sailboats narrowly miss each other, not to mention the nearby swimmers. It was one big regatta of incompetence. I sat on the lifeguard tower, trying to keep track of everyone and think of the nicest way possible to ask an obese dad not to do a cannonball off the dock when someone else's kid was dog-paddling right under him.

I scanned the family dynamics splashing around me. There were dads merrily tossing their sons in the air and moms who applauded wildly when their little boy showed how he could dive off the raft. And then a canoe floated by with a red-faced father sitting in the front but facing backward toward his wife while their son glumly sat cross-legged between them over the boat's keel. The gruff dad—who was holding the paddle incorrectly—was browbeating his wife for not paddling properly as they slowly drifted toward the swimmers. "No, Betsy, paddle *forward*! Wait, *backward*, I mean! What's wrong with you, do you see where we're going?" Chas, who had just dislodged a kayaking dad's boat from the rocks around the motorboat dock, yelled, "Excuse me, sir? You need to get out of the swimming area, and actually you're sitting the wrong way. You're in the front, not the back. You need to turn around." If the wife took any solace from this, she didn't get much time to enjoy it, as the father then yelled, "I wouldn't have to sit this way if I could trust you to paddle!" His son sat, chin down, likely wondering if he could stay at camp all year long.

The waterfront was alive with this mix of parenting styles. Lefty brought his dad and two brothers, one older, one younger, down to the dock. The four looked identical, just incrementally smaller. Judging from their radiating glee for being together, the boys clearly idolized their dad, and the feeling was reciprocated. While their dad took off his shoes, his three sons all jumped into the water, yelling, "Come on in, Dad!" in the exact same cadence, but descending timbres.

Later, when I switched places with Helen and stood on the dock, a wide-chested father strode up to me, his gangly twelve-year-old Coyote son meekly following behind him. "Yer the swimming counselor, is that it?" he said, squeezing my hand with a grip that was half life insurance salesman, half bear trap. His son stood behind him, his willowy mom's arm around him protectively. "How's my son doing? He gonna get through level five?"

His son was a nice, funny kid, although he came to lessons reluctantly and was often more interested in trying to do underwater backward flips than honing his strokes. I imagined this was the kind of freewheeling attitude that did not go over well with Daddy Ironpaw. "He may," I said. "He's been working hard, so it looks good." You always wanted to prop up a kid in front of his parents, no matter how much you had to stretch the truth. There was no test at the end to prove whether you had been exaggerating; this was summer camp, not SAT prep.

The dad reached behind him and yanked his son away from his mom, who gasped a bit. The phrase "You *coddle* the boy" was probably uttered in their home once a meal. He threw his arm over his son's shoulder, less an act of chumminess than a restraining tool. "You've got ten days left," he said, looking his son in the eye. "You *can* pass out of this thing. The only thing left is to ask, Will you?"

The Coyote's body seemed to constrict before my eyes. "Yeah, Dad."

"Great then." The Coyote stepped back toward his mother, who put both arms around him, softly saying, "I bet you'll do it, too."

The father turned to me. "Tell you what, if you can get him out of five by the end of the year, there's a brand-new Mercedes in it for you!" He flashed the grin of the humorless, the kind that told me that while he was technically kidding, a new iPod wasn't out of the question if I could promise him results.

I returned to the cabin before lunch and found it choked with moms and dads unveiling care packages of magazines and camping equipment and refolding their sons' clothes. I introduced myself to them all, silently marveling at the wonders of the genetic code: Trumps' parents were equally rotund, with the kind of physiques made for matching sweatsuits. And Marquee's dad made the exact same dramatic arm gestures as his son, just with a wider wingspan.

Every area was occupied with hair-touslers and sheet-straighteners except Mudge's. The only Bear whose parents didn't come, he lay on his bed, staring at a book but never turning the pages. After I made the rounds, greeting parents (except Afty's, whom he gloomily led out the door without introducing them to anybody), they all filed out, leaving Mudge and I alone. I went over to his bed.

"Your folks coming today?" I asked.

"Nope," he said, not looking up. "They're traveling. Couldn't make it."

I squeezed out an empathetic wince, then went back to my area, where I made sure there were no moms left, and then changed out of my bathing suit. I heard the first bugle call for lunch blow and made to head across camp, where there'd be a special buffet for the families who stuck around. "Hey, Mudge, you going down to the Dining Hall?"

He dropped his book and heaved himself out of the bed with great effort, making feeding himself feel like a favor to me. "I *guess*."

We walked out together, in silence at first. We passed the tennis courts, where a father was still out there, volleying with his son. "His serve stinks," said Mudge.

"Why don't you tell him?" I asked. "Actually, let's both go down there, I'll hold him, you hit him over the head with a racket. He'll think twice about serving badly after that."

If his usual smirk was 25 percent smile, 75 percent contempt, the one he flashed now was nearer to 50/50. Astonishing. We arrived at the Dining Hall steps, where everyone gathered, sons hopping on their dads' backs or teaching them the various hand-slapping games kids played waiting for assembly or lunch bugles. I walked over to Reg. As I took a step, Mudge blurted out, "I'm going to eat lunch with you because there's no one else around."

I stared at him. What a touching statement. At that moment, the bugler climbed to the top Dining Hall step and blasted his meal-call toodle into the crowd, and everyone swept through the swinging doors. "All right, Mr. Sunshine," I said. "Thanks for the opportunity. Let's eat."

On a stretch of tables at the far end of the hall, the kitchen staff had laid out fresh salads, multiple variations of bread, and cold-cut platters that would shame any deli. The parents appreciatively *oohed* as they speared roast beef and turkey onto their plates; the Eastwind food was always good, but people had such low hopes for summer-camp food that just the fact that the deli meat wasn't gray was a PR coup. We came up in line behind Reg and slowly edged toward the food, following the pace of his clunky sneakers.

"Mudge will be joining us for the meal," I said to Reg, pointing next to me. "Don't forget to thank him."

"Thanks then, mate," said Reg. "We owe ya one." Mudge gave another 50/50 smile. We filled our plates and wandered the packed room until I saw open seats next to Chas. He had done his part to impress the parents by taking a shower for what might have been the first time this summer, but his wild, thick hair resisted brushing. It stood up and out as if someone was operating a giant fan underneath him. The Dining Hall was even louder with hopped-up parents there; so much for the mellowing effect of grown-ups. The thunderous atmosphere had an energizing effect on us, and we spent the meal razzing each other and joking at a frantic pace, with Chas accenting the silliness with his circus skills—spinning a plate, juggling french fries, etc. Mudge remained mostly silent as he ate, sitting in his usual ramrod posture, his chest puffed out as a physical billboard reminding everyone that he was the most perfect specimen around. He occasionally grunted a laugh, the only kind he'd deign to release, lest he lose the upper hand.

Chas balanced his last potato chip on his nose, then flipped it into his mouth and announced, "I'm off for more. I'm not gonna let these parents outeat me."

Mudge uttered his first words. "You *like* this food?"

Chas looked confused and scratched his head. His fingers vanished up to the first knuckle. "I'm trying to figure out if that's a negative comment or not."

Ha! Now Chas saw that I was dealing with no ordinary killjoy, and that this needed a thoughtful approach. Unfortunately, at this moment I was so caught up with our joking mood that what tumbled out of my mouth was not a teaching moment, but reflexive sarcasm. "I think I can help out with this," I said. "I've spent a lot of time with Mudge, and I've learned the nuances. When he says, 'Do you *like* this food?' he's legitimately curious as to whether you like the food. But when he says, 'Do you like *this* food?' it means, 'You have such bad taste that you'd probably like soup made out of my underwear, but don't get your hopes up because I wouldn't even give up a torn pair of tighty-whities for the likes of you.' So you see, it's complicated."

"Ahhh, I think I see now," said Chas, who never met a riff he didn't like to build on. "So what about something like, 'Do you think your shirt isn't ugly?' Would that be negative?"

"Good question, good question," I replied. "It really depends on the mouth placement on that one." I reached an arm around Mudge's head and put a finger on his upper lip. He flinched—he was the kind of guy you could imagine yelling, "No one touches the Mudge's face!"—but then relaxed. "If the corner of the lip is raised this much"—I pulled it up to a comical sneer—"then it's fair to assume he finds your shirt ugly. But anywhere in this region"—I waggled it up and down a little lower, and he remained surprisingly pliant—"that means, 'Your sense of fashion fills me with delight. Although you as a person still disgust me.' " I let go of him. "Mudge, if you ever need me to translate for anyone else, say the word."

I nudged him in the side and winked. He smiled. Forty percent contempt, 60 percent genuine mirth. I looked up and saw that Chas was smiling too, his eyebrows raised in a "See?" expression. Having inadvertently followed Chas' philosophy, Mudge and I were now bonded a little more tightly, but not in the healthiest of ways. If he teased Wind-Up again, would he be more receptive to my counseling techniques, or just ignore me until I got down to his level and mocked his ability to mock? I thought of the browbeating dad who had offered the Mercedes and wondered if a relationship based on sarcasm was any better than one based on unrelenting, harsh judgment. Was I making things worse?

I'd heard about junior high teachers who gave their students sacks of flour to carry around for a week to give them a sense of the responsibility of caring for a kid. This summer I'd been given sacks of kids. I just hoped I wouldn't drop one.

CHAPTER TWENTY-FOUR

IT WAS HELEN'S DAY OFF, SO ANNE AND I DIVVIED UP THE LEVEL-5 KIDS WHO came down third period. "My three guys come with me," I hollered, walking toward the end of the dock and perusing my clipboard. Every lesson began with a quick math problem: scan the checkoff lists of the random grouping to find the common denominator of what everyone still had left to learn. Once I settled on the sidestroke, I turned around and saw no one behind me. My trio was still on the dock, taking their shoes off as slowly as if they were dismantling a bomb. I stomped back. "Hey, you guys coming?"

One of them—a precocious thirteen-year-old who carried himself like a sixty-five-year-old Catskills comedian—looked up at me. "Do you mind?" he said. "We're having a very private discussion about our periods."

I hated when wiseasses were legitimately funny. "Your time of the month for swimming has arrived, so let's go." I was aware that they were looking over my shoulder. I turned and saw a small, awkward Lion strutting down the dock, his towel draped over his shoulder, and on his head lay a fresh, newly cut Mohawk. Reg had recently given himself the same hairstyle, but it fit with his wardrobe. It didn't make the same statement for this Lion, clad in a blue Eastwind T-shirt and a green bathing suit. The Mohawk wasn't straight; whoever had shaved it must have been reading a magazine while doing it since it curved over the top of his head like a parenthesis. Plus, he had thick, curly hair, which did not lend itself to a Mohawk; it curled over like a sleeping cat. All in all, Sid Not-So-Vicious looked like someone had crocheted a cabin's worth of dust bunnies together and rubber-cemented them to his head. And he couldn't have seemed prouder.

You could set your clocks by when campers began experimenting with their own hair. One of the great things about camp was it freed the boys from stifling societal pressure for a couple of months. The flip side of that was that sometimes society was right: Just because girls weren't around and freedom was in the air didn't mean a fifteen-year-old should take a razor to his head.

That night I had cabin duty. I was playing Snatch with some of the boys when British Sean came in. "Time out, everybody look up from your tiles for a second," I said, turning to Sean. "What's up?"

"A few of us are thinking of going to the movies tomorrow night, you in?" he asked. "*Terminator 3* is in town."

Anyone attempting to smuggle a thoughtful, independent movie into this town was frisked and turned away at the border. "Awesome," I said. "I'll see you in the Office as soon as I've walloped these guys." He left. "All right, eyes down . . . now."

Marquee wandered over. "You're going to see *Terminator 3*? That's dumb. Why don't you guys go see *Charlie's Angels 2*?"

"Because it looks idiotic, and I heard *Terminator* was good and . . . GARTER!" I snatched Trumps' GREAT by adding an R.

Marquee snorted and looked around with an exaggerated expression that was somewhere between "Can you believe this guy?" and "Can I get a witness?" I was once again struck by how much self-confidence fit into a guy whose feet barely touched the floor when he sat on a cot. "Oh, right. So I guess you *don't* want to see Drew Barrymore, Cameron Diaz, and Lucy Liu in hot tight pants."

"STURE!" yelled Lefty, reaching for my REST with a U.

"Not a word, Webster's," I said, slapping his hand away.

"It is too!" he yelled.

"Use it in a sentence."

He thought a minute. "Josh is a big hairy dope, I'm *sture* of it." He blew kisses to the imaginary crowd cheering his crackling bon mot.

I snorted and grabbed the tiles back. "Anyway, Marquee, I don't want to sit through ninety minutes of crappy movie for two minutes of tight pants."

"I'll take the two minutes, right, guys?" Everyone agreed that idiocy was a small price to pay for tight pants on cute girls. Ergo, I was a homo.

"Fine. Tomorrow night when I'm out at the movies, you guys can all go to sleep with your tiny two-minute erections. DUVET!" Bam, Lefty's DUET was mine.

"Bullshit! If that's a word, 'sture' is a word! What the hell is a duhvett?"

"*Duvet,*" I said, very slowly dragging his tiles one by one in front of me. "It's a comforter for a bed. I'll use it in a sentence: Lefty will need eight *duvets* tonight to keep warm after the cold chill of loserdom seeps into his bones."

"I'd rather be a loser who likes hot chicks than a hairy ape who likes to see robots fight! Now flip a tile so I can come back."

It amused me that somehow I had become the butt of their jokes about questionable sexuality. I had a fiancée: I was two months away from owning a legal document that proved I was attracted to women. That made me the straightest guy in the cabin . . . who didn't have a mattress in the back of his van, that is.

One Snatch rout later I rousted everyone up to the bathroom to wash up as I picked out a David Sedaris story to read them. They had been going over well recently; the last time I had finished one, there was a moment of silence in the dark and then Action said, "Are these stories written by a girl?"

"Nope," I said.

"Are some of them written by a girl?"

"Which ones?"

"The ones where he talks about his boyfriend."

"Nope. All are written by a man."

He thought for a moment. "So he's gay?"

"Yep. Does that make the stories any less funny?"

"No," he said quietly. "I was just wondering."

The enlightening moment lasted 0.6 seconds, until Marquee yelled, "Action's a fag!" Well, baby steps.

Tonight, as I lay on the bed waiting for them, I felt relaxed. It had been a good day; clear, sunny, 80 degrees, a little swimming during the day, some refreshing trash-talking at night, and now, a cool breeze coming through the screens wafted the smell of the pines around us. The familiarity of it all was calming. Kids making dirty jokes, guys giving bad haircuts. It was a good world indeed.

As they came tumbling back into the cabin, Lefty and Marquee were in the middle of a conversation about their high school social lives. ". . . and we have dances about every couple of months that are *awesome*," Marquee was saying. "My friends and I get totally hyper on Coke and just go crazy on the dance floor."

"We don't have that many dances in my school," Lefty replied, throwing his toiletry kit onto his top shelf from the end of his bed like a foul shot. "Mostly I just hang with friends and watch movies."

What a safe, well-behaved life. That's about what I was doing at that age; in ninth grade, stories wafted by me at school about guys drinking Schnapps when their parents went out, or the keg parties held at an upperclassman's house, but it felt like it was going on in a separate world from me. Another preconception of the kids today was dashed: that they were growing up faster and faster. "So you guys don't go out to big parties?" I interjected. "I'd imagine there's a lot of guys in your school who just want to drink and do drugs."

They stared at me blankly. Perhaps they were suspicious: that question coming out of an authority figure's mouth sounded like the lead-in for an invitation to a Bible study group.

"No," said Marquee. "I guess there's guys out there doing stuff like that, but it's pretty dumb."

The Fog wandered over. "Yeah," he said, the whispery voice of responsibility. "I see some kids drinking, but it's really stupid because that can only lead to taking drugs, which is the dumbest."

Wow. It was as if Nancy Reagan was hiding underneath their bunks, passing them script notes. They were still mama's boys at fourteen, just like I had been. But back then I'd snicker at the antidrug public-service announcements with my friends just to seem rebellious; these guys probably murmured, *No, we have no questions about our brain on drugs being like fried eggs, and we'll take our brains hard-boiled from now on, thank you very much.* To generalize from them to all fourteen-year-olds would be wrong, I knew that. These were sheltered, upper-middle-class kids who liked to go to camp, for God's sake. There were probably kids this age spending their summers smoking pot or crack or worse, but I preferred to dwell in the reassuring little sector of the big bad world in which kids thought only dopes did dope.

I read them a story—what the hell, two, just for making me feel so good—and then wandered down to the Dining Hall, where I fixed myself a late-night bowl of Cheerios and watched two CITs shine flashlights right into each other's eyes to see who would look away first. My instinct was to put money on the burly CIT with the three-D-battery Maglite, but go figure, the nerdy one with the AA halogen light emerged victorious with his hardier pupils.

I wandered up to the Office to call Christine. Chas and Reg sat at their usual spots at the conference table with their laptops. Sean wrote out a letter longhand. I was going to the Staff Lounge less and less frequently, having found that I got along better with the younger staff once I stopped trying so hard to fit in with them. Chas had been a counselor here for so many years that he had seen every possible permutation of Staff Lounge shenanigan, so he stayed away out of boredom. Sean and Reg were regulars at the Office, too, and I enjoyed it as a hangout for the socially inert.

"You win your game?" asked Sean.

"Did I *win*? The day those little punks outspell me is the day the alphabet weeps."

"Testify!" yelled Chas, absentmindedly scratching his balls with the hand that wasn't clicking on his e-mail.

Reg's fellow Antelope counselor—he of the uncomfortable karate demonstration—came in and glanced at a photo array Reg was organizing on his computer. He documented everything. "Come on, bro, erase that one," said Karate.

I leaned over Reg's shoulders to see a picture of Karate sheepishly holding a small black object at arm's length. He was giving the camera a look that said, "Why must there be a photographic record of this?" Reg stiff-armed Karate to keep him from hitting the delete key, and then ignored his pleas not to tell us the story.

The night before, the two of them had entered their cabin to find the kids huddled over something. One of them had pulled a small transistor out of a disposable camera and was trying to explain how they could turn it into a Taser. Karate, an electrical engineer, declared this a dangerous object that kids should not be playing with. He snatched it away and, in doing so, gave himself a massive electric shock. To hear Reg tell it, Karate's entire body seized up as if someone had jabbed a Popsicle into his anus. He threw it on the bed and stared at it, gasping.

"I told you that was dangerous," he said as all the kids stared at him. He bent back down to look at it. "You've gotta be careful how you handle it." He picked it up again, gingerly, and turned it over in his hand.

ZAP! Another Rumpsicle. "DAMN IT!" he yelled. It happened two more times before he declared that this was unsafe for anyone to touch; he tossed it in his laundry bag, announcing that he would throw it away in the morning before it hurt anybody else. This morning, Reg had watched him wake up, stretch, reach into his laundry bag to get his electronic nemesis, and then, of course, ZAP! One last prebreakfast convulsion.

When he finished, I wondered if there would ever come a time in my life when I would not be laughing at that story. Chas, Sean, and my whooping sounded more like hysterical screaming than laughing, and Karate just sat there, blushing. When we all finally eased into quiet tittering, all it took was for someone to yell "ZAP!" to once more throw us all into conniptions.

After about an hour, the word "zap" finally lost some of its effect, and, seeing that it was ten thirty, I decided to call Christine, who was now in L.A.

"Hey, Sweets," she said. Behind me Chas must have found a way to reinvent the zap wheel because everyone was roaring again. "Sounds like good times at Camp Eastwind tonight."

"Reg just told us a hilarious story about somebody hurting himself."

"Yep, that would make your night, all right," she said.

I was in a cheery mood, and I told her all about the funny little things the campers had done today and the gorgeous weather and the Snatch game and how I'd even been getting along better with Mudge now that we understood each other in a weird, mutually mocking way. Then I blabbered on about the talk I had with my cabin tonight and how impressed I was by their innocence. "I haven't felt this relaxed in a while," I said. "Just hanging with smart kids, everybody having a good time, no stress."

She told me about her job and L.A. life. I listened and laughed, enraptured with her ability to infuse everyday anecdotes with witty observations. Her descriptions of, say, her hotel's overly accommodating concierge who, after being politely corrected for mispronouncing Christine's last name, just blinked and mispronounced it the same exact way for three days running, or the desperate attempts by her fellow cyclists in spin class to seem indifferent to a celebrity spinning among them, both said more about Los Angeles than the entire staff of Fodor's ever could.

I had been in a great mood before calling her, and now hearing her voice made me feel even better. "This may sound crazy," I said. "But what if we came back here together next summer? There are a couple people here with their spouses."

"You're kidding."

"No. Come on, you went to camp, you loved it. It's not such a bad place for adults." I hunched over farther to hear her over Chas' yelling. "We'd have each other for adult conversation, but I think you'd enjoy getting to know these kids. Plus, it's a sweet location to hang for the summer. We always talked about getting a summer house, and until we can afford it, it's the next best thing."

"You're not kidding?" She laughed a laugh of finality. "No, we're not going back next summer."

"But I thought you loved your camp?"

"I did, back then. We're going to be starting a family, starting a whole new life. And if you go freelance, what about our health insurance? Wait, why am I even getting that specific? This is silly. Did someone spike your Kool-Aid?"

"Fine. Crush my dreams." She was coming to visit in three weeks, after her L.A. job was over, and when she got here she wouldn't be so adamant. The lake was like crack: The first dip was for free, and then she'd be hooked for life. "So what's up with the wedding?"

She'd been very busy working with her mother on the planning, and she sounded remarkably upbeat as she filled me in on the startlingly elaborate details for the festivities. For someone who had wanted a small wedding, this was turning into a ride at Epcot Center. The menu was a fusion of Thai, Chinese, and Vietnamese dishes served family style, and would be eaten with chopsticks. Large, round paper lanterns would hang throughout the tent, and at the end of the meal, everyone would receive a Chinese restaurant–style takeout box, inside of which would be a fortune cookie with a personally written fortune and a small, pocket-sized Buddha trinket. "What do you think?" she asked.

"Wow," I said. I loved when her stories were filled with details, yes, but did a party need so many? There would be a lot going on at our wedding, and very little of it felt like it had anything to do with me. I chose my words carefully. "One thing: You know we're not Asian, right?"

I hadn't chosen carefully enough. There was a moment of aggravated silence. I knew this pause: It was always accompanied by narrowing of her eyes and clenching of her jaw. "Do you really think I'd do something that was in bad taste? Do you think my judgment is that poor?"

"No, no, I'm sure it's good!" And like a moron, I continued to explain myself. "It just all seems a little . . . I keep coming back to the word 'Asian.'"

"What do you have against Asian?"

"Nothing, that's just it. I respect Asians. Love 'em to bits. Love 'em to Asian bits. So much that I feel weird about this, it seems like we're co-opting their culture to play dress-up. I listen to this Asian theme, and I think we're one step away from banging a gong, wearing kimonos, and saying, 'Ancient Chinese secret, eh?'"

"It's not an Asian *theme*, it's a wedding with Asian *accents*!" she shouted. "There's a big difference."

"What about the Buddhas? That's someone's religion, and we're giving them out like yo-yos at a bar mitzvah. If I was at a wedding in China and found a Jewish star in my goody bag, I'd be pretty weirded out." Silence. "Christine?" More silence. That was the trouble with talking to someone on a cell phone in L.A.: you couldn't tell if she was quietly simmering or had just lost her signal. The quiet continued long enough to convince me it was a technical glitch: if it had been the silent treatment, I would have heard angry breathing.

As I waited for her to call back, three CITs, bored with their Dining Hall flashlight fun, rolled into the Office in a big trundling mass of titty-twisters and punched arms. One gangly, hyperactive CIT was the pestiest of them all; he filled the very specific role of likable but annoying little-brother substitute for the staff. He could always be seen coming up behind a counselor and hovering over his shoulders, pitching insults in a nasal bark until the staffer grabbed him and threw him in the nearby lake, stream, or mud puddle. Most of his conversations ended not with a period, but with a splash. Tonight, he and his friends broke apart through the Office doorway, taking a divide-and-conquer approach to annoying us. Two grabbed at Chas's and Reg's laptops, while Pesty asked Sean if he was done with the communal computer. *No? How about now. No? How about now.*

Of course, that's when the phone rang. Just as I reached for it, Pesty leaped over me to grab the receiver first. "Camp Eastwind!" he crooned, twisting himself up in the phone cord as I grabbed for it. "Who's calling? . . . What? Who would marry *him*?" I grabbed a stapler, flipped it open, and brought it to his forehead. "All right, all right, he's right here! Here's your *lover*!" He handed over the receiver and then went through a spastic attempt to disentangle himself from the cord, eventually stumbling and falling to the floor, cracking his friends up. He was so used to every interaction ending with him being thrown down that if no one followed through, he did it to himself.

"Sorry about that," I said, scooching my chair into the corner and jamming a finger into my free ear.

"I really love that you're worried about the proper etiquette behind using Buddhas and *that* was your secretary."

And then we went back into arguing about the Buddhas and the theme—sorry, *accents*—with her telling me again that I needed to trust her taste, especially after all my talk convincing her she should make this wedding her own and not just a generic celebration. "I can't *believe* you're micromanaging this now. You're just scared that anyone will think it's weird or 'different.' But no one will, they'll love it."

"All right, I get it, it's all good. It's just the Buddhas—"

"It's not just the Buddhas!" she shouted. "It's anything new! You're talking about us going back to camp for good. This was a great experiment for you this summer, but that's not our life anymore. Why are you so scared of change?"

Scared of change? Here it was again. I was getting married, wasn't *that* a leap? She was the one who was so scared about throwing a wedding, and just because I questioned using a sacred icon as the equivalent of a JOSH AND CHRIS 4-EVA souvenir napkin, I was the scaredy-cat? This was insanity. . . .

And then: *Frrrrrappppp*. Behind me erupted the most extraordinary fart I'd ever heard. It was percussive, explosive, with a startling amount of moisture. It was the ideal to which all whoopee-cushion designers aspire. I whipped around reflexively to see Chas leaning back on his chair, legs spread apart up on the table, a look of surprised pride at the work of his own ass. It hung in the air for a moment, with everyone staring at him in a mixture of shock and idolization. That delicate half-second seemed to linger forever. And then everyone else erupted in unison.

Bwahhhahahahahahahahaha!

Were I not engaged in a battle for my pride I would have been laughing too, but instead I bit my lip and tried to continue the conversation and ignore the noise. Where were we? Oh yes, that I was afraid of change. I, who sat wearing a T-shirt, sandals, and gym shorts that still had crusted spaghetti sauce on them from dinner. I, who that morning had giggled when a thirteen-year-old made a joke about periods. And I, who was now sitting in the same Office where broken wind had reigned as the evergreen equivalent of "Who's on First" since long before I last sat here fifteen years ago.

"All right," I said. "Keep the Buddhas."

CHAPTER TWENTY-FIVE

AT THE END OF JULY, THE HIKING STAFF MET SECRETLY TO DECIDE WHICH handful of new initiates would be welcomed into the exclusive Eastwind Mountaineers. Members of this revered club were anointed with a sacred green bandana that, as tradition had it, must never be washed; in the days leading up to bids, an anxiety crept into the eyes of any hiking camper who pined for a filthy rag to call his own. For those interested in mountain climbing, it was the ultimate honor. No matter how many years ago they were initiated, most adult Mountaineers still knew exactly where their green bandana was stored and would probably divorce their wife if she washed it. Other activity clubs came and went, picking a different-colored bandana and trying to give it the same mystique. But none had the staying power of the Mountaineers. In 1984 I was initiated into the Eastwind Canoeing Club and given a blue bandana, and eagerly brought it this summer only to find out the club didn't exist anymore. I also had a purple bandana from the first year of the Eastwind Photography Club, which barely lasted a few summers; if the photo counselor was trying to infuse his activity with a weighty, Mountaineers-like manliness, perhaps he should have picked a different color.

Wind-Up wanted a green bandana more than he wanted a second

mouth to keep talking while he was chewing dinner. I actually pitied Mitch, who, as a member, had a say in who got in and who slept next to Wind-Up. He was besieged every time he walked into the cabin.

"Soooo, Mountaineer choices come soon, Mitch old buddy old pal . . ."

"Leave me alone, Wind-Up, I don't want to talk about it."

"Righty right, righty right, you don't have to tell me twice. You want to keep your secret, but you can just give me a hint. Just one tiny hint. Just a wink, maybe, just a peep . . ."

"Seriously, Wind-Up, if you don't shut up about this I'm going to take my green bandana and stuff it into your mouth."

"So *your* green bandana, not *my* green bandana. I'm intrigued by your choice of words."

The suspense was starting to bother me, too. From what I'd heard from various trip leaders, Wind-Up could be a slow and maddening presence on a mountain; out in nature, it was hard to get lost in your thoughts when he was telling you every last one of his. But what he lacked in tranquility he made up for in guileless enthusiasm. On a mountain, it was better to have someone who couldn't stop rambling about all the joys in his life— be they his dad, the Phillies, or that leaf he just picked up—than to have a malcontent who opened his mouth only to whine about his hiking boots, the food, or Wind-Up not shutting up about that damn leaf.

The "bids" were expected to go out early Saturday morning. By Thursday, Wind-Up was a wreck. I'd wake up in the morning to see him pacing the cabin, muttering, "I bagged most of the four-thousand-footers, but I did miss Mount Katahdin and Crocker. Could be a factor, but you never know . . ."

"Shut *up*, Wind-Up!" groaned a roused Mensa, but Wind-Up just kept pacing.

Wind-Up, who was usually out of camp for more than half the week on trips, constantly trailed behind on his swimming-lesson quota. The morning before bid day, I corralled him at breakfast. He was sitting next to Lars, the burly lead hiking counselor who was Wind-Up's idol, and also the most influential voice behind the Mountaineer nominations. "You didn't think you could escape, did you?" I said, crouching next to Wind-Up's chair. "I'm gonna pick level four for swimming this afternoon, and you're gonna raise your hand."

He swung his head toward me—too close, as was his wont—and laughed, spraying a mist of chewed eggs into my face. "Come on, Josh, give a guy a break here! Let's pretend you never saw me, like I'm out on a mountain."

"Wind-Up, you ducking your swimming lessons?" boomed Lars.

"Swimming stinks! No offense, Josh." He leaned toward his hero conspiratorially, as if the two mountain men would put the puny water boy in his place. "What do you need swimming lessons for when you're on the summit of Mount Adams, am I right? I didn't see any lakes on the whole Presidential range—"

I interrupted him. "I'll see you second period. Lars, raise his arm for him, will you?"

For second period, Eastwind's rowdiest level-4s descended on the dock, all shouting the tasks they needed to pass. My nerves were frayed by attendance, and as Anne and Helen attempted to break them into groups and I checked off names while sitting on the bench, I was aware of Wind-Up's face orbiting centimeters from my own. "OK, OK, I'm here, mark me down, mark me down." When I did, he cartoonishly backed away toward the path. "You go back to your class, now, don't you worry about me, I'm right behind you . . ." He snarfed at his own sneaking-out shtick.

I needed silence, and I was only going to get it one kid at a time. "Wind-Up, you'd better start paying attention, because Lars asked me to tell him how this lesson went. He said that they're making their final decisions on the Mountaineers, and they're factoring in swimming ability."

He guffawed. "Ha ha, very funny. I think you're trying to trick me, Josh, but I was not born yesterday!"

I faked my most serious gaze. "I'm not kidding. He says he needs to know people can be counted on not to drown when he stops at a swimming hole on the way home from a trip. He's going to factor in what I tell him very carefully. So are you ready to swim?"

He suddenly looked ashen, and he stepped back, slowly shucking his

T-shirt and shoes and murmuring to himself, "So swimming lessons *are* important, okay, it is what it is, we'll just have to do our best and hope Josh and Lars are all right with this, I'll just swim like I've never swum."

Seeing him so dampened, I felt like a bully, using his most cherished dream as leverage. And it was a lie, to boot. All through his lesson he looked a little frightened in his intense need to have the best swim lesson ever. It didn't make him a better swimmer, but it made him quieter. When he got out of the water, I said, "Good job, Wind-Up," and meant to tell him when the bugle blew that I was just kidding about Lars. But two of his classmates started grabbing at my clipboard, and by the time I fought them off, he was gone.

In fourth period, Le Goob came down for level 5. The name was short for "lugubrious," because of his sad eyes and woebegone posture. He was taller than his peers and walked hunched over, his shaggy blond hair hanging over his eyes. He was Teenage Josh version 2.1.

He came down to swimming often, and all of his strokes were smooth; his only problem was that he was afraid to dive. I had never had him as a student, but I had seen him during many periods standing on the edge of the crib with Helen, legs quivering as he stood with arms pointed out in front of him, chin tucked in, never fulfilling the promise of his ready position.

Today there were four other kids down with him who all had only the butterfly kick left to pass, so I quickly volunteered to work with Le Goob. He was at camp for only one month, so he'd be going home on Monday. "So we're down to the wire, huh, Goob?" I told him. "Good, I like the pressure. Today we dive! Tomorrow we flip!"

"I don't dive," he mumbled.

Josh Jr. would not go home a loser on my watch. I took him out to the raft, where we sat on the sunbaked wood. "So what's the problem?" I asked.

"I don't dive."

"Don't or won't?"

"Both, I guess. Can't."

"That's crap. You can. And you will."

We started with him trying to dive from a standing position; when that was unsuccessful, we moved backward down the ladder of dive difficulty, having him crouch, then kneel, then stand on the raft's ladder, water up to his knees, so he just had to flop forward. Nothing made him feel comfortable, and we couldn't go much lower without having him dive when already underwater.

By the end of the period, he was getting angry at himself, so we sat together on the edge of the raft. I asked him about his town, his school. He told me a familiar tale of feeling like he had no friends, feeling useless. Why had it taken me this long to really get to know him? He should have been my project from Day One; *him* I understood. We were still out on the raft when the bugle blew. "All right, Goob, I gotta do Free Swim tower duty. You'd better go back in."

He was about to slide into the water but stopped. "Can I sit out here with you while you lifeguard?"

"Sure." I climbed the tower, while he sat on the second rung of its ladder, happily serving as my lifeguard proxy: If I'd said "Jump," he'd have said, "How high?" (And then clarify, "You did say 'jump,' not 'dive,' right? OK then, how high?") With him leaving camp so soon, the next day would be his last opportunity for lessons. It wasn't much time, but it would be enough.

When I settled into my cot that night, I remembered that I had forgotten to tell Wind-Up that I was just kidding about conferring with Lars. The Mountaineer bids were supposed to come out the next morning, and we'd all know soon enough if he got in. Lars traditionally surprised new initiates by surrounding their beds early in the morning and waking them—and everyone else—with a rowdy fight song.

I woke up at six fifty and groggily flipped over to look toward Wind-Up's side of the cabin. I had never heard a song. He was up and dressed, sitting on the end of his cot with his Phillies cap on. All he lacked was a baseball mitt and a single tear and he'd look like a son waiting for a deadbeat dad who would never come to take him to the promised big game. Head on my pillow, I continued to watch him as he stayed there, immobile. Ten minutes passed, and I heard reveille blow. No one ever made a move to get up until the next bugle call, which was fifteen minutes away. He looked over, saw I was awake, and tiptoed toward my cot.

"What's up?" I asked.

"It's a big morning, yes sir," he whispered, but I could barely make out his words. Speaking softly was anathema to him, and when he tried to whisper it came out sounding like he was attempting another language. He then mumbled something unintelligible about Lars. To me it all sounded like the mournful wail of the betrayed chatterbox.

What a shitheel I was. "Oh, man, Wind-Up, I'm sorry. And look, I didn't say anything to Lars about your swimming, that was just a bad joke. I would never have done anything to hurt your chances."

He still didn't seem to be listening. "You had me scared, but when I saw Lars this morning, I was like, 'Phew!' " Huh? I was confused. "Guess they decided to do something different this year," he went on. "I was waiting for the big song but they just snuck up and that crazy man Lars put his hand over my mouth, and whispered, 'You're in, Mountaineer.' Pretty darn sneaky, that Lars. I'll get him for that, oh you bet I will." He opened his fist, and a green bandana that he'd squeezed into a tight ball expanded in his palm. Hot damn, he was actually in.

I shook his hand mightily, thrilled for him and marveling at his placid, quiet reaction to the whole thing. Was the Mountaineer membership so mighty that its impact could silence even Wind-Up? If Lars had known that, he might have initiated him the day he arrived.

The other Bears started waking up. "You get in?" mumbled Marquee.

"Yup, you're looking at the newest member of the Mountaineers." He stood up, now speaking at a normal volume. It was still difficult to understand him, but this time because he was trying to form words while his mouth hung open in a gaping grin. "Gonna tie this here green bandana right around my head, not too tight . . ."

The other guys yelled congratulations, which woke everyone else up, and soon everyone was shouting and hooting at Wind-Up. The cheering returned his mouth to its characteristic speed. "Yeah, the bandana will get a little dirty, but that's the Mountaineer way. It's like my old pal Lars always says on the trail . . ."

■

Le Goob came down second period, and Helen and Anne let me work with him alone while she took the others. "Your jumping days are over today," I told him.

"I can't dive," he stated. Any progress we'd made yesterday was forgotten. Now he was back to his *Green Eggs and Ham* stubbornness. He would not dive in with a fox, he would not dive in without socks.

We swam out to the raft, and I made up for the lack of support I gave Wind-Up yesterday with an inundation of positive reinforcement. Every time a dive turned into a jump at the last panicky minute, I treated it like it was an Olympian effort. When he got frustrated and moped his mantra "I can't dive," I stared into his eyes with as much soulful meaning as I could muster and said, "You listen to me: Le Goob *can* dive." I'd always mocked movies like *Good Will Hunting* and *Ordinary People* in which an unorthodox psychologist could undo years of internalized guilt by simply repeating a phrase like "It's not your fault." And here I was doing the same thing, only aquatically.

At the end of second period, Le Goob was still true to his word: He couldn't dive. And so we made an appointment for fourth period, his last chance. We had only an hour. Back on the raft, I delivered my best fourth-quarter, down-by-six pep talk. I stacked metaphors on top of life lessons and slathered it with hyperbolic praise and cliché: This was the first day of the rest of Le Goob's life, and when he did this he would go back to school knowing he could do *anything* and he'd prove that anyone who doubted him just didn't know Goob. Then I moved on to a first-person "I can relate" story, telling him about how I—an adult!—went through the same thing just a couple of weeks ago as I stood with my cabin on a bridge far above a river, terrified to jump. To make my point, I changed the ending to one in which I faced my fears and leaped, figuring he was only here for two more days, so what were the odds he'd fact check? It was the only relatable story I had, so a little inspirational exaggeration was appropriate.

Nothing worked. Soon, only five minutes remained in the period. No more talking, just diving. I had him kneel on one knee on the edge of the raft. "You are going to lean forward and just fall in the water. I know you're scared about falling on your stomach, but you will not get hurt, do you hear me? I will not *let* you get hurt. Do you trust me?"

"Y-yeah." With his arms outstretched by his ears, forming a barrier over his face, I could barely hear his nervous murmuring.

"Are we going to do it?"

"I think so."

"Can Le Goob dive?"

"I don't know."

"Le Goob can dive! Are you ready? One . . . two . . . three . . . GO!"

That was my "It's not your fault" moment. As Le Goob slid jerkily into the water, everything changed. His head popped up out of the water, grinning. *Did I do it?* Oh, yes, you did it. Having finally landed one punch through his barrier of fear, he tore it apart, diving again and again, quickly moving up from one knee to standing, and by Free Swim he was doing flips off the diving board. *Le Goob can dive, Le Goob can dive!*

That would have been a good movie.

But instead, we kneeled at the end of the dock for five minutes, with Le Goob caught in an endless loop of "I'm ready . . . no, I'm not ready, hold up, hold up. OK, now . . . no, not now," his entire body rigid as his phobia fought off his desire to leave level 5 behind. The toot of the Free Swim bugle drifted over the lake. "Le Goob, it's now or never."

"OK, OK, OK," he stammered, lifting his arms purposefully, letting them hover there. He leaned forward, but just as he was almost going head first, he lurched backward. *"Damn it!"* he yelled, stood up, and jumped into the water, lingering beneath the surface longer than usual, as if savoring the quiet uterine calm before resurfacing to face his own weakness. His eyes were glum when he finally popped up, but there was a stubbornness to his glare. It told me, "Now do you believe I can't do it?"

Helen was on the dock, holding back an anxious mass of Play-Swimmers waiting for me to get up into the tower. I mustered some enthusiasm afterburners and told Le Goob he had tried his hardest, which I was proud of him for, but we had to stop. I watched him forlornly trudge through the water back to the dock, as if he was so beaten down by this that he was now afraid to do the strokes he had already mastered.

I wrangled Helen and Anne after Free Swim: I wanted to pass him anyway. Screw the Red Cross, he'd passed all the other qualifications easily, and he'd pass them again even more quickly next summer and be stuck unhappily and pointlessly refinishing his lesson quotas because of one fear. They agreed, and after dinner I grabbed Le Goob when I saw him leaving the Dining Hall. I had expected to find him a destroyed mess, perhaps whipping himself on the back with a switch, but he was jostling amidst a mass of friends happily on their way to Ultimate Frisbee.

Perhaps this afternoon hadn't been traumatic for him; perhaps he took some solace out of having his own low self-image confirmed. Indeed, he looked more shaken when I walked him down to the dock and told him we were passing him without his having to dive. He looked down at his shoes and got very quiet. "You proved something out there," I said, grabbing hold of both his shoulders. "You were terrified, but you never stopped trying. You kept coming down period after period. You're a great swimmer, and you're a great kid. When you start school, remember that. And next summer, know that Le Goob *can* dive. And I'll bet Le Goob will dive."

His reddening eyes fluttered like moth wings as he stood and stared at me. I stuck out a hand; he gave a weak handshake back, mumbled a thanks, and then skulked away to join his friends.

So two campers passed milestones that day. One was rightly welcomed into his dream club on his own merits, after I stupidly made him doubt he would; as for the other, I purposefully twisted the rules to let him leave on an up note. Both would go home accomplished. But neither made me feel completely triumphant. Perhaps those moments of purity only do happen in the movies.

CHAPTER TWENTY-SIX

THE JUNIOR HIGH AT WHICH TREVOR TAUGHT STARTED ITS SCHOOL YEAR ridiculously early, so he packed up his climbing ropes and death-defying slide show and went home on Saturday night. I feared this meant it would be just me and Mitch left, but Frank assured me a replacement was coming. At the end of Sunday's Rest Hour, our new counselor arrived, throwing open the screen door so it banged against a cot with a crack that made the boys' Snatch tiles bounce.

There stood Charlie. He was sixty-seven years old, a lawyer who had just retired but refused all notions of relaxation. His nephews had attended Eastwind and he'd visited often, and decided that a summer working here would be a great way to indulge and share his recent love of rock climbing. He was thin and muscular for his age, with a twist of unkempt gray hair resembling a toupee that had been thrown into a dryer and then put on backward. With a duffel slung over his shoulder, a loop of climbing rope through his arm, a helmet draped on a finger, and metal carabiners clipped to every belt loop, he looked like he arrived straight from a photo shoot for a special "You can do anything!" issue of *AARP* magazine. Before the door slammed behind him, I could see a canoe paddle sticking out of his car's back window and a kayak on his roof. I assumed his parachute and bullfighting costume were still in the trunk.

He dumped all his actionware onto the floor and scanned the cabin, as if looking for a wall to climb. All the boys stared at him quizzically. To them, it must have looked like Frank had swapped out the current Trevor for a much older model he'd been keeping in the storage shed.

I stood up, hoping to jolt them out of their mass gaping. "Hey, welcome to the Bears," I said, extending an arm. "I'm Josh."

"Hi, Josh! Charlie! Say, this place is great, just great. Just look at that cove out there."

"Yeah, it's—"

"And the trees are fabulous. Say, I was thinking, maybe I could string a zip line from the trees right into the lake."

"Um, that really seems like something you should run by Frank . . ." I said, a bit bewildered.

He had already pushed past me and was reaching up to grab a rafter. "We could put a chin-up bar here, all the kids could do chin-ups. Really get an exercise plan together! You guys like chin-ups?"

They all looked at each other in confusion. "Again," I said, "that'd be a Frank thing . . ."

He looked at the back windows. "Those clotheslines are awfully low, I'd like to get them up higher, get the clothes away from any animals."

Yeah, and maybe we'd put the cabin on a giant rotating platform so we could all have a view of the lake. In fact, why not just put the cabin on wheels so we could drop everybody off at their activities each morning like a carpool? "Hmmm, well, these are interesting ideas, Charlie, but I *really* think you should bring these to Frank."

The bugle signaling the start of third period blew, and the cabin slowly filed out past Charlie, eyeing him warily. He blurted out good-byes to every one as they passed by, and when the door shut behind Afty, Charlie's head jerked around, everything in his field of vision alerting him to something that could be made better. I didn't like it. After spending a month here, I didn't want to change anything; part of that was routine, and part of it was exhaustion. I just wanted to catch my breath and not disturb any momentum I'd built up. I felt like Jimmy Buffett breaking in an overeager bass player with ideas about how to rejuvenate the act: "No, we will *not* experiment with a ska vibe. We will play 'Margaritaville' just like the record and I will bring out a fake parrot and the crowd will cheer and we will all cash our checks and go on to the next city. Save that ska shit for the jam band in your mind."

The next day I woke up before the reveille bugle. Charlie was out—probably trying to build an elliptical machine out of pine branches and acorns—and Mitch and the boys were still sleeping. I went up to the bathroom to wash up and returned to find Charlie back and sitting on Lefty's bed, reading him selections from a collection of nature essays on animals. Judging from Lefty's disoriented look, it had been the most startling wake-up call of his young life. Charlie hadn't realized that fourteen-year-olds needed at least a three-minute period of adjustment after being jolted awake before they could appreciate being lectured on the ocelot.

When he finished the essay, Charlie stood and slammed the book. "Fascinating animal, the ocelot! Now, off to breakfast. Let the summer begin!" and stormed out of the cabin.

After Charlie let the door slam behind him—jolting Mitch awake—Lefty turned to me, blinked twice, and said, "Seriously, who is that guy?"

Dewey and the Fog, both one-monthers, left for home that day. The cabin seemed to readjust from a slight tilt when Dewey's parents shuttled his weighty collection of sci-fi books out of his area into their car. The Fog, whose meek voice had grown to nearly conversational levels over the course of four weeks, was again deathly silent as he dragged his trunk to his dad's car. All the effusive farewell hugs and shoulder punches from his fellow Bears only made him more quiet. He was off to a family vacation to California, but not even a trip to the moon could make up for the fact that his best friends would keep having fun without him.

Two new campers would be arriving to take their place for the summer's second half. I hoped our additions had similarly mellow temperaments to Dewey and the Fog. A month ago, I had boundless energy to be understanding and to sensitively discipline and befriend troublesome kids. Four weeks later, not so much. And if the upcoming visit from Christine went anything like our last conversation had, my ability to remain upbeat would be on the wane.

The new Bears arrived that afternoon, and it quickly became apparent that the camp gods had not just laughed at my request for easygoing campers, but had hung it up on a nail by its underwear. First came Countdown, whom I so named because while he appeared well-behaved, I could tell that it was only a matter of time before he made trouble. He had a pug nose, jug ears that waved out from under a mop of fine, dark hair, and the mischievous eyes of a boy who was always wondering how he could get your bed up on the roof as soon as you left the cabin. He laughed with an infectious Woody Woodpeckerish snicker that made me reflexively flail a hand over my back to check for a KICK ME sign.

And then came Kid ADD. I had become well-acquainted with attention-deficit disorder in the past month. At the beginning of camp, the nurse had circulated a list of every camper's medical ailments, and the page had been littered with the repeating acronyms ADD and ADHD (attention-deficit/ hyperactivity disorder), as well as one I'd never heard of before, HAAD (hyperactivity attention deficit). I'd been told that was just like ADHD, except more hyperactive: *New and improved ADD: now with more arm-flailing!*

"Are kids really that much more hyper than they were fifteen years ago?" I had asked Mitch.

"Nah," he said, picking at his flip-flop. "They've just got a name for it now. Pills, too."

With easily one fifth of the campers sharing these diagnoses, I had initially chalked this proliferation up to today's nervous parents jumping for any pharmaceutical cure-all that would make their kid perfect. But over the course of last month, as I tried to deal rationally with some of these kids after they failed to take their medicine, I wondered whether we should just grind Ritalin directly into the macaroni and cheese to blanket everybody: better safe than sorry.

But nothing had prepared me for Kid ADD. He could make the most scattered boy from my first month here look like he was meditating. He was compact and pockmarked, with wild, curly red hair that reflected his inability to do anything in a straight line. His usual stream of conversation went like, "What time is lunch? Who took my red hat? I got winners in backgammon! That your fishing rod? Do you have a soccer ball? Why isn't anyone going to lunch?" After being tricked several times into attempting a response to his questions, only to find him uninterested in the topic by the time I got to my first verb, I figured it would be better to save my energy and not answer him at all. Unfortunately, silence was the only thing that focused him, so when he threw out an unanswered question, he'd dwell on it and repeat it. And, in a crushing catch-22, the only way to free him from his record skip was to start an answer, and then he'd be on to something else.

"When's lunch? Come on, tell me, I'm hungry! Did we miss the bugle? Should we head down now? Come on, Josh, tell me! I don't have the schedule memorized yet."

"Lunch is at twelve thir—"

"*WHERE'S MY RED HAT?*"

Over and over again I fell for this. It was the conversational equivalent of Lucy pulling the football away from Charlie Brown.

I assumed Kid ADD's constant chattering would eventually become ignorable white noise, like a humidifier. Except a humidifier doesn't run around the room, pulling things off your shelf and asking about them. By the time I sat up to wave him away, he was already somewhere else, and when I finally relaxed again, he was back. It was as if all the mosquitoes that had been swarming around my head all summer had bunched together into a five-foot, four-inch mass and put on a boy suit.

The noise level in the cabin grew steadily when he was around, since everybody had to shout to be heard over him. On his first night, Kid ADD pushed himself into the middle of a Snatch game and demanded to know the rules. Mudge, Lefty, and Action ignored him, and to do so they needed to talk louder to drown him out. Determined to have his question answered, he went them one decibel louder, only to have them trump him. This shrill one-upmanship escalated until Lefty finally screamed, "God damnit, you try to spell words and grab someone else's by rearranging them . . ." And just like that, of course, Kid ADD was gone, pestering Mensa and Countdown to show him their tennis rackets, leaving the Snatch players stuck hollering at each other in their uppermost registers.

The din became untenable. *"HEY!"* I yelled. *"Everyone quiet down now! It does not need to be this loud in here!"*

"Does this fan work?" Kid ADD had materialized into my area and was playing with my tiny fan. I grabbed it out of his hand, slammed it back on my shelf, and pointed for him to go away. As he zigzagged away, the door swung open and Charlie came through and sat on my bed.

"I checked with Frank and was surprised that he wasn't that interested in the zip line. Something about kids hitting rocks. Say! What if we moved all the rocks? We could build an enormous fort out of them, high enough for someone to sleep out on the water!"

Exhausted and irritated, I left Charlie to put the kids to bed. It was Sean's thirtieth birthday and he had demanded a big blowout at the Staff Lounge. Though I was always thrilled to welcome someone else into his thirties—it made me feel like I had lured a counselor over to the dark, cranky side—I wasn't that interested in partying. I was too distracted with thoughts of Christine's upcoming visit. She was coming home from L.A. tonight and would be here in two days. I'd made a reservation at a nearby hotel for three nights, making sure I didn't have cabin duty during that stint so I could stay with her.

Her flight arrived in New York at nine thirty P.M., so I headed to the Office to call her at ten fifteen. She sounded winded when she picked up.

"Hey, you're home!"

"Yes. I'm home." The dark tone of her voice was a hybrid of anger and misery and anger. No affection, really. But did I mention anger?

"Hooray?" I suggested.

"I just got in, I'm starving, they didn't give us *anything* to eat on the plane, and I've got a million things to do."

This was neither warm nor fuzzy. At best it was cold and rashy. It was time to abort before things got worse. "Why don't we talk tomorrow. I just wanted to say hi and that I'm looking forward to seeing you." That would have been the perfect way to end it, had I ended it that way. Instead,

I added, "One last thing: I was wondering if you knew when you were coming up on Thursday?"

"When? *When?*" It was as if I had just jabbed at her Achilles' heel with a shrimp fork. "Do you know how much I've got to get done before I come to see you?"

"Yes, of course, I was just trying to plan—"

"I'm trying to plan too. *Plan a wedding!* I've got to unpack here, then repack, get up tomorrow, go to Chinatown, pick up some sample paper lanterns, take Amtrak up to my parents', go look at the venue the next day, meet the caterer, borrow the car, and drive up to see you."

"Look, I'm sorry, but—"

"Why did you make me come up this weekend? This is crazy! I just got home!"

Now I was angry. "First of all, we haven't seen each other in six weeks. I thought it would be good to see each other again, seeing as we're *spending the rest of our lives together*. Second of all, I *suggested* this weekend, and you never said it would be a problem. If you had, I would have said, 'Fine, next weekend.' "

Sean burst in, clearly already a little drunk. He yelled, "Come on, you laggard! We've got beers to drink!" I just stared at him with a look of pain and bent over into my corner of apoplexy. He grimaced and backed out.

"You should have known it would be a problem!" she shrieked. "*I* wasn't thinking!"

I tried to untangle that logic but was left with a knot of rage. "Let me get this straight: For the rest of my life, I'm not only going to be blamed for my shortsightedness, but for yours, too?"

I felt confident I had the upper hand with that one, but quickly lost it when she swerved the argument into a comparison of what we both had to do in the next few days. Her: reroot self after being away for a month, and finalize an entire wedding. Me: stand on dock, and possibly eat s'mores. The more we argued, the more tired we both got, until she finally suggested we both hang up. "I'm sure it'll be great to see you. I'm looking forward to it, I am. I'm just *really* stressed now and can't believe I have to be up there in just two days." I wanted to tell her to make sure she included that sentiment in her wedding vows, but wisely opted to stay quiet and just said good night. We hung up, my head screaming. I had gone from look-ing forward to seeing her to never ever wanting to go home again.

Sean gingerly walked back in to find me pounding the conference table with both fists like a Viking drum.

"Hey, mate, I'm just about to turn thirty," he said. "Should I turn back?"

CHAPTER TWENTY-SEVEN

CHRISTINE WAS SUPPOSED TO ARRIVE IN THE AFTERNOON, SO I WENT TO THE office during clean-up period to make sure she hadn't e-mailed me a change of plans. It wasn't inconceivable to me that the last twenty-four hours of frantic wedding errands would have broken her, making her light all the paper lanterns on fire and head back to New York. But there was no such message.

As I was signing off, Mitch came in. We hadn't talked much in the past couple of weeks, which was surprisingly easy even though we slept just five cots away in the same giant room. We were cordial, but our inability to find things to talk about had naturally divided the cabin into two jurisdictions when we were both there, and we rarely crossed to the other's side. We'd occasionally exchange pleasantries, but it was nothing that lasted very long and was usually cut even shorter by a Wind-Up soliloquy on tree bark or orange peels and I think we were both relieved for the interruption. Our longer conversations were usually about something Mitch was really interested in and I wasn't. Like now. He sat down at the table and launched into a dissertation on a new motorboat he was just reading about made especially for wakeboarding. I had never wakeboarded; sharing a table with Reg made me familiar with the lingo, but I didn't know

216

what any of it meant. When he asked kids if they wanted to learn to go "toeside goofy," I didn't know if it was actual terminology or Aussie vernacular or some sort of new foot product for the clinically insane that he was sure would make him millions. I knew even less about motorboats, but Mitch proceeded to go into great detail about how these boats' sterns filled with water to make the back drag more, creating more wake. On and on he went about the wonder of this creation, with no perception or care toward the fact that he might as well have been listing his fifteen least favorite cold sores for all the knowledge or interest I had in the subject.

I nodded through his excited dissertation until he finally ran out of horsepower to discuss. We sat in silence for a minute. "What are you up to?" he asked.

"Actually, my fiancée's coming into town today."

"That's cool," he said, putting a bare foot up on the table. On the ball of his foot, a flap of skin from a popped blister blinked at me. "You should take her out to celebrate, maybe down to Portland. There's this bar there that's a blast." He picked at his big toe in thought. "Damn, I can't remember the name at all, but every time I get up there I go. Great jukebox, and they've got every kinda beer you could want, and there's bras hanging from all the rafters. It's like a big frat party."

"Hmm, sounds cool," I said, even though the only thing that could make this less appealing would be if with every third beer the bartenders gave you a free lecture about wakeboarding boats.

"I'm drawing a blank, sorry about that. But if it comes to me today, I'll tell you, you should bring her there, she'd love it." He smiled beneficently as he got up to leave. Yes, me and my foreign-film-loving, Asian-wedding-accented, male-dominance-wary fiancée would stage our passionate reunion in the shadow of a female bartender in a leather halter pouring Jack Daniel's down the throat of a Delta Chi brother celebrating his twenty-first birthday. And Christine would swoon as Billy Idol's "Mony Mony" blared on the jukebox while the sisters of Alpha Xi Delta chanted "Get laid, get fucked!" Maybe Mitch should be our wedding planner, I snorted to myself.

As if I had any better idea how to connect with her these days.

■

That afternoon I had two new ten-year-old Raccoons down for basic level-3 instruction in fourth period. They could have been a comedy team: Little Ig and the Giggler. Physically and behaviorally, Little Ig reminded me of a tiny Reverend Jim Ignatowski from the TV show *Taxi*. Both he and his namesake had unkempt, thick, brown hair and were prone to staring off into space, slack-jawed, but while the TV character's odd, parallel-universe behavior was due to a life of drug use, it just came naturally to Little Ig. He and the Giggler became fast friends in their bunk, and they went to most activities together. The Giggler was in a constant state of merriment about jokes only he could hear. His default demeanor was googly-eyed chuckling, but as soon as something remotely entertaining occurred around him (and by his standards, this could include someone walking by and saying "Good morning"), he staggered around in hysterics, spitting out phrases like "What is going *on* here?" in between guffaws. His laughter actually sounded like "*yuk yuk yuk!*", which I had always assumed was a convention that existed only in comic strips.

Their personalities made them a good pair. When Little Ig stared at a tree and then slowly poked at a leaf, this was A material to the Giggler. He clutched the sides of his own head as he weaved behind Little Ig, drunk with mirth—"*Yuk yuk!* Now he's with, *yuk yuk*, the tree!"—and Ig spacily smiled back, happily assuming the Giggler was getting the same thing out of the tree that he was. Neither of them really understood what the other was talking about, and they were blissfully indifferent to it. It took a lot of mutual confusion to create that kind of chemistry.

The day's rudimentary instruction was rhythmic breathing, the basic respiration for the crawl: Exhale with your face in the water, then turn to the side so your mouth comes out of the water to inhale. With these two it was a daunting challenge. I directed them to chest-high water and had them hold on to the dock with both hands and dunk their heads down between them. The age-old mnemonic for this exercise was to tell students to imagine that first they talk to the fishies (face down in the water, blowing bubbles), and then they listen to the fishies (head turned sideways, ear in the water). Little Ig got sidetracked asking what he should say to the fishies, while Giggler was just tickled about getting to submerge. To him, the lake was one giant pie to smack his face into. Getting them to focus on the task was like trying to get a guy with his head on fire to sit still for a haircut. I could only get out a fraction of instruction when they'd both interrupt, saying, "Like this?" and drive their heads into the water and start spluttering. When they came up to gasp for air—which proved in itself that no, the calm breathing exercise was not done *like this*—all I could get out was, "Close. Just don't forget we *talk* to the fish—" before they'd both yell "Like this? Like this?" and plunge in for more variations on a wrong theme. Within minutes we had our give-and-take whittled down to its purest form: "Like this?" *Splash, splutter.* "No, try—" "Like this?" *Splash, splutter.* "No, try—" "Like this . . . ?"

I wondered how Christine would react if she showed up during this cycle of futility, watching her fiancé leaning over two ten-year-olds begging them to listen to fishies. Encountering such a perfect illustration of how much more adult her worries were than mine would present her with a dilemma: how to choose between an eye-roll or a pitying chuckle? Just thinking about it made my toes curl inward, embedding themselves in my sandals. I bet that wasn't how Mitch got his blisters.

This whole day was starting to feel futile, which gave me a bad feeling. The Giggler and Little Ig's attempts to breathe bore so little resemblance to swimming that I was surprised they weren't holding tennis rackets. With only a few minutes to go, I stood up, intent on ending with a victory. The easiest and quickest thing to pass was Jumping into Deep Water. I brought them over to the sailing dock, gave them both life vests, and had them both leap off. This they were able to master, but to be fair, gravity did most of the work.

When walking back to the swim dock, I said, "Congrats, guys, you passed that."

"Hooray!" squealed the Giggler. Apparently "hooray" and "yuk yuk" came together in the goofy-vernacular twin pack.

"So we're out of level three?" said Ig. "We can go out to the Raft?" Threes weren't allowed out there without a life jacket.

I said that no, they had just passed one part of level 3. There were many more to go but if they kept coming down to lessons they could learn everything.

"I *hate* level three. That's why I don't like coming down for lessons," said Ig.

I was going to explain the concept of a catch-22 to him, but figured I'd be more successful explaining it to his life jacket. Instead, I sat them down and told them that things would go much faster in lessons if they listened to their teacher more. "Do you understand?"

"Yes," said the Giggler.

"Uh-huh," said Ig.

"Really?" I asked. "What did I just say?"

Pause. "I don't know," said the Giggler. Little Ig wandered off to look at sand.

And then I heard my name. I squinted up along the shoreline, where I saw flecks of color passing through the trees that stood as the barrier between the lake and the shore path. Christine flashed through a brief clearing, wearing a skirt with a summery design of lobsters. Hey, I *love* lobsters! was my disconnected first thought. And then there she was, stepping carefully over roots, waving and grinning wildly. Not the kind of forced smile you gave to someone just so you could get close enough to smack him in the head with a wedding-planner binder. Not the kind of grimace you gave to the man you tied your life to and have now caught losing an argument to a pair of ten-year-olds. Just a grin. A happy, happy grin. And I returned it.

I'd always heard the romantic cliché "my heart swelled" but assumed it was just metaphorical. It was like "seeing stars"; as a tall person, I'd cracked my head on the tops of countless door frames and low air ducts while walking at full speed, and all I saw was my own blinding fury at short architects. But "swelling hearts" I could suddenly vouch for. When Christine rounded the last turn off the path and was there on the dock standing before me, I felt my chest expand; my blood started to rush faster, as if someone had just released a kink in my arteries. My breath grew short, and I made a note to apologize to the Giggler and Little Ig, because it turned out breathing wasn't always that easy. I was experiencing the most romantic panic attack ever.

I immediately reprioritized: I *liked* lobsters, but I *loved* this woman.

And there, on the shores of the lake where I'd experienced countless uplifting moments in my life, I was raised even higher. As long as my heart was swelling, I thought it OK to run through the romantic cliché manual: We ran to each other, we embraced, we kissed. Over and over again. The bugle for Free Swim blasted, but it might as well have been angels trumpeting our great love, and the kids who swarmed the dock were our cherubim and seraphim. One small difference: Instead of lifting us to a cloud of inamorata, they whined about who was going to check them in to swim.

"So this is camp," she said.

"If you think this is romantic, wait till I show you the wood shop." The cushion of her thick hair, the gentle nudge of her high cheekbones, the scent of her skin that I had always thought was her entrancing unique musk but eventually learned was just Dove Powder Fresh deodorant. This was her. This was the her that had faded away as we stubbornly argued for six weeks about catering and vows and bands and where we'd live and then retire to. We were fighting to defend worldviews we'd honed before we'd met, back when getting married was just a hypothetical.

Now, finally, we were back in the present together, a land where all past arguments were decreed idiotic. We were going to have the best life ever.

I felt a tap on my arm. I released Christine and looked down to see Little Ig holding a pair of flippers that were at least four sizes too big.

"Since I passed out of level three, I can swim out to the raft, right?"

I had rented a room at an old, sagging resort that sat across the lake from camp, but tucked farther into a bay and out of sight so I didn't have to worry about Kid ADD floating by on a sailboat and demanding to know what time dinner was.

We spent our time in a rotation of ebullience, giddiness, and ecstasy, interrupted only by sleep and bathroom breaks. Even when we discussed the wedding, a topic I'd assumed would euthanize our good vibes, both of us were excited. Just before she'd left Rhode Island the wedding invites had arrived from the printer, and feeling our names and the wedding date embossed onto card stock had made it more real to her. It was no longer something to fight, it was something to embrace. She was happy about the food, the decorations, even her dress. The Christine on the phone would want to throw this Christine in front of a train.

When I returned to camp Saturday morning, Christine drove to visit her old camp an hour away and returned for the ultimate date night: a burger at the beach cookout and a ticket to the second Staff Talent Night. I again took to the stage for "Nicknames," refreshing the older campers' memories of theirs and assigning one to all the second-session boys, and Jim, Zach, and Dwight reprised their messy fake-hands restaurant sketch. The show had everything; in the middle, all the lights went out for a moment and some camper yelled out "Penis!" to much applause, and for a closer, the nature counselor led the crowd in a goofy song about a talking potato that had the whole room shouting along. When it was over, and Christine and I headed back to the resort for our last night together, I babbled ecstatically about what a pure evening that had been. There was an innocence to the fact that no matter what else was going on in the world, in that room there were kids roaring at guys wearing funny hats and teenagers who weren't inhibited about singing a foolish song. She laughed at me.

"It was fun," she said. "But I don't know if I'd ascribe such great meaning to it. It was camp. That's what camp is. What did you expect?"

"Why are you being so cynical about my joy in not being cynical?" I said. "It doesn't happen very often."

"Are you kidding me? It's been happening all summer. For the last six weeks I've listened to you drift off into a reverie every time a kid does anything short of spraying everyone in your cabin with an Uzi."

This was the kind of conversation that I remembered from our phone calls. Although it didn't have the same vengeful bite now that we weren't disembodied voices.

"You need a little more time here." I patted her hand. "You'd be surprised what a summer will do for that city-girl skepticism. One good shot of bug juice will clear it out like a dose of ipecac."

She grabbed my hand back and leaned over and kissed me on the cheek. It was far warmer and more tender than the hard plastic of a phone receiver. "I love the idea of not being cynical. But I think after this we're both done with camp. I love it, too, I just visited mine today, for God's sake, and I love what camp did for me and you. But we gotta get married and move on. Camp'll be here where we left it when we're ready to drop our kids off."

I sat for a moment, trapped between two instincts: to sulk or to keep driving all the way back to New York. "What if our kids don't want to go to camp?" I asked.

"With our DNA? They'll be born ninety percent pottery clay, ten percent swimming flipper."

The next morning I was due back at camp and Christine had to go home to New York. I'd see her in just over three weeks. "Keep your eye on the mail, you'll be getting your invite soon," she said as we kissed good-bye. "Don't forget to RSVP. And no, you can't bring a date."

The Sunday afternoon all-camp activity was Staff Hunt, a campwide hide-and-go-seek match where all the counselors were the prey. Some of the more ambitious counselors dressed in camo gear and climbed up into trees. I was feeling lost and unmotivated, so I crawled under the Antelope cabin, my face pressed against an old trunk that reeked of mildew and dirty camper. But not even that smell could erase the sense memory of Christine's powder-fresh scent, so Dove and yet so unique.

CHAPTER TWENTY-EIGHT

SINCE THE BEARS HAD TWO NEW MEMBERS, A SECOND UNIFYING CABIN TRIP seemed in order. Once again Mitch declared that he'd plan the whole thing; when he had done that last month I had felt useless, but this time I just sat back and reveled in the rare, Halley's Comet–like event of Mitch Taking Initiative. Our destination was Old Orchard Beach, a touristy spot just north of Kennebunkport, which Mitch promised would have, in his words, "plenty of girls for you weenies to strike out with."

Charlie had another trip scheduled that day, so Mitch and I packed the ten Bears into one stretch van, an arrangement that was only slightly less deafening than the inside of a paddy wagon after a race riot. Everyone sat shoulder to shoulder, exchanging his strategies for nailing a beach babe, while Countdown desperately tried to rally support for a mass mooning of a toll collector. Wind-Up had been strategically herded into the seat over the wheel well, which led to a nonstop travelogue of the various pains in his ass every time we hit a pothole. And in the backseat, like a period at the end of the van's incredibly loud sentence, sat Kid ADD, his nose just peeking over the backseat like Kilroy. His wild helmet of curly red hair obstructed the bottom of the rear window, even more so when he excitedly bounced up and down, screaming at everyone to repeat what they said to make sure he was in every conversation at once. And all the while, Mitch and I sat next to each other in the front in silence.

When we left camp the sky was a glorious pure blue, but as we neared the coast the skies quickly darkened ahead, as if a storm was rushing at us from the opposite direction in a game of weather chicken. I wondered how we were going to kill an entire day at the beach in the rain. With the addition of Kid ADD and Countdown, the collective patience of the cabin had plummeted. The Bears now got bored when there were endless options, so I could only imagine the horror if there were none. Just as we neared the coast Mitch directed me off the main road. I followed his pointed lefts and rights as he circled us through all the Maine towns located just inland. I quickly grasped that the plan was to kill time. The boys stayed busy arguing in the back, but after three hours in the van, while driving through the nondescript town of Arundel, Kid ADD reached his breaking point. "Shouldn't we be there already?" he hollered from the back. He pulled himself up so his hair pressed flat against the van roof. "I want to get *out!*" A couple of other voices agreed.

"Relax, ladies, we're just seeing the sights," said Mitch.

"What sights?" whined Trumps, who was mashed on a seat between Mudge and Lefty, both of whom were being pressed into their windows by his girth. "I just see houses and lawns and junk."

"Just houses?" I said over my shoulder. "Arundel is a historical landmark." We drove past a self-storage building. "That's the very first self-storage area in America. The redcoats built it to store their muskets." At a stop sign, an antiques store stood on our right. "And you know who first opened up that antiques store? Ben Franklin. Well, then it was just a furniture store, but nobody ever bought anything so they eventually became antiques."

"No way Ben Franklin lived here," huffed Mudge.

"You're so full of it," howled Afty. "Josh doesn't know what he's talking about!"

"Where else would he live?" I asked. "Arundel's only, like, *the* kite capital of the world."

As we swung through Biddeford, I announced it as the birthplace of paper towels. (The town's original name was "Bountyville" until the factory moved, I explained.) West Scarborough was where they shot the third Star Wars movie. And Goodwins Mills was where Abraham Lincoln grew up. "That's bull!" yelled Marquee. "He grew up in Indiana." He sunk back in his seat. "We had to learn that for social studies," he muttered, lest any of his cabinmates think he was some sort of brainiac.

"Though he was born in Kentucky," said Mensa.

"Whatever, Brainiac," said Marquee.

Then Mitch spoke up. "You're both wrong," he said. "It was here." I looked over at him, but he was staring out the window. I was surprised to find him playing along. "We're passing his house any minute. I know it because it has a front door."

Were we teaming up together? Yes, it looked like we were. "Did you guys know Lincoln invented the game of kickball on his front lawn?" I said. "Yep. He and Thomas Edison did together. They were neighbors. They formed the World Kickball League."

"You used to get extra points if you knocked over a stovepipe hat," added Mitch. "They called it 'a stovey.'" He turned his head from the window and gave me a sneaky smile. We *were* teaming up together! The army of grudges toward him that I'd built up instantly started to back down in the face of his palling around. *Hey, wait, we could still be friends!* How very eighth-grade girl of me.

Finally, after exhausting every town, we had to drive to the beach. It was only 68 degrees and misting; we could say that Abraham Lincoln invented kickball with a straight face, but there was no way we could fake that this was good beach weather. We wandered with everybody over to the beach hub, an assault of arcades, bumper cars, and more fried dough than you could shake a corn dog at. "Watch 'em a second," growled Mitch, plunging into the arcade. He came back out with pockets bulging with quarters. "Everyone gather around. I'm giving you all two bucks to go crazy with. We're gonna meet back right here in an hour, got that?" To kids who hadn't seen money or flashing lights in five weeks, getting eight quarters was like winning the lottery, and they happily dashed off into the arcade. It was a terribly anti-Eastwind outing, but what else could we do after coming this far? That was the thing about Mitch; he listened to Frank's rules, and then he promptly followed whichever ones jibed with his own perspective. And though it sometimes clashed with my follow-the-rules rigidity, the kids always came away with a great memory. "Let's get some chow," Mitch said to me.

We entered a brew pub packed onto a pier and ordered some nachos. This was our first time communicating more than "Who's got cabin?" in weeks. The melted cheese and beans were our social lubricant, and he regaled me with more tales of past counselor and camper chicanery. Unlike his motorboat and mountain-climbing lectures, this I was interested in. No matter how moldy the gossip, it was still fascinating. The restaurant was dense with cigarette smoke and deep-fryer fumes, but it all smelled like bonding to me.

After an hour, we gathered everyone and headed down to the beach. It was still drizzling, but we ate our lunch outside anyway. We weren't alone on the sand. There were plenty of families who had decided that if they paid for a beachfront hotel, they were going to enjoy the beach, damnit. Parents wearing sweatshirts huddled under beach umbrellas reading paperbacks while their kids packed pails with thick, moist sand. The weather dictated they should be miserable, but nobody seemed that way. The Bears didn't seem to mind the lack of sun, either. Countdown tried to dump sand down the back of people's bathing suits—fun in any weather—and Lefty and Action even ran into the water. Finally, it was time to get back in the van. Even though the sun mockingly reemerged just as we drove away from the beach, I considered the trip a success. And then Action yelled, "Hey, Mitch, can we go jumping?"

Asking Mitch if he'd take you jumping was like asking a sadist if he'd mind kicking you in the groin. He adjusted our route, directing me back to his favorite bridge.

The Bears seemed to have gotten braver as the summer progressed. After past conquerors Action and Mensa quickly jumped again, Lefty slowly swung his legs over. He yelled back at me, "If I die, tell Christine I'm sorry I couldn't steal her away from you like she begged me to," and leaped, screaming all the way down. Mudge, Marquee, and even, to my surprise, Afty followed after some deep hyperventilating. When it looked like momentum might sweep everyone over the bridge, including Wind-Up, I quickly dispatched him down to the rocks below to act as watchman for the jumpers. If he did jump, I wasn't convinced he could swim himself out of the plunge, especially because he'd reemerge from underwater with so much to talk about.

Up on the bridge, Kid ADD trembled with excitement, alternating between marveling at how high they were and harassing Trumps and Countdown, the only ones other than himself who hadn't jumped yet. "You gonna go?" he said to Trumps, who was noticeably quiet, hanging back from the edge. "What's the matter, you got no sack?"

"I don't see you going," spat Trumps.

"I may go," he said, craning over again. "I did this last year on another trip."

"Yeah? Well, I did it last week," Trumps said, rocking from foot to foot.

Countdown straddled the rail, trying to work up the courage to get both legs over. "You gonna jump, or just hump that thing?" said Mitch, grinning over at me. I smiled back weakly. Countdown was the kind of pest who just asked to be razzed. Literally. Just the other night he sat on the end of my bed while I played backgammon with Mudge, goading me into mocking him. "Let's go, Mr. Funny, let's see that funny-man humor. Come on, funny man," he said, not stopping until I finally put down the dice and teased him about what he was wearing. His shoulders bobbed as he giggled, and when I finished, he said, "That all you got, Mr. Ha-ha?" and I had to once again call a time-out from the game and give him crap about his stinky area. I rationalized that it wasn't negative attention since I never went after anything he'd be sensitive about, like his protruding ears—which was why I wasn't comfortable mocking him for teetering on the edge of the bridge. But then again, it would be a chance to continue the bonding process with Mitch.

Trumps stood next to me. "I did jumps like this like three times last week on another trip," he told me, a little too loudly.

"I'm sure you did," I replied.

"I just don't feel like doing it today."

"Sure. So don't do it."

We stood silently, letting Kid ADD's badgering of Countdown fill the air. Trumps nervously played with the string on his slumping bathing suit. "Are you gonna do it?" he asked.

"Nope."

"How come?"

Mitch climbed over the edge of the bridge next to Countdown. "I can't wait all day," he said, jumping off. As I watched him vanish over the edge, I realized I felt none of the pangs of regret over my cowardice from last month. Just the deep desire to stay there on the bridge.

I turned to Trumps. "Because I don't feel like it either. And it scares the crap out of me."

He looked up at me suspiciously, but when he saw I wasn't making fun of him, his features relaxed. "Yeah," he said.

Yeah. Screw this fear-conquering bullshit. When did that become so important? I understood it when it hampered your life, like not being able to fly or leave your house. But why did anyone have to skydive or cliff-jump? I'd heard the proselytizing of the adrenaline whores: Confronting your fears was all about "living life to the fullest." But by whose definition? After years of living alone in an effortless world of sleeping until eleven A.M. on weekends, eating out of take-out cartons, and relaxing on a couch that I had finally gotten permanently molded to my prone, TV-watching body, I was about to get married and start a family. And holy fuck indeed, that leap was a lot bigger than this bridge. Christine and I might go through dark times of bickering about divergent life choices and panicking about bank balances, but I was gambling that we would get through all that. And in a few years we'd find ourselves on a family vacation, playing in the sand on a beach with our kids—maybe even when it was drizzling—and to me, *that* would be living life to its fullest. Leaping off this bridge was supposed to show me what I could do in life? I knew what I had to do in life, so why not skip the agonizing metaphor?

We both watched as Mensa and Action took their third leaps past Countdown, and Mitch reappeared at the bridge, Wind-Up close behind, announcing it was time to go. Countdown looked pained, and his ears glowed red. You could see him search inside himself for the bravado that would lurch him over the edge at the last moment, and, realizing that he had left it back at camp, he slid back onto the road. "Too bad!" taunted Marquee. "The guys who did it are the Sexy Six, and you're not in it!"

"Well, neither am I," I announced. "I guess we're the Fantastic Five." I high-fived Trumps, Wind-Up, and Countdown, and went for Kid ADD, who backed away.

"No way!" he yelped. "I did it before, so I'm in the Sexy Seven."

"Fine, the Fantastic Four, then. A quartet of studs who women find irresistible for our dedication to not killing ourselves." I stole a glance at Mitch, expecting to see his face splashed with scorn and girding myself not to care. But it was devoid of expression. He just shook out his T-shirt, pulled it over his head, and started back to the van amidst the dueling chants of "Sexy Seven!" "Fantastic Four!"

CHAPTER TWENTY-NINE

AT THE BEGINNING OF THE SUMMER, IT SEEMED INCONCEIVABLE THAT YOU would ever grow weary of supervising fun, but, magically, after one kid too many asked you the same question one too many times, suddenly you were ready to go home. At the six-week mark, the escalating grouchiness of the whole staff was palpable. The camper impersonations in the Staff Lounge got a little more acidic, the disciplining remarks a little sharper.

One chilly afternoon as the Free Swim bugle blew, Helen and I sat on the swimming benches, hopeful that no kid in his right mind would opt for a dip today. Helen was curled up in a baggy sweatshirt and running tights, attempting to blend in with the dock to make sure no one saw her. But there was one Coyote who came down every Free Swim, no matter what the weather. I'd thought that part of the fun of Free Swim was the mass participation, but he was just as happy flopping around by himself in a swim mask, a glum lifeguard sitting on the tower staring at him. And sure enough, down the path he came.

"C'mon!" she protested. "You've got to be kidding me, it's freezing in there!"

"What? I like it," he said, kicking off his shoes.

It was Helen's day to sit in the tower, but she didn't want to swim there.

I recommended she get a boat to row out and clip it to the lifeguard tower. At that moment, Zen Richard happened by. "Don't tie it to the tower," he said sharply. "You have to tie it to the inland side of the raft."

With mock anger, I said, "Oh, sorry, *Mr. Dock* says we have to go inland."

He turned and gave me a vicious glare I'm sure Buddha would not approve of. "On the tower side the boat'll bang against the dock and chip it, wiseguy," he growled. "And then I'm out there all winter trying to buff the marks out. You want to be out there all winter?"

I put up my hands. "Whoa, man, I'm sorry, I was just kidding. Inland is fine."

His shoulders relaxed slightly. "Sorry for snapping. You know: six weeks."

If six weeks could break the most placid man in New England, what chance did the rest of us have?

Back in New York, my apartment was my sanctuary from my busy life. At the end of the workday, I could return home, ignore the phone, and lie on the couch watching TV or reading, the only aural interruption being a car horn on the street outside. And even that I could ignore, knowing that no matter how bad the traffic outside, the aggrieved driver would never drive up the stairwell of my building, smash through my door, and honk in my face to get me to go outside and make the other cars move faster.

I had no such refuge at camp, and I desperately needed one after a long day of begging kids to swim. Some nights when I had no activities after dinner, I grabbed a book and wandered the camp in search of a quiet reading spot, as mythical a goal as finding a clean camper. I sat down at Birch Grove, and after cracking open my novel, a scrum of kids burst out of the woods, involved in a convoluted variation of tag in which the spot I was sitting on was home base. So I ducked behind the Grove, to a pastoral rock outcropping into the lake where my friends and I used to hang out at age fifteen and pretend we were too good to be with everyone else. When I arrived, I found three Lions there, pretending to be too good to be with everyone else. The Staff Lounge was too filthy to consider an oasis, so I wandered in circles around camp in a futile search for silence, the grip on my book growing tighter the closer it got to bedtime, when I was due to return to the cabin for duty.

As soon as I stepped into the cabin, I became the unwilling referee for every disagreement. I served as the human dictionary for Snatch arguments and as the enforcer of all privacy issues ("You're in my area!" "I am not, my feet are just past the bedpost line." "But you're leaning over the edge. Jooooooosh!"). No matter how hard I tried to avoid getting sucked into silly problems, it was impossible in an open cabin that was nothing but beds and shelves. And then there was Charlie, who regularly bounced up to me to propose a new brainstorm for improving the summer. Alas for him, enthusiasm was a zero-sum game between us, and I had lost all strength to be polite. One muggy morning he approached me with his idea to ban towels at the showers, except on cold days. "This morning I took a shower and let myself air dry as I walked back to the cabin, and found it quite delightful," he said. Six weeks earlier I might have indulged him with a rousing debate of the pros and cons of having damp, naked kids skulking through camp, but instead I just said, "I'm not sure everyone else needs to feel the wind rustling through their nutsack," and turned back to my book.

But of everyone, Kid ADD was the biggest threat to my patience. Someone finally taught him Snatch, and he adapted the a-broken-clock-is-right-twice-a-day strategy to the game. Whenever a tile was flipped, he shouted out every combination of the open letters, figuring one had to be a word. If no one paid attention to him on the third try, he'd just grab the tiles and feign certainty. "PNOD . . . NOPD! . . . DONP! It's donp!"

"Don't touch those!" shouted Mensa.

"Donp is a word! *Donp . . . is . . . a word!* Josh! Is donp a word?"

"No."

"You don't know *anything.* Donp's a word." When they finally pried the tiles out of his hand, Lefty yelled "POND!" and picked them all up again.

"No way, no way! Pond isn't a word!" yelled Kid ADD. And a new tile was flipped over and he started all over again. "FRE! FER! ERF! Erf is a word. *Erf . . . is . . . a word!*"

The slightest problem obsessed him, and he couldn't pay attention long enough for me to help him solve it. One morning I awoke to him pulling all his clothes out of his shelves. "Where is my sky-blue sweatshirt? *Where is my sky-blue sweatshirt?* Which one of you dicks took my sky-blue sweatshirt?"

Reveille hadn't yet blown, and the Kid's frenzy was met with a chorus of "Shut *up*s" by his fellow campers. One might have slipped out of me as well.

"I won't shut up! I had a sky-blue sweatshirt and now it's gone!"

All day long he talked about the sky-blue sweatshirt, refolding all his clothes and then yanking them back out again in an endless cycle of searching, as if a giant sweatshirt might somehow have gotten stuck in a pair of socks. I was surprised to see him stick with one issue, but that concentration only extended to the big picture of "Sweatshirt lost, me want sweatshirt back." When I asked him to retrace his steps to where he last had it, he wouldn't reflect longer than to say, "I last saw it on my body, because it's my favorite sky-blue sweatshirt!" One moment he was convinced someone stole it, then someone buried it, then someone threw it in the lake. No matter what the theory, it was my fault for not finding it. "Why aren't you helping me? *I need my sky-blue sweatshirt!*"

Mitch was on a day off, or just elsewhere—I'd ceased to be able to tell the difference—and so, by default, I was in charge of solving the Case of the Missing Sky-Blue Sweatshirt. My only oasis was in the middle of the night, when the cabin was quiet and I'd dream of finding the sweatshirt, yanking it over Kid ADD's head, and pulling the string on the hood so tight that no sound could come out.

That Wednesday night it started to rain, which was a relief. I loved the occasional rainy day. Instead of teaching swimming, Helen and I stationed ourselves in the Dining Hall to supervise board and card games. Rest Hour was extended, and the dreariness mellowed everybody enough that they actually sat still. The lake went calm and glasslike and cross-camp walks relaxed me as I was lulled by the hypnotic dapple of raindrops hitting the leaves above. Everything looked greener and smelled fresher. Until it went on for a few days.

On Friday it was still pouring. There were occasional teasing moments of sun, but dark clouds quickly paved over that brief spot of brightness and resumed dumping rain. After forty-eight hours of their favorite outdoor activities being closed, the campers got antsy. Counselors were devitalized even further by the glum weather, and would have been happy to nap. But the boys didn't nap. They just paced and thought about new things to break and new ways to break them. And an absence of distraction just freed up more time for Kid ADD to obsess about his lost sweatshirt. The mood got more desperate; a few days earlier, Charlie and I had promised the guys a cabin trip down to the Campfire Ceremony pit to light a blaze and make s'mores. But when the promised date arrived, it was raining too hard, and I said we'd have to postpone. There was an angry rebellion. They wouldn't accept that my depriving them of chocolate was not a malicious act, and, growing increasingly angry and belligerent, they demanded their s'mores. Hearing myself explain for the third time that rain plus fire equals no s'mores, I stormed out, leaving them with Charlie. The next morning, returning from breakfast, I found two Starburst wrappers sitting on my bed. As candy was verboten in camp, this was the ultimate tropical-fruity sign of disrespect for my authority. I held them in my hand and glared around the cabin, but no one met my gaze.

On the third day of rain, the cabin started to stink. If the first day of rain smells like nature is being fed and nurtured, the third smells like nature got fat and crapped itself after eating too many bags of Doritos. The culprit was mildew, a rank, pervasive stench that smelled like dirt gone bad. It wafted out of the wet shoes that never dried and the damp clothes twisted into small balls and either stuffed into the campers' laundry bags or tossed under their beds. Afty, who slept next to me, was apparently born without sinuses, as he never noticed that the sopping-wet shorts and T-shirts he crammed into his bag smelled like a mixture of feet, old olive loaf, and an un-air-conditioned morgue. And, his bag was made of a mesh fabric. Mesh! Who made a laundry bag out of mesh? Did the same company also make chain-link diaper pails? Afty hung it from a nail on his shelves at a perfect height so the swollen, stinking sack dangled right next to my sleeping head like a giant pouch of ass potpourri.

I had adjusted to and embraced living in a grubby world, but now I hit my wall of patience. All of my usual adult fussiness returned. I was obsessed with controlling the cabin smell. When I entered and sensed the presence of something newly putrid, I stormed into everyone's areas, leading with my nose, and sniffed up and down their shelves to discover what was responsible for this unholy stink. I became the Hercule Poirot of moldy bathing suits, unable to rest until I'd discovered the guilty garment and triumphantly walked out of the cabin with it dangling from the end of a broomstick, depositing it out on the drying line, where it never would. The campers just gave me weird looks.

"You smelled their *shelves?*" asked Christine over the phone that night after we'd compared our days.

"You don't understand, it's awful," I moaned. "I'd prefer a cabin full of skunks to what I'm living with now. And I'm the only one who seems to mind. The only smell these guys notice is when someone farts. And then they applaud." I had recently discovered the only private phone in camp, an extension in the kitchen pantry, accessible at night. I sat in the dark on a drum of flour, my knees at chin level. The constant damp had made my own Teva sandals go bad, and the mix of rubber and foot sweat proved a worthy combatant against the gentle scent of freshly baked goods. Ugh, now I was one of *them*.

I shifted on my makeshift seat so the plastic raised circles on the flour lid didn't make a permanent imprint in my ass. I groaned as I slid around, trying to find a comfortable position. "You all right over there?" Christine asked.

I sighed and rubbed my eyes. "I'm sitting in the dark marinating in my own and everyone else's filth," I said. "And to think I could be sitting with you."

"I miss you too," she said tenderly. "I can't wait to see you. But you need to try to hold your nose and enjoy the rest of your time. You've always wanted to do this, so don't wish the time away faster."

I went back to the cabin around midnight. Charlie had cabin duty, and I crawled into bed, pulling my lamp close to me to read. I heard the creaking of a bed on the other side of the cabin. Slow, shuffling, horror-movie footsteps approached in the dark. My small circle of light reached only just past my bed, and I watched as two white, spindly feet entered it, and slowly the rest of the body emerged with it. It was Charlie, looking wildly disoriented as he stood in a white T-shirt that extended just past his crotch in a parody of a baby-doll nightie. He hovered for an endless moment, squinting dazedly at me, all of his hair pushed to one side of his head.

"Oh," he finally said. "It's you." And then he turned around and slowly shambled out of my light. When he faced the other way, I saw that he was pantsless, and his T-shirt rose up over his air-drying ass. His pale, puckered butt faded away in the dark like the ghost of sagging future, and I heard him lay down on his cot. He let the silence settle in and then broke explosive wind, unmuted by underwear. I'm not sure Christine had factored that in when she told me not to wish away time.

By the next wet day, the tiny stream of water that normally snaked down the slight slope of camp to the lake had turned into a frothy river, and kids in yellow slickers crouched on its banks, racing leaves down the flume. I walked around in a permaglower, sick of board games but not wanting to go back to swimming. Mitch showed up for Rest Hour and joined in a game of Snatch while I lay on my bed reading a magazine. It figured that the one day he showed up for active duty there'd be nowhere dry for me to go.

Everyone was relatively mellow, lounging around the cabin in small groups. For a glorious moment, Kid ADD had forgotten about his sky-blue sweatshirt. Trumps and Marquee, whose beds were next to each other, were having a fervent conversation about Marquee's fishing rod. I was vaguely aware of their voices rising, the tenor shifting from excitable to angry. Let Mitch deal with it for once, I thought. I couldn't really see what was going on anyway with all the damp towels hanging from the rafters.

"*I'm sorry, I'm sorry, I'm sorry!*" The rest of the cabin looked up at once to see Marquee covering his head with his arms and staggering into the aisle, pleading with Trumps, who loomed over him, wildly and clumsily throwing punches. Movies trained you to think that all fistfights were macho yet reasoned, an interchange of measured, rewardingly acoustic roundhouses; it had been a long time since I'd seen a real brawl, but this one reminded me that they're actually short, frantic, graceless affairs.

Trumps's face was frozen in a red grimace. He jerkily swung his thick arms, and there was no resounding *whack* when they hit his cowering opponent's back, just dull thuds as Marquee bent farther and farther over, trying to fold in on himself to get out of the situation. Mitch and I leapt up to split them apart. In a schoolyard the other Bears would have formed a circle and cheered, but here they sat quiet and discombobulated in their places. *A fight? At camp? Now* that *can't be right.*

Mitch grabbed Trumps around his heaving, lumpy chest and dragged him out of the cabin, while I led a shaken Marquee over to the corner. His showy personality normally made him seem much bigger than he was, but now, as he blinked feverishly, repeating that he was fine as his body gave an occasional seismic quiver, he looked tiny and brittle. He stammered that Trumps had been admiring his fishing rod, but then wouldn't give it back. When Marquee had tried to pull the top of the flexible rod toward himself, he accidentally let it go, and it twanged back, striking Trumps in the face. I always suspected that the fury I saw simmering inside Trumps when he lost a game of cards had the potential to boil over. It was surprising it had taken this long.

As I calmed Marquee down, the bugle for third period blew. Everyone reluctantly filed out of the cabin, their eavesdropping curtailed. Marquee's resolve crumbled as they left, and he shuddered and cried, furiously wiping his eyes with his forearms, as if it didn't count as crying if the tears never reached his cheeks. I waited for him to compose himself, and he took a deep shuddering breath in, muttered he was going to Wood Shop, and took off out the door.

That afternoon, I was in the Dining Hall for my fourth straight day of board games, and Bears came and went, asking me about what happened. "You think they'll fight again?" asked Afty.

"Marquee better put up more of a fight next time," said Mudge.

"I heard Marquee poked him in the eye with a fish hook," said Countdown.

"Damn, that's cold," said Lefty. "He tries that with me, I'll serve up his head with my tennis racket at the courts."

"I'd light a match and fire bug spray at him in the Trips Room. *Whooosh!*" said Kid ADD. What was this, summer-camp Clue? I gave everyone the same talking points: It was an accident, and there would be no more fighting. But it didn't do much to contain the palpable agitation spreading through the cabin. Now the guys would start choosing sides, the arguing would get louder, and I'd have to be on constant alert for somebody putting somebody else's head through a screen. It would be up to me to deal with it all, because Charlie would be too busy suggesting new ways to fix the screen with spider silk and God knew Mitch wouldn't be around. It would be hell. No, worse than hell, because at least when you burn in hell, it smells like a campfire.

At the end of fourth period I begrudgingly returned to the putrid cabin, prepared to find it either deafening or on fire. As I got closer, I could already hear yelling, but I was surprised at the content. "BIFE? . . . FIBE . . . BEFI! . . . BEFI! Befi is a word! *Befi is a word!*" A rousing game of Snatch was humming, with Kid ADD, Lefty, Action, and, surprisingly, Trumps and Marquee, who sat right next to each other. I looked to my right and saw Mitch lying down on his bed, filling out some paperwork.

"Do you see this?" I said, pointing over at Little Yalta. "How the hell did those guys get to be friends again?"

He looked searchingly at me for a moment, trying to figure out what I was talking about. Boy, was he tuned out. Couldn't even remember a cabin fight. Then his eyebrows raised as it clicked. "Oh, those two guys? After Rest Hour I had to go into town to get some new tires for a van. So I grabbed them both and made them come with me, asked 'em a bunch of leading questions on the drive down there, then left 'em in the van together while I got the tires. When I came back, they were chattin' it up." He put his pen in his mouth and talked around it. "I knew they'd make up."

I was stunned and impressed by the effortlessness with which he solved this. But I felt a great void where my martyrlike sense of superiority used to be. What right did he have to be a great counselor?

As I returned to my bed, Kid ADD stood up mid-turn to accost me. "Hey, Josh, check it out." He pointed with both hands to the sweatshirt he was wearing. "The sailing counselor found my sky-blue sweatshirt, no thanks to *you*."

I looked at his newfound garment, and all the relief I'd momentarily felt from a peaceful cabin was now replaced by simmering frustration. "That sweatshirt," I said through gritted teeth, "is green."

He looked down at it for a moment, frowning at all its forest greenness. "Well, it said 'sky-blue' on the label. And now I've got it." He blew a rasp-berry at me and sat back down at the game. "Hold up, hold up! What do we got, F . . . E . . . R . . . B? Ferb's a word, isn't it? Josh, is ferb a word?"

I would never make it through two more weeks.

CHAPTER THIRTY

I TRUDGED THROUGH WEEK SEVEN, COUNTING THE PASSAGE OF TIME IN LES-
sons. "Nine more periods until my day off," I'd tell Helen. "And then six
after that until Sunday." Then she replied with her count, and the exchange killed about fourteen seconds. And then time went back to creep-
ing by in a sludge of kickboards, backstrokes, and meals. One day Jim, the
ex-biter who had been a swim instructor two summers earlier, asked to
take a break from teaching tennis to come give a lesson at the dock, for old
times' sake. I watched him splash and hoot and yell and cheer and inspire
the kids. His energy shamed me, but anyone could play that game for one
period. I had been Mr. Chips for the first couple of weeks. Now I was
every burned-out high school science teacher I'd ever had. All I lacked
was a desk to put my feet up on, an unfiltered cigarette, and tenure.

I got one unexpected shot of adrenaline after lunch when I went to
gather the cabin's mail at the Office. Countdown had been bugging me for
a couple of days about his dad sending him a package, but it hadn't arrived yet, and today he tailed me again. I made Countdown stand outside
while I joined the other staff by the mailboxes, but when I saw a rectangular package with his name on it, I called him in to open it under close su-
pervision.

"Just keep your hands where I can see them," I said in my best cop-show voice. "Open 'er up." He tore open the brown paper to reveal a shoebox. I put a hand on his chest and gently pushed him back a step. I removed the top and pulled out some crinkled-up newspapers to reveal a flashlight and a skateboarding magazine underneath. Eyeing Countdown suspiciously, I held the flashlight up to my ear and shook it. He rolled his eyes. I picked up the magazine, flipped through its pages, then waved it by its staples, subscription cards drifting to the floor. At this point the other counselors surrounded us, all of us glorifying in our modicum of authority. I patted down all the newspaper, then decisively held the box out for him. "All right, you're safe. Enjoy your package."

He held out both hands to receive it, and just as I laid it in his palms, the skinny arm of Dwight the pottery counselor reached for the box through the wall of watching staff. "Check for a false bottom!" he yelled. Just as I was thinking, That's ridiculous, he scooped his hand down into the box, prying up a perfectly cut rectangular piece of cardboard with his fingernails. When he flipped it up, the whole staff bent over the box and saw six packs of M&M's and Reese's Pieces. From the collective gasp we all let out you would have thought we'd uncovered a human head. Our mouths hanging open, we all turned to stare at Countdown. He looked back with the nervous expression of a border-hopping illegal immigrant who just emerged from a secret tunnel to have a patrolman blast a searchlight in his face. And as the staff's facial expressions shifted from surprise to smug victory, he made a decision: *It can't end here*. He yanked the box to his chest and dashed out the door.

"*We got a runner!*" I yelled, bolting after him. Reg took off after me while the rest of the staff stood on the porch cheering. "Where you going, Countdown? Where you gonna hide?" I hollered, six steps behind him as he careened down the hill toward the lake and veered down the shoreline path. My arms and legs pumping faster than they had in weeks, I yelled back to Reg, "High road, high road!" Like fighter planes in a precise formation, he split off toward the Possums cabin, and I could see him paralleling us through the trees to head off Countdown. It all felt like an action film. I rehearsed Schwarzeneggerian candycentric puns for when I caught him. *Sorry to Starburst your bubble! Don't cry over spilt Milky Way!*

As Countdown tore down the dirt path, his toe caught a root and he tumbled onto the ground. With his arms tightly embraced over his box of candy, he didn't have the chance to flail, he just landed with a thump, did a rough somersault, ended up back on his feet, and continued to run. To his right he saw Reg outpacing him, destined to block him at the dock. With no exit, he veered right, into the woods between the two paths, and quickly became ensnared in the bushes and branches. He stopped, looked around, and tossed the box off to the side.

"Really?" I huffed, hands on my knees as I caught my breath. "*That's* your exit strategy?" Reg jogged up and we high-fived. He plowed into the bushes and picked up the box, as Countdown sheepishly extricated himself.

"Nice run, mate." He clapped Countdown on the back and handed him back his magazine and flashlight while passing me the candy. "If I hadn't headed you off, I bet you'da made it all the way to Canada."

I fondled the candy lasciviously. "Ooh, the staff is gonna love eating these," I moaned. "Don't be sad, though. I'll bet if you sniff the flashlight you can still get an M&M contact high."

"You gotta admit I was close," he said, picking dead leaves out from his sandals as we walked away.

"Close only counts in horseshoes and Hershey bars," I shot back as we walked away. "You should have asked your dad for those." I wasn't angry at all. I was grateful to Countdown for the little dash of intrigue, no matter how childish. I would toast him with peanut-butter filling when we shared his candy up at the Office that night. And maybe I'd thank his equally sneaky dad personally when he came for the upcoming Visiting Day.

When the parental deluge began again three days later, I found myself once again lifeguarding on the end of the dock, attempting to distinguish between drowning dad and just-bad-swimmer dad. After a couple of hours, Action came up behind me. "Dad, this is my counselor, Josh," he said. I had missed meeting his parents last month, and I was now facing a smiling man with equally bad taste in clothes. His ill-fitting bathing suit had a yellowish pattern that I thought existed only in Petri dishes; I assumed he and Action must have taken father/son shopping trips to Color-Blind Junction and Color-Blind Junction for Boys.

We exchanged hellos and, as a good counselor, I gave a quick synopsis of all Action's positive traits and achievements as he blushed and his dad beamed. That taken care of, the two leapt into the water with a Frisbee, starting a game of catch off to the left of the splashing masses. Back and forth they tossed the disc, with Action coughing on inhaled water every time he leapt forward with a *kerploosh* to catch a throw that fell short. I went back to surveying the other swimmers, but my eyes kept coming back to them. They never tired of their game. Thirty minutes, an hour, ninety minutes, they were still there. Were they putting me on? Action was fourteen. This was the age when boys ignore their parents and choose grunting as their preferred method of communication. With his mature physique and beginner's mustache, Action looked like he'd hit puberty hard enough to break it. Of the hormones that triggered the "my parents are such idiots" reaction in teenagers, he probably had twice the average. And yet here he was, gleefully soaking in every moment with his dad with no sign of impatience or sullenness. How did they pull this off?

Two men excused themselves as they climbed up the ladder in front of me to get out of the lake. I had seen them earlier playing in the water with a precocious Raccoon, a tiny, blond moppet reminiscent of every ten-year-old actor brought in to cute up an aging family sitcom. I was surprised he hadn't arrived with a catchphrase and a laugh track. There was a taller and less telegenic visiting boy in the lake with him; they looked around the same age, and from the foursome's interaction I gathered that he was the Raccoon's cousin and one of the men was the Raccoon's father, the other his uncle. The men dripped back to the benches to fetch their towels, while the cousin swam up to follow them. The Raccoon followed him, protesting that he wasn't done swimming yet. As the two boys climbed the ladder, I got distracted by a kayak that was sliding backward into the swimming area, much to the confusion of the father inside who was *sure* he was paddling forward. As he held his paddle up toward me with a frustrated look that said, "Get me a new one, this one is obviously broken," I saw the Raccoon's cousin lurch past me back into the water with a squeal. I'd seen enough horseplay over six weeks to recognize when someone had been pushed. I turned to see the Raccoon standing next to me, smirking down at his cousin, who had just bobbed to the surface. His face dripping, it took me a moment to realize that he was crying. The Raccoon simply leaped back out into the water over him and started wading back to the raft.

"Hey, come back here!" I yelled, while trying to help the sobbing cousin out of the water. The Raccoon kept heading forward, absentmindedly splashing with his hands. When the cousin got out, he walked dejectedly back toward his father.

"What happened, buddy?" asked the boy's dad.

Unable to form words through his blubbering, the cousin pointed back to the water and then made a pushing gesture. The Raccoon's dad joined them on the dock. Once parental figures were involved, my authority vanished, so I just eavesdropped while scanning the water. "What? He pushed you? No, he wouldn't push you," said the uncle. The dad yelled out, "Hey, son, you didn't push your cousin, did you?"

The Raccoon turned back with a practiced look of innocence. I could practically hear his eyelashes batting from where I stood. "No way!" He turned around and went back to splashing.

"See?" said his uncle. "He didn't push you." The cousin froze with his mouth open, paralyzed by betrayal. I resisted the urge to slap him on the back of his head to kickstart his protestations. "Come on," said the Raccoon's dad. "Get dried off, you probably just fell in." He turned out to the water. "Hey, buddy, we're gonna get ready to go to dinner, so come on back in a few minutes!" The cousin shuffled and snuffled back to fetch his towel, wearing the aggrieved look of the perpetually blamed.

Action and Action Sr. still played on. *There* was a dad who did things right. Who was he? What was his secret? I looked at my watch, saw it was time to end the Free Swim, and blew the whistle, waving everyone back in. What were their secrets, I wondered, as sopping dads paraded past me with their kids? How did they make good kids? How did they make brats? Like Lefty: How did he get to be the funny, confident, and kind kid that he was? I had thought I'd like to have him as a good friend, but someday I wouldn't mind having someone like him as a son.

This was not the Visiting Day I used to know. I used to survey the celebration, comparing dads to mine. Now I was comparing them to the dad I'd like to be.

CHAPTER THIRTY-ONE

CAMP CARNIVAL WAS TRADITIONALLY THE LAST SUNDAY OF THE SUMMER. Each cabin spent all morning building its own booth for the afternoon celebration. The Bears had been arguing about it for the whole last week. On Saturday they had reluctantly given in to Countdown's idea to play "Name That Tune" with a hip-hop mix CD he'd brought. His plan was to sit at a table with my portable stereo, playing snippets for kids to guess what song it was. The CD only had ten songs, so not only would it be a very uninteresting sport, but it would get old very, very quickly, the rap-music equivalent of "Guess which hand the rock is in?" So I suggested an alternate idea that I knew would work, since I had done it my last two summers at camp: a rudimentary dunking booth. It combined the skill and aim of baseball pitching with the schadenfreude of seeing other people get wet. The Bears loved it.

I knew this was the sort of project Charlie would thrive on. As I didn't have any campers swimming across the lake Sunday morning, I was desperate to enjoy one late sleep, so I outlined the logistics for him on Saturday night, hoping he'd take the lead and get working on it the next morning while I slumbered. It was more a dousing booth than a dunk tank, as we'd balance a bucket of water above a victim and players would throw tennis balls at a target that would knock the bucket over, drenching whoever was underneath. All we'd need for this basic apparatus were two planks, a target, a bucket, a rope, a hinge, a chair, and yards of rope and duct tape. While I explained it to him, I repeatedly interjected that this should be kept *simple*. Without that important parameter, Charlie might easily think my plan could be bettered with the use of pullies, a water-wheel, and a Van de Graaff generator.

At seven fifteen on Camp Carnival morning, I heard Charlie get up to start recruiting dazed campers to help him. Although I was grateful for his motivation and the extra bit of sleep, the ensuing noise rendered it all moot. The dunking site was just down the road in the Senior Cove, and the sounds of Kid ADD and Trumps arguing over who would get to fill the bucket while Charlie banged nails into the tree were the opposite of a lullaby. My permanent state of crankiness was now boosted with sleep-deprivation. If I could get through the day without either suffering a brain hemorrhage or taking someone's life, it would be a triumph. I went to get breakfast and had been sitting for only fifteen minutes before Kid ADD burst in, shouting at me and my Cheerios that Charlie needed my help right that moment.

I arrived, grumbling, at the Senior Cove at nine fifteen, just as a bedraggled Sean stalked out of his Tigers cabin, located just twenty yards away from where Charlie was hammering and the boys were screaming. "I'm going to kill your fucking cabin," he growled as he passed, his eyes still red. "At seven thirty they start that shit." Charlie was on a tall ladder, busily tying a plank to the tree.

"Ahhh, there you are." He climbed down after tightening a knot. He proceeded to go through in great detail what they'd done, how they'd done it, what worked, what didn't. Fine, fine, I thought, just finish it up. "So it looks like we're in good shape," he said. "And so I leave it to you, as I promised some boys I'd meet them down at the waterfront." And with that he passed me the duct-tape baton. I couldn't really be angry with him, as he'd been working for two hours. I could be angry at Mitch, though. I hadn't even seen him in the cabin for the past few days.

Okay, I thought. Two more days, two more days, you can do it. I inhaled deeply and raided my reserves of patience and enthusiasm as I set about hammering, knotting, taping, and painting our contraption. I mined my memory to avoid past failures, starting with finding a sturdy branch to tie the bucket to. On my first attempt at building a dunking booth in 1986, we had an unfortunate test run with a CIT. When the full plastic bucket was knocked loose, the branch snapped loose as soon as the line went taut. The bucket came straight down, never tipping over, so its bottom (weighted with five gallons of water) landed with a dull thud on the CIT's head, followed shortly by the branch. After balancing on his skull for an interminable second, the bucket slowly rolled forward, pouring all the cold water onto his lap. Prefacing a splash with a near-concussion made it a far less whimsical contest.

Only a handful of Bears had shown up to help, and they floated in and out of the project between showers, mumbling about other things they needed to do. Even Wind-Up, whom I could always count on to orbit around a captive set of ears, had vanished. Kid ADD was the one constant. Ironically, his dedication to the project made it go far more slowly. Whatever step we worked on, he was always demanding to jump five steps ahead. And he quickly drove away the more shakily committed Bears by yelling at them for not doing a task right that he himself had no idea how to do. I tried to calm myself by running a mantra through my head as I gripped the hammer: *Hit the nail, not the child, hit the nail, not the child.*

Eventually, just me, the Kid, and Lefty were left, and an unexpected teamwork developed. Lefty knew enough to ignore the Kid, and with no one to boost him to higher decibels by yelling back, Kid ADD plateaued at a tolerable level. After a while, his ricocheting patter seemed a fair price for his legitimate enthusiasm for the project, since it was lacking from everyone else. Every so often he got so excited about our progress that he threw his arm around me, and at that moment I'd remember that under his hyperactivity, this was a good kid. And then, before the warm moment had a chance to cool off, he yelled in my ear, "Can we fill the bucket now? I get to fill the bucket!" I explained that the bucket wasn't tied to anything yet; he asked again if he could fill the bucket, and I changed my mantra to *He's a good kid, he's a good kid, he's a good kid* . . .

After two and a half hours, we finished making a contraption that was functional, albeit ugly, the planks barely visible underneath its swaddle of tape and rope. The Kid, Lefty, and I stood back to admire it. "We're gonna totally dominate the carnival," said Lefty, and then the Kid begged me to let him sit under the bucket when the booth opened. Not only had he earned it, but he was the perfect target: Whoever was under the bucket needed to goad the throwers, and I knew his voice would never get tired.

After Rest Hour, the games began. All the classic, simplistic games were offered by the other cabins: ring tosses, whistling contests after eating peanut butter; spraying out lit candles with squirt guns. But ours was by far the most popular. Lefty stood on the ladder with a hose, resetting and refilling the bucket every time it got knocked down, and Kid ADD made a phenomenal target. He had found a fantasy land in which his shrill shouting was not just sanctioned, but encouraged. And since he was shocked into silence every time he was doused with cold water, the people knocking the bucket perched over his head got to live in a fantasy land where they could make him stop shouting. Soon the line for our booth stood fifteen kids long, and the other Bears drifted back, eager not only to drench Kid ADD but also to share in the reflected glory.

For forty-five minutes the booth ran seamlessly. I delegated my campers to be ticket-takers, and Wind-Up loved the job of fetching errant balls that missed the tarp we'd hung as a backstop because it gave him the chance to throw them back in the style of his favorite Phillies outfielders. Every time Kid ADD got dunked, it provoked a roar of applause from the waiting crowd. But he was shaded by the trees, and, perched on a metal folding chair in a bathing suit, his feet in a growing puddle, he started to look cold. When I saw his shoulders trembling, I pulled him from the game. And that marked the end of my good times.

When he had been under the bucket, he focused on the throwers. Freed from his chair, he now focused on all of us. He screamed about how he should fill the bucket . . . no, he should take tickets . . . no, he should get the balls! And how whoever was doing any of these tasks was doing it wrong. Meanwhile, everyone else fought to claim the dunkee's chair. I picked Mensa to take the position, which enraged Trumps and Mudge, who wouldn't accept any other duties. Kid ADD tried to climb the ladder to claim the hose job, while Lefty clutched the tree, yelling at him to get down and stop shaking the ladder. Afty, in a protective mood, ran to try to yank Kid off. And through this anarchy, the kids in line impatiently waved their tickets and argued over who cut in line. My head pounding, I looked around for any relief. In the distance, I saw Charlie through the crowd at another booth, a spray of Saltine sand and peanut butter chunks shooting from his pursed lips. And where the hell was Mitch?

As if on cue, a car beeped behind me. I turned to see Mitch's van backing down the camp road, his attached boat trailer heading for the lake. He got out of the van and noticed our booth for the first time. Bemused, he cut in front of the line, threw a ball, and dumped a bucket on Mensa. Laughing, he continued on toward the waterfront. Minutes later I heard a motor on the water and saw Mitch's boat putter around the edge of the cove toward the beach, driving right up on his submerged trailer. Agape, I watched him shut it down, hop out, attach it to his trailer, then get in his van and slowly drive away.

That motherfucking boat-driving motherfuckingfucker. He didn't help me out one bit on Camp Carnival, and then had the titanium balls to lovingly pack up his funcruiser right in front of me? The very joyriding motorboat that all summer marked him as the "cool counselor"? Was it an oversight that he hadn't also backed over me with his van? I was on fire with rage, nearly popping the tennis balls as I handed them off. I was through being his scapegoat. Only two more days left at camp? Fine. He was going to perform every cabin duty until the last camper left. And then some. He was gonna read *me* a bedtime story, make *my* bed. Maybe I'd start a fight of my own so he could mediate *my* ass. Goddamn chore-shirking, cliff-jumping, kayak-flipping bastard.

The last thirty minutes of Carnival crept by, my back tense with coiled frustration, and after Frank sat under the bucket for the ceremonial dunk-the-authority-figure finale, I sharply ordered the Bears to dismantle and clean up our booth as quickly as possible, as I had something important to do. When the last plank was brought back to the Wood Shop, I stormed around the camp, asking everyone I passed if they had seen Mitch. By the tennis courts, I bumped into Chas, who said he'd just seen Mitch down by the dock. Seeing me hyperventilate, he tried to calm me down. That was exactly what I didn't need. After two months of being cowed, I was going to have my say.

I stormed down to the waterfront, and there he was, sitting alone at the end of the motorboat dock. I could only see the back of his head and his shoulder as he relaxed shirtless on a wood deck chair. Tanning? *Tanning?!* That was all I needed to help me lose all freak-out inhibitions. Forget jumping off a bridge, telling him off would be the great achievement of my summer. I stormed down the length of the dock, reveling in the surprised look in the eyes of the campers who stepped aside like frightened villagers. Yes, avert your eyes, I thought. *I am going to vanquish the evil lord who has kept you in his sway for so long, and expose him as nothing but a CHEAP FRAUD! And you shall have a new king, one who stays off bridges and always drives at the speed limit, and, hey, who's up for a nice safe game of gin rummy? Mind the cards' sharp edges!*

"Mitch!" I shouted. He turned to look at me. I could see he was doing paperwork. "You *really* fucked me over today." I liked the force in my voice. Each word was testicular, round and hard with a little hair on it. He looked surprised, as well he should have. "I've been covering for you all week. All goddamn week. And today, you didn't do a damn . . ."

I walked in front of him. No more grumbling behind his back, I was going to stare him in the eye, because that's what men did. I had not, however, planned on his being naked. He must have just come out from a spontaneous skinnydip, and now, without a towel, he was using the Charlie method to dry off. My big dramatic moment, and I was now facing a quizzical Mitch staring at me, his clipboard placed on the chair's armrest, giving me a full view of his penis, lying in his lap like a sleeping hamster.

". . . thing?"

Nothing will confuse and disarm your anger more quickly than being confronted by an enemy's scrotum. "Umm . . ." I tried to relocate my simmering resolve, but all I could find was a desire to find him a pair of shorts. It was unfair, now it was two against one. "You just . . . you kind of screwed me by . . . uh . . . I was left doing Carnival all on my own."

"Oh," he said. "Hey, I'm sorry, man, but I had a crazy week, and now I've got all this paperwork to finish."

"Yeah, I had a crazy week, too," I said, regaining my balance, albeit with far less of the apoplexy. "And I've got paperwork, too. And I was still up at nine putting that damn dunk tank together." I remembered the ultimatum I had planned on giving him. "I've had the cabin pretty much all week, so tonight and tomorrow night you're gonna take it."

He winced and then looked at me apologetically. "Uh, dude . . . I'm leaving tonight."

"What?"

"Yeah, I've gotta get home to get ready for the school year, I didn't tell you?" I just stared at him. "That's part of the reason I'm so busy now. Frank really screwed me over, since he's demanding this shit before I get out of here, even though he originally told me he didn't need it right away." He gave me a conspiratorial, working-man "Can you believe the fucking boss?" look. "Ummm, let me think. How about, uh, I can leave later tonight and put them to bed, you'd just have to be back at eleven. That work for you?"

I threw up my hands. "Fine, cool, you get them tonight, whatever." I walked down the dock to the beach, as he yelled one more "Sorry, dude!" to my back. Had this been a victory? I wasn't sure. Even if it ended up being pointless, I had stood up for myself. I showed Mitch I was not one to be walked all over . . . at least not for more than seven weeks and five days. So at least I could go home with that. Yeah. Take that, world! You don't mess with . . . uh . . . me . . . and . . .

I stopped by the tennis courts and shook my head. Who was I kidding? The whole thing was idiotic. My big shining moment involved arguing with a naked man about who would cover a summer-camp cabin. It illuminated around eighty connected strands of foolishness, most of all the pointless competitiveness I'd felt with Mitch all summer. So much time wondering, Does he think I'm not cool enough? Not brave enough? Not tough enough? He wasn't thinking any of those things. He wasn't my nemesis; he didn't really care what I did, as long as it didn't get in his way of enjoying a stress-free summer. At forty-two, he was still able to spend his camp sessions the way I thought I was going to spend mine: carefree and childlike. In that way, anyway, he was a better man than I.

I slowly walked back to the cabin, passing Chas on the way. "Hey, man, how'd it go?" he asked. I just burst out laughing.

CHAPTER THIRTY-TWO

THE NIGHT AFTER CARNIVAL, WITH SEVENTY-TWO HOURS LEFT UNTIL GOING home, I sat up at the office taking a refresher course on the summer via the massive photo files on Reg's computer. It was a study in the number of creative ways campers can use staff as a jungle gym; every picture was of a boy happily clinging to the back or front of a counselor, waving at the camera while simultaneously trying to wrestle him to the ground. The giddiness level remained high through all eight weeks' worth of photos. The only way you'd know they weren't all taken on the same day was by watching the campers' hair expand from a fresh-out-of-school short cut to a enormous hairy hydrocephalic mass.

From right outside the Office I could hear some loud good-byes. Katia then entered the room. "Oh, friends, I am to leave and so sad!" She kneeled down next to Reg. "Will you be missing me?"

"You going home early, Katia?" said Reg, keeping both hands on his computer. "What's that about?"

"I must see America!" she squealed, leaning in toward him, making one last impression on his side with her breasts. "And I have ride. Mitch say he take me with him!"

Of course he did.

After she left, Jim came in. During the camp season, he was so consistently excited to be there that he entered every room like a talk-show host bounding out onto the stage. Today he seemed a little flatter. He saw the end of camp coming, and he didn't like it. He glanced over Reg's shoulder and watched some photos go by. When Reg hit the last photo, taken of his campers lumped in a pig pile just two hours ago, Jim was quiet, then ventured a question. "Reg," he said. "Did you have a good time this summer?"

"What, you kidding? Gotta be the best. The best."

"What about you, Josh?"

The real answer was complicated. The beginning had been painful, but then I tasted its old greatness, but then came the revelations and acceptance of just where I was in life that made everything so conflicted and . . .

"Yep. The best," I said. This was still Jim's home. Every other season was just an obstacle to get through to get to the next camp summer. He didn't need to be introduced to a world in which Eastwind was complicated. Eastwind should never be complicated; when it got that way, that was the sign to move on.

Jim seemed reassured by our answers, but he still hovered awkwardly like he had something to ask. Finally, he blurted out, "You guys coming up to the Staff Lounge? It'd be a lot better if you two were up there." He looked pained. "This summer needs that. It feels like there's been no . . ." He interlaced his fingers to make the international symbol for cohesion.

I had barely been to the Staff Lounge over the past couple of weeks, but it didn't occur to me that anyone had noticed. I thought it was for the best for everyone; I had grown tired of trying to imagine it as my Staff Lounge of old, and by staying away, the adrenaline-disciplined who made it their outpost wouldn't need to play the very extreme sport of trying to relate to me. It seemed to work out better for everybody. I didn't want to trample Jim's summer ideals, but this time I couldn't oblige him. "Sorry, it's just . . ." I shrugged. "But maybe we'll be up there later. Great summer, man."

As he left, his hopes for last-minute unification dashed, Reg restarted his photos and we both laughed all over again at the memories, pointing at kids and rehashing each moment. The summer hadn't ended yet and the blemish-buffing nostalgia process had already begun. Assistant Director Roger walked in and watched the photos for a few moments, alternately gasping, *tsk*-ing, and letting out barks of laughter. In the middle, he turned to me. "Well then! Maybe you'd like to see some other pictures that you might remember?" He brought me into the storage closet and pulled open a filing cabinet. Inside were year-marked folders dating all the way back to the 1950s, each stuffed with black-and-white prints salvaged from the photo shack at summer's end or donated by ex-campers. On the second-to-last day, I had finally found the visual proof that long, long ago, I existed at Eastwind.

I grabbed the '80s files and brought them back to the desk, eagerly flipping through each year. In 1980 and '81, the faces were just vaguely familiar. I appeared only in the background of some group shots, a skinny kid with an enormous head of thick hair and a glinting grille of orthodonture. Most of the others sparked incomplete memories: Was that kid the one who could fit his body through an unstrung tennis racket? Or was he the guy who was forbidden from playing any more Dungeons & Dragons until he spent at least three periods outside? But as I got into the late '80s, I recognized just about everybody, if not by name then by anecdote. And I was everywhere. There were shots of me as a Bear, navigating trust falls with my two best friends. There I was on the archery range wearing too-short shorts, and there on the dock teaching swimming in a too-short bathing suit. And then a shot of Rocco and I performing a camp rap at Staff Night 1988, waving our arms in our best white-boy interpretation of late-'80s hip-hop style. I couldn't remember any of our lyrics, but I assumed we rhymed "Sunday shower" with "rest hour," because that was about as far as our rhyming skills would have taken us.

One staged photo from 1986 showed a group of us standing outside the infirmary with the nurse, all in a state of exaggerated injury. One of my favorite counselors and I held a stretcher on which rested a camper with a bandage around his head. Rocco stood behind me with a broken badminton racket hanging around his neck. An old friend whose name I couldn't even remember had his eyes crossed with a fake arrow through his head. This had clearly been a carefully orchestrated gag shot, but I had no memory of it at all. There were other shots like this as well, where I remembered the faces but not the situation that at one time had been so important to record. I thought I recollected everything from my camp days. What else had I forgotten? And, twenty years from now, would I look at a photo of Reg and me gleefully stuffing our faces with Countdown's hidden candy and wonder what that was all about?

I needed to avoid the same mistake this summer. I went to bed determined to soak in everything in my final hours. I would not spend my last days looking at my watch, waiting to get back to Christine. I knew I'd have the rest of my life with her; I didn't want to berate myself the next July as I watched Rorschach blots of perspiration spread on my shirt while I waited for the subway, thinking, You were living twenty yards from the Senior Cove, and you didn't savor it, you asshole?

Monday morning I dwelled on everything, attempting to wedge it so forcefully into my sensory memory that years from now, I'd be able to close my eyes and conjure up everything about Eastwind. I dug my toes into the Senior Cove sand, listening to the *shlup*, *shlup* as tiny, dwindling waves from a faraway motorboat's wake flopped onto the shore. I served breakfast with gusto, inhaling the room's scent of twenty-dozen scrambled eggs. I jumped in the water for every last lesson, swimming with the kids and just floating on the lake between periods, watching the last boats go by. During Free Swim I stood on the tower, looking down on the screaming, hooting kids who did flips off the diving board or clutched their chests like they'd been shot and fell off the side of the crib. And then I went back to the cabin to revel in the sounds of a cabin of fourteen-year-olds tearing around in circles and celebrating the last moments of what had just been declared the Best Summer of Their Life—just edging out the summer before, which had just edged out the summer before that, which had just edged out the summer before that. Fifteen years later, maybe they wouldn't remember every moment; Lefty might find a picture of me and call up the Fog and say, "What was that tall counselor's name again? Remember how he used to scream about how smelly the cabin was?" And then they'd talk about how, hey, wouldn't it be cool if they both went back for another summer? And that urge, just like mine, would prove that though they might not remember every counselor, camper, period, meal, and Free Swim, they remembered what was so special about this place. And, I thought, as I watched a merry pig pile form on top of a gasping and laughing Action, no matter what the rest of my life held, so would I.

CHAPTER THIRTY-THREE

"WHOSE GREEN TOWEL IS THIS?" I GOT NOTHING. "DOES ANYONE RECOG-nize this? Someone brought it, so someone's gotta take it home."

No one listened to me, they just kept packing. Rest Hour on Monday was when the campers had to face the reality of the end of camp. They'd be gone the next day, whisked away in a convoy of buses and parents' cars. Nobody seemed particularly concerned about leaving anything behind, as evidenced by my inability to disseminate the hulking heap of bathing suits, shirts, socks, and towels that I'd gathered from the drying line behind the cabin. Item after item received blank stares from the Bears, until I scoured it for a nametag, then threw it at the head of its ignorant owner. "Oh yeaaaaaah," he'd say as he peeled it off his face, only recognizing his own property when it was pressed against his eyeballs.

The trunks that had been stored under the cabin for eight weeks now crowded the aisle, lids yawning open, waiting to be stuffed with poorly folded clothes. The mood was rambunctious, an affected overexuberance that worked as a defense against the dawning reality that another Eastwind summer had ended. By the end of afternoon Free Swim, everyone was done packing, and the cabin felt both more crowded and emptier than it had all summer. Most of the shelves were cleared, but trunks and suitcases were stacked up across the floor, fragile pottery mugs and birdfeeders placed on top for proud handoffs to parents. The beds now had sleeping bags spread out on bare mattresses, as the blankets were packed away.

For the past month, before assemblies, the boys had lingered around the cabin until the last possible moment. But tonight they stampeded out the door as soon as the first bugle blew, because tonight was Banquet, the eagerly anticipated final-night extravaganza. I entered the Dining Hall with my cabin to find it festooned with streamers, fancy tablecloths (by which I mean there were tablecloths at all), and, most important, bottles of soda. Forbidden all summer long, tonight cola was in endless supply, a paradise of carbonation. The overture to the evening was the fizzy rush as fifty two-liter plastic bottles of Sprite, Coke, and Orange Slice were simultaneously yanked open. For a moment I thought the boys weren't going to drink them, they were going to pour the soda over their heads and just *be* with it.

For this meal we sat grouped by cabin, and the twist of Banquet was that the counselors who had always been the meal dictators were now the delegated waiters, an authority-figure switcheroo that never failed to tickle the campers. The staff performed an age-old shtick, leaning out of our chairs as Frank prepared to release the waiters, and then we bolted for the slide, shoving each other out of the way to get our cabin served first. The Bears were determined to make sure Charlie and I never sat down, scooping fistfuls of french fries out of the basket I'd just returned with and sending it right back to me: "More fries, slave!" It was everyone's role to be as negative as Mudge, telling me I wasn't moving fast enough, and that unity of exaggerated complaining gave Mudge the biggest smile I'd ever seen on him. The sugar and adrenaline made everyone hyper, including me. For a moment I knew what it was like to be Kid ADD, as I swiveled from fetching more fried chicken to flicking Action's ear, to shouting to Wind-Up to pass the corn, to ducking as Marquee threw a handful of corn at me.

The Dining Hall was thunderous. Chas led his cabin in increasingly meta chants, like "We are table seven, who the hell is table eight?" even though our tables weren't numbered. When the other cabins tried to formulate a response, they just ended up pounding on the table with their fists. Charlie leaned forward mischievously and said to the Bears, "Hey, guys, how about we do, 'Beans, beans, the musical fruit, the more you eat the more you toot'?" Everyone ignored him except for Wind-Up, who shouted it out on his own.

After the final dessert had been cleared, it was time for the culmination of the evening and the summer, the bestowing of awards. In true everybody's-a-winner fashion, each activity had some to bestow. Even if you were the most sedentary, underachieving of all campers, chances were that you had done something right that qualified you for notice. Swimming was the most predictable, as we handed out the Red Cross cards we'd spent all afternoon filling out for anyone who passed a level. But after us came leather, windsurfing, sailing, canoeing, archery . . . everyone. Serious notices of achievements were bracketed by many goofy awards, like the Mountaineers' "Nasty Backpack," given to the camper with the least interest in hygiene on the trail, won by a delirious Wind-Up, whose acceptance speech couldn't be heard over the deafening applause. That was probably no accident.

After Banquet, as the caffeine highs subsided, everyone proceeded to Campfire Ceremony. I received my little paper bag of charcoal from Frank, a handoff that came with the unspoken promise that I would someday bring it back. I tucked it in my shelves when I returned to the cabin, which was alive with the usual chaos, jacked up even louder by the repressed sadness of another summer ended. Kid ADD couldn't find his sweatshirt, but at least now he knew it was green, and I found it wedged under Trumps' duffel bag in only fifteen minutes. As he grabbed it from me, he smiled, and we shared a moment that lasted only until he noticed Lefty setting up a game of Snatch on a trunk. "Hey, I'm gonna play! I'm gonna play!"

It was late, but I thought the boys deserved extra time for their last night together, so I went to my bed and pulled out some Eastwind stationery to finish one of my last camp duties, writing my camper letters. It was an Eastwind tradition for the counselors to divvy up their cabin's campers and write their parents closing missives about their sons' summers. They were report cards of a sort, going through each boy's favorite activities, standout accomplishments, and other sundry personal progress, a parting note to reinforce what a great summer the son had. We were also told to touch on any troubles the boy might have had over the summer—bullying, insubordination, laziness—but only if it was a huge issue or had been a problem in the past that was getting better. Even then, I kept that part short. Parents were paying for their kids to have a good time, not to be analyzed and criticized. When you bought a ticket for your child to go in a haunted house, you didn't want a ghost to come out afterward to tell you your son was insufficiently frightened and rudely inattentive to the swooping vampires.

I was responsible for writing about Lefty, Marquee, and Afty. Afty seemed in a good mood tonight as he watched a final Snatch game—after loudly volunteering himself to sit out because he "never won, anyway"—but he darkened when he walked over to his bed and saw me working. I capped my pen and tucked away the letters. "What's up, Afty? You bummed to be going home?"

He eyed me like I was holding a Taser behind my back, his eyes in shadow behind his limp bangs. "Are you writing cabin letters?"

As a camper, I was never particularly concerned or aware of the final-letter process. It never occurred to me that I was being judged for my ability to have a fantastic summer. But Afty was always aware of being judged. "I was, why?" I replied.

"Are you doing mine?" He fixed me with an accusatory glare.

"It doesn't matter. Mitch, Charlie, and I split them all up."

"If it doesn't matter, why don't you tell me?" His face further tightened.

"Don't get so worked up, it's really not important."

"Just tell me. I know it's you, and I know you're going to write something bad, so I want to know."

"Okay!" Never before had someone worked so hard to confirm the worst news about himself. "You win! I *am* writing it. And you know what?" He glared at me, waiting for the inevitable critique. "It's gonna be good. I was *happy* to have you in the cabin this year."

His face abruptly loosened. "All right," he said. "Jeez, that's all I wanted to know." He grabbed his toiletry kit and wandered out to the bathroom. I give up, I thought, and stuffed the pad away and wandered the cabin, getting in some last precious moments of good-hearted abuse with the guys: accepting a farewell "Tall Doofus" from Lefty, giving Countdown a parting "superdork," reminiscing about the many, many times I had trounced them in a wide range of games. Sometime since the '80s, signing the walls multiple times had been banned, so I found a blank space, stood on the edge of a cot with a black Sharpie, and, as per the new tradition, wrote out the names of the 2003 Bears.

"Your handwriting stinks," said Mudge, eyeing every letter I wrote.

"I think I'll miss you most of all, Scarecrow," I replied. He gave me a smile that was only 8 percent smirk.

When Charlie and I finally got everyone in bed, I turned off all the lights and made everyone go around the room, talking about their best moment of the summer. Kid ADD broke in, "I got one, I got one! Jumping off that bridge on that river!"

"You never did that," said Mensa. "I only remember that because it was the Sexy Seven, see, and the members included—"

"Shut up, not on the cabin trip, but on another trip, ask anybody!"

"All right," I said. "Kid did it. Who's next? Wind-Up?"

"Come on, Josh, you don't even need to ask, do you, buddy? I think this bandana around my neck says it all, don't you? Although there are runners-up, I'd have to say—"

"Give me the list tomorrow, Wind-Up, we gotta get to everybody," I said. "What about you, Mensa?"

He thought for a moment and said it was learning how to kayak, or maybe the first time he got up on a windsurfer. I waited for Kid ADD's interjection, but he was quiet. Apparently, his mouth had jabbered to the point of exhaustion, and he had abruptly fallen asleep after his bridge declaration.

"That sounds like a good summer," said Charlie. And after a moment of thought, Mensa agreed that it was. Around we went: Action loved his Mount Washington overnight trip, because he got to cook the dinner. Marquee had caught the biggest bass of the summer. Countdown's attempt at candy-smuggling foiled, he settled on making it through the highest challenge on the ropes course. Afty had made a dish for his mom at Wood Shop that "turned out all right, I guess." Mudge had made it to the quarterfinals of the camper/staff tennis tournament. Lefty had bushwacked for three miles following a compass on an orienteering trip.

"I can't pick just one," said Charlie, his voice loud in the dark. "I was just so thankful to you boys and camp. You gave an old man a chance to feel young again. I didn't know if I'd be useful after retirement, but this summer, I felt like I was." It made me forgive all his daffiness. Maybe I just came back too soon. Age sixty-five, that would have been the time to do it.

"What about you, Josh?" asked Lefty.

I thought for a moment. It was like when Jim asked me if I had a good summer. The real answer was hard to explain, so I took the second-best answer I had. "I think right now is my favorite," I said. "You guys were a great cabin. And to hear that you all had an awesome time, and are all going home having accomplished something, that makes me know this summer was a success."

"Hey, Josh?" asked Countdown after a quiet pause. "What's that song that Guns N' Roses sings that's all about oral sex?"

"And with that," I said, "we go to sleep." I fumbled around in my area for my flashlight. Just as I stood up to leave the cabin, Afty sat up.

"Hey," he said. In the shadows I could see him fumbling in his shelves and then handing something to me. I took them and flicked on my flashlight. They were ten folded stationery note cards, with a vivid color photograph of a different Eastwind vista affixed to the front of each one: a dramatically jagged lake sunset, the Bears cabin shrouded in shimmering trees after a rainstorm. These were the images I had seen in my head for the previous twelve summers when I sat imprisoned in a city office building. Every moment Afty hadn't been crafting his chair, he had been in the photo shop printing these. "I had extras," he mumbled. "You can have them, I guess." He paused. "Thanks for being my counselor."

"Wow, these are amazing," I whispered. "I don't know whether to send them or frame them. Thanks." I turned them over in my hands. "And thanks for being my camper."

He blinked and then lay back. "Yeah, well, whatever."

At the beginning of the summer, I had envisioned my Afterschool Special as having a more theatrical, demonstrative conclusion, one worthy of a goopy title like "The Boy Who Learned to Feel," or maybe, "An Ego Flowers in the Bears." Instead it should be called "The Begrudging Gift That Might or Might Not Have Had a Deeper Meaning." But I liked its script all the same.

CHAPTER THIRTY-FOUR

THE EXODUS BEGAN AT SIX THIRTY THE NEXT MORNING, WHEN A BUS HAULED thirty boys—including Countdown and Mudge—from the New York/New Jersey/Connecticut area back to their waiting parents.

After mock-frisking Countdown to see if he stole my wallet, I turned to Mudge. "It was a pleasure," I said, extending my hand. "Have a great year."

"School sucks," he replied.

"Go on, get outta here, you're gonna make me cry, ya big lug," I said, whacking him on the shoulder.

The other riders walked a gauntlet of good-bye hugs and handshakes into the bus, and when it finally rumbled up the road, they all waved out their windows as if trying to get the vehicle airborne. The rest of the day was a slow, maudlin evacuation as parents arrived, filled their minivans, and drove away, each leaving the camp one camper quieter. Occasionally a car would grind past up the gravel road, and I'd see a camper slumped over in the backseat, wiping away a tear at the thought of leaving. The Bears emptied out, and I felt a warm pang as Lefty, Action, and the rest slowly said good-bye. I'd miss them. Less so on rainy days, though.

Wind-Up's dad arrived around ten and confirmed that chattiness was hereditary. Chummy and garrulous, his father kept me trapped for twenty minutes with a sneak-peek travelogue of the end-of-summer mountain trip he and his son had planned. If Trivial Pursuit ever came out with a "Wind-Up Family Trip Edition," I would dominate, now knowing the answers to such questions as, "What is Wind-Up's dad's favorite brand of tinned beef?" and "Name three gas-station chains the Wind-Up family will fill up at over their dead bodies." I was stunned to see Wind-Up tug at his father's sleeve and say, "Come on, Dad, we gotta *go*."

"All right, all right, let's move, your mom is waiting for us." I tried to envision her, but all I could see was a giant set of wind-up chattering teeth in a hairnet. I shook Wind-Up's hand, and he jumped into the passenger seat, idly caressing the new bandana tied around his neck. His dad grabbed me by the shoulder to give one last, concise word. "Thank you, all of you guys. You have no idea what this summer meant to him."

All the campers were gone by three, and the staff rushed to clean up their activity areas. That night was the much-awaited Staff Party, the annual bacchanalia at which the staff could enjoy camp as they'd dreamed of it all summer long: without campers. We all gathered down by the dock to swim and await the kitchen crew's arrival with trays of shrimp and home-made hummus and other delicacies that would have been wasted on the campers. A canoe was filled with ice and soda and juice, and two kegs were rolled out onto the beach. The weather was ideal, the mood boisterous. The farewell vibe made everyone emotionally hyperactive; the laughter was extra loud, the reminiscences spiked with added fondness, the this-was-a-great-staff pronouncements especially earnest.

With all of our heartfelt bonding finished along with the food, the kegs were brought over to the Senior Cove for the traditional debaucherous conclusion. Frank surreptitiously vanished at that point; even with his staff now relieved of duty, he preferred not to see them at their most slur-ring. Sean brought down his amp and guitar from the Theater, along with a drum set for Lars, and the two began jamming as a campfire was lit on the beach. A tradition of last-night nudity had been initiated since my de-parture, and suddenly the fire was surrounded by fifteen hopping, naked coworkers, bravely staring down the conventional wisdom that thrown sparks and exposed penises weren't a good match. Even Anne and Helen stripped down to join the big naked dance number, but I remained clothed in the prude section of the party, sitting with the uncomfortable Eastern European kitchen workers on a picnic table, sipping my beer. It didn't count as peer pressure if I was out of everybody's peer group.

The night went late, and I had only vague memories of stepping over a couple of counselors passed out facedown in the sand as I staggered up to my cabin. I had a fitful evening of drunken dreams interrupted by hourly staggers down the cabin steps to pee, and was woken at eight when Charlie decided to load up his car to get an early start on the road, letting the door slam behind him with every load. It seemed an appropriate wake-up call for my last morning of cabin living.

After a final dip in the lake to jar my brain awake, I went to the Dining Hall, where a few quiet staffers nursed their hangovers over bowls of cereal. We greeted each other with the weak smiles of people who couldn't recall if they'd recently done something embarrassing. It was anticlimactic facing each other after the previous evening's long good-bye, like we'd summed up our deep friendships in a tearful farewell at an airport gate, ready to board a plane to parts unknown, only to have the flight delayed.

After eating, I returned to the Bears to pack and load my car, during which time everyone else woke up. Ready to go, I made a good-bye loop past Jim, Zach, Chas, Helen, and Sean.

"Happy marriage, brother," said Sean. "Nice seeing you off to adulthood."

"I'll see you there soon enough," I said. "I'll save you a seat. I'll make sure it's padded because I know how brittle your bones are."

"Fuck you, I'm still a young 'un."

"You can play electric guitar all you want, but you're still thirty," I said. "Good luck figuring it all out."

I found Reg sitting on the dock, taking in the lake one final time. I'd invited him to the wedding two weeks earlier and he'd assured me he'd like to come, but as he'd be traveling around until the end of his visa, he had no idea if he'd be near Rhode Island. "Wow, I'd be honored, mate," he had said. "Tell you what, I'll try my best to be there, should work out, but if I can't, don't worry about it." Just as there was no way I could comprehend his improvisatory future, he couldn't comprehend my world where head counts for caterers were of the utmost importance.

But today he slowly stood up from the dock chair and shook my hand. "Thought about it," he said, "and I'll be at the wedding. No worries." This was a relief, and not just from a price-per-plate perspective. I had walked away from camp with a close friend, and that's what summer was always about. And as an added bonus, since we'd be reuniting in just a few weeks, it relieved us both of the pressure of trying to define this new close friendship in a big "final moment."

I went up to the Office and found it empty. I picked up the phone and called Christine. "They asked me to be winter caretaker, so I'll just need nine more months," I said. "Can you stall the wedding band?"

"If you're not here by the end of the day, I'm marrying the keyboard player," she said. "Move your ass. I need someone to grow old with, and I'm running out of time."

I hung up just as Frank entered the Office. He seemed looser than he had in weeks, temporarily free from the burden of worrying about kids' lives. I thanked him for allowing me to come back. "Hey, thank you," he said. "Think there's anything I can do to convince you to come back next summer?"

I laughed. "Well, I guess you never know," I said, then stopped myself from playing the polite card. "Actually, I think I do know: I doubt it."

"Figured," he said, and we shook hands. Like men do.

ACKNOWLEDGMENTS

THIS BOOK WAS NOT A STUNT. IT CAME OUT OF A VERY REAL, LONG-STANDING desire to return to "Eastwind," mainly because of the profound impact that two men—Nick Latham, who sadly passed away just as I was finishing this book, and Bill Ricker—had on my life. For me and my peers at camp, these men shaped us for the better. With our memorable summers together, they gave me the backstory for this book, yes, but they also planted the seeds for the self-confidence I would one day need to actually write it. And many thanks to Chuck and Laura Mills and Bill French, not just for allowing me back to "Eastwind," but for running it with the same integrity and strong values so a new generation of boys can have what I had. All five people were of great help to me with their history lessons and reminiscences, and the book also gave me the opportunity to reconnect with and have my memory refreshed by great old camp friends, especially Bobby Linscott, Rich Baumel, Maria Latham, and Brandt Ricker. And then there are my new camp friends, Cameron McGrane, Rob Wilby, Andy Sapora, Cara Schadel, and Jesse Hershman, who helped me remember every meal and wibble. And to the rest of the staff and campers of 2003, thank you for sharing your summer. You gave me hope that even if I changed, camp, mercifully, never would, and that's the way it should be.

I am grateful to my agent, Lydia Wills, who encouraged, protected, and kicked me to make this book come out the way I envisioned it. She always told me the truth—even the bad news—and for that I'm grateful.

At Hyperion, my insightful, patient, endlessly dedicated editor Peternelle van Arsdale will always have my awe and gratitude. When I first heard her regal name, I never imagined she would once give me the note, "I don't want you to think I'm all about the poop jokes . . ." but truly dreams can come true. I was also fortunate to get the unerringly perceptive input of Leslie Wells and Will Schwalbe, as well as the energizing help and support of Bob Miller, Ellen Archer, Jane Comins, Sally McCartin, Katie Wainwright, Beth Dickey, Miriam Wenger, Laura Drew, Phil Rose, Rachelle Nashner, Navorn Johnson, Linda Prather, and Linda Papastavrinoudis. And thanks to Rich Freeman, Mitch Smelkinson, Karen Glass, and Derek Evans, for seeing the story's potential beyond the page.

At *Entertainment Weekly*, Rick Tetzeli, Henry Goldblatt, and Kristen Baldwin gave me the freedom and encouragement to pursue this project, and Brian Anstey's artful aid saved me at an extremely panicky moment. At the *Boston Globe*, Nick King and my journalistic idol, Neil Swidey, first allowed me to tell my summer story in their pages, which got everything going. And thanks to the great friends who helped me throughout the process: Katherine Schulten, Dan Snierson, Brian Raftery, and Gillian Flynn gave incisive early readings and encouragement, and Karen Valby saved my ass with a thoughtful and precise read-through at a critical moment. And while I was at camp, Dave Hamilton and Nancy Sidewater served as my tether to the outside world by keeping me entertained with a steady mailed supply of news clippings and office gossip, which made my return to society that much smoother.

I thanked camp for molding me, but to give them all the credit is unfair: while they took care of me for one month of the year, my parents, Dick and Linda, handled the rest. Their lifetime of nurturing, reassurance, support, and—the magic ingredient—nagging drove me to get off the couch (my mother's favorite battle cry) and pursue this project. I must also thank my in-laws, Jim and Ann Schomer, for their enthusiasm and understanding when I skipped town three months before marrying their daughter.

As for my daughter, Lila, hopefully she was too young to note that her dad spent much of her formative year muttering to himself about page and word counts, but her sweet nature always quickly made me forget them. And as for Christine, this book would never have been done without her, and I don't just mean for the argument fodder. The most bolstering, loving, inspiring woman I've ever met, she was a brilliant sounding board and a constant cheerleader whom I leaned on all the way to the finish line.

We once realized that she and I might have attended the same camp social years ago, but any romantic notion of us sharing an official first dance as teenagers was dashed by the reality that we were both wallflowers. But that's OK; it was definitely worth the wait.